LILLIAN HELLMAN

A BIBLIOGRAPHY: 1926-1978

Mary Marguerite Riordan

Scarecrow Author Bibliographies, No. 50

The Scarecrow Press, Inc.
Metuchen, N.J., & London
1980

Library of Congress Cataloging in Publication Data

Riordan, Mary Marguerite, 1931-
   Lillian Hellman, a bibliography, 1926-1978.

   (Scarecrow author bibliographies ; no. 50)
   Includes index.
   1. Hellman, Lillian, 1905-   --Bibliography.
I. Title.
Z8395.52.R56   [PS3515.E343]   016.812'52   80-16147
ISBN 0-8108-1320-3

With thanks to

Carroll

ACKNOWLEDGMENTS

I wish to thank Sol Behar, Acquisitions Librarian, Anglo-American Collections, University of California, Berkeley; Ann Roberti, Frances Surina, and the other librarians of City College of San Francisco; Peggy McLoughlin, Emmanuel College Library, Boston; Ann R. Sharry, S. N. D. , Emmanuel College; Jane Herzog, Genevieve McNulty Riordan, and Al LaValley, Limelight Bookstore, San Francisco, for their help and suggestions; and, Editta Sherman, Carnegie Hall, New York, for her photograph of Lillian Hellman. Their generosity and graciousness were significant in my completing this bibliography.

TABLE OF CONTENTS

PREFACE

The completion of a bibliography such as this makes clear
the need for a reappraisal of Lillian Hellman's works now
that her memoirs have enlarged her place in American literature. Looking over the variety and quality of her work, the
recurrent themes that make us ultimately reconsider and re-
fine our thinking about our underdeveloped human natures,
about the integrity essential to the health and development of
the individual or situation or nation, seeing the fine quality
of the craftsmanship and the artistry of her work, we quickly
recognize the talent, the vigor, the vision that Lillian Hellman presents. Had she done nothing else but write the plays,
she would have a secure place in American drama as a major playwright. Lillian Hellman has brought to the stage the
best of the American tradition in the theater and has provided audiences with profound recognitions of what it means
to be human. These glances at life she recasts very special-
ly and in a personal context in her memoirs, expressing her
great concern for the moral, the concern that life could be
better, the insight that in spite of our eventual wisdom life
takes its toll and it does go on.

The reader of her work early recognizes what Louis
Kronenberger writes of as the "realistic mind and the heroic
spirit, working together" in his introduction to The North
Star (B7) through reading her plays and her memoirs. But
one learns a great deal about the scope and range of that
mind and the magnitude of that spirit by turning to the biographies written by Doris V. Falk (F66) and Richard Moody
(F152), the taped material (E34, E35, E36, E37, E38, E40),
the list of people whom she has known, and most profitably
to the letters in public collections located throughout the
country--granted, not in nearly the numbers the reader is
greedy for, but a sufficiency, such as in the Archives of
American Art (E7) or at the University of California's Bancroft Library (E24) or at the Houghton Library (E14) or at
the University of Washington (E30), certainly at the University
of Texas at Austin (E28)--to read of her capacity for friendship, her enormous dignity and pride, her independence and

spirit, the woman of character, wit, fierce courage, unre-
lenting intellect, compassion, the wise survivor, appreciative
of life, and always grateful for finding sufficient will in others.

Controversy has marked many periods of Lillian Hellman's public life: The Children's Hour, her anti-Fascist
activities, her strong Soviet allegiance, the HUAC hearings,
Scoundrel Time, and most recently the Diana Trilling episode
with Little, Brown. Too, she has been willing to jump into
controversy when it was not her own personally, to support
and to protest, as in the support of Robert Lowell's refusal
of President Johnson's invitation to the White House Festival
of the Arts and in the filing of the suit for the release of
the controversial Richard M. Nixon tapes during the Watergate hearings.

Often it is through the controversy that we read the
character of Lillian Hellman, the willingness to take the side
she prefers and then adhering to it indomitably; the convic-
tion she is right after she has made up her mind; the out-
rage when matters or people become aesthetically displeasing
or vulgar. In his review of Dead End (H559) Peter Galway
writes she "is aware of beauty in the heart of ugliness."
And it seems that her aesthetic view of life is that out of
which her indignation, courage oftentimes, compassion, sense
of justice come, and gives the spine to her morality because
the quality of human acts comes into play. In any case, as
Doris Falk concludes her biography: "Whatever we may think
of her politics or temperament, we must rejoice in the ener-
gy, ingenuity, and skill of the performance."

When a library's resources are limited, perhaps the
most ready, even though abbreviated, approach to getting a
good sense of Hellman's work and the extent of her accom-
plishment is to turn to Bill Moyers' interview (E37), her own
reading of Julia (E38), and Kimball King's short but fine lecture (E40), most readily available by writing to the companies listed.* The Paris Review, Writers at Work interview by John Phillips and Anne Hollander (G157) is generally

---

*Addresses for the recording companies are given in Section
E. Addresses are also included for libraries and institutions
holding materials of interest when those addresses might not
come easily to the reader's mind.

held by libraries and is a fine supplement to the cassette
tapes.

When one's library resources are not limited, perhaps
the most helpful works that reveal Hellman personally as well
as her thinking and the stature of her contributions are the
Margaret Case Harriman early profile (G79), Jean Gould's
chapter (F83), the critical biographies of Doris V. Falk (F66)
and Richard Moody (F152), and Harold Clurman's introduction
to Moody's biography.   Jacob Adler's monograph is excellent
for the abundance of information (F3), although he seems to
shift in his final opinion of Hellman, first building to the view
that she is absolutely superior as a playwright, then shifting
to a more cautious rating at the conclusion of his piece.
The newspaper articles too are interesting and helpful.   Caroline Moorehead's Times (London) article (G137), Nora Ephron
(G57), Judy Bachrach (G14, G15), Kathleen Brady (G25),
Stephanie de Pue (G48, G49), Gloria Emerson (G56), Jo Ann
Levine (G112), Seymour Peck (G152) are but a few of the
telling articles.

Politically interesting material is readily found especially in Sections F and G (G115, G121, G133, G150, G198,
and F193) and in Section H under Scoundrel Time.

The dates used in Sections A and C are performance
or publication years; in Section B, the release dates.   In in-
stances of conflicting or uncertain dates, when no other more
recent or reliable source could be found, the biographies of
Doris Falk and Richard Moody were used to resolve the mat-
ter.

In Section F, page numbers are supplied to give the
user of the bibliography information about longer references
or when Hellman is not listed in the index.   For those en-
tries without page number, the Hellman reference can be located in the index of the book.   In Section H, individual
works are listed alphabetically by genre.   Page numbers are
also supplied if Hellman is not to be found in the index.

When the title of a newspaper or periodical article
gives enough clue to the general contents, usually no annota-
tion is given for the entry.   The citations under The Big
Knockover in Section H are reviews of the book and about
Hammett, but are included because some mention of Hellman
is made in the article.

Because the New York Times Index is readily available, special indexing of Times' reviews is not made for this
bibliography, although, of course, the Times' reviews are
listed in the appropriate sections.

Materials in periodicals and newspapers in Canada and
in England are included to the extent that they have been in-
dexed.

Even though the search for materials has been exten-
sive and comprehensive in libraries on both coasts and the
bibliography has been compiled most carefully, I look forward
to the revised edition to be certain it is absolutely complete.
Then perhaps it will be known whether in fact Lillian Hellman
did write the letter listed as D23 and the review of Valley
Town (D16).   Too, perhaps additional scholarship will have
discovered how many short stories Miss Hellman did write
and publish or if there is a significant number of unpublished
stories in her possession.

CHRONOLOGY

1905
20 June   Lillian Florence Hellman was born in New Orleans to Max Bernard and Julia Newhouse Hellman

1911   moved with parents to New York; spent six months in New York and six months with father's sisters in New Orleans each year

1922   graduated from Wadleigh High School

1922-24   attended New York University

1924   toured the mid-West and the South with mother; attended Columbia University one semester before going to work for Liveright; met Julian Messner, vice-president of Horace Liveright, Inc.

1924-25   manuscript reader/editorial assistant for Liveright; worked with T. R. Smith, editor-in-chief, Manuel Komroff, Louis Kronenberger, Beatrice Kaufman, Bennett Cerf, among others; Liveright accepted her enthusiastic recommendation to publish William Faulkner's Mosquitoes

1925
31 December   married Arthur Kober

1925-29   book reviewer for the New York Herald Tribune

1926   went to Paris because of Kober's work; wrote for the Paris Comet, an Anglo-American fortnightly that appeared October 1927 to January/February 1930

28 November   appeared in print for the first time as Lillian
                 F. Hellman, a book review of Our Doctors
                 by Maurice Duplay, New York Herald Tribune
                 Books (she dropped the "F." in the tenth and
                 final review, June 2, 1929)

1927
19 June   reviewed Mosquitoes for the Herald Tribune

1927-30   theatrical play reader for Leo Bulgakov, Har-
                 ry Moses, Anne Nichols, Herman Shumlin;
                 discovered Vicki Baum's Grand Hotel

1929
summer   went to Germany to study for a year at Bonn,
                 but changed her plans after discovering the
                 anti-Semitism there

1930   moved to Hollywood; met Dashiell Hammett;
                 Sophronia Mason died

1930-32   scenario reader for MGM in Hollywood at
                 $50 per week; friends with Laura and Sidney
                 Perelman, Nathanael West, and William
                 Faulkner

1931   met Dorothy Parker at a party given by Wil-
                 liam Rose Benét, after moving back to New
                 York with Dashiell Hammett

1932   divorced from Arthur Kober; collaborated
                 with Louis Kronenberger on unpublished play
                 Dear Queen

1933
September   short story "I Call Her Mama Now," signed
                 Lillian Hellman Kober, published in The
                 American Spectator; renewed acquaintance
                 with Herman Shumlin at party given by Ira
                 Gershwin; later went to work for Shumlin as
                 reader; read William Roughead's Bad Com-
                 panions at Hammett's suggestion; "Closed
                 Doors, or, The Great Drumsheugh Case" be-
                 came the basis of The Children's Hour

1934
January   short story "Perberty in Los Angeles," signed

Lillian Hellman Kober, published in The
American Spectator; Hammett's last novel
The Thin Man was published and dedicated to
Lillian Hellman

20 November   The Children's Hour, dedicated to D. Hammett, directed by Herman Shumlin, opened on
Broadway at Maxine Elliot's Theatre for 691
performances (banned in Boston, Chicago,
and London)

1935   returned to Hollywood to work for Sam Goldwyn at $2500 per week; met William Wyler;
wrote first screenplay The Dark Angel with
Mordaunt Shairp; began writing screenplay for
first film version of The Children's Hour, to
be titled These Three (which Goldwyn had
bought for $35,000); met Dorothy Parker
again in Hollywood and became life-long
friends; helped to revive the Screen Writers'
Guild; attended dinner given by Mrs. Ehrman
in Beverly Hills for Gertrude Stein and Alice
B. Toklas (Hammett, Charlie Chaplin and
Paulette Goddard, Anita Loos also were
guests); mother died

1936
3 March   film These Three, directed by William Wyler,
released in New York

June   returned to New York from Havana before
going on to Tavern Island

November   The Children's Hour performed privately at
the Gate Theatre Studio in London

15 December   Days to Come, dedicated to Julia and Max
Hellman, directed by Herman Shumlin, opened
Broadway run at the Vanderbilt Theatre for 7
performances

1937
January   founded, with Archibald MacLeish and Dorothy
Parker, Contemporary Historians to back
Joris Ivens' project to go to Spain to make a
documentary; collaborated with Archibald Mac-
Leish on the story for The Spanish Earth, an

appeal for the cause of the Spanish Loyal-
ists--eventually left the project because of ill-
ness

13 January   the U. S. State Department warned citizens
against serving in Spain

winter   returned to Hollywood to do screen version of
Sidney Kingsley's Dead End for Samuel Gold-
wyn

summer   finished first version of The Little Foxes

30 July   returned to New York

24 August   attended opening of Dead End, directed by
William Wyler, at the Rivoli Theater in New
York

25 August   sailed on the Normandie to attend a
theater festival in Moscow and to have
a pre-Moscow visit in Paris (Alan
Campbell and Dorothy Parker were on
the same crossing); Dorothy Parker
introduced her to Ernest Hemingway,
Sara and Gerald Murphy; saw James
Thurber and Otto Simon in Paris

October   arrived in Valencia to tour the war zone

20 October   drove to Benacasim with Gustav Regler to
visit the base hospital

22 October   driven to Madrid; spoke to the people associ-
ated with The International Brigade, visited
hospitals and nurseries; saw Hemingway

5 November   returned to Valencia

11 November   flew to Barcelona; trained to Paris

13 December   reviewed Thomas Job's adaptation of Barchester Towers for Time

1938
March   attended private showing of The Spanish Earth
at Frederic (Florence Eldridge) March's, held

to raise money for ambulances (Alan Campbell, Dorothy Parker, F. Scott Fitzgerald, Hammett, Jorvis Ivens, Ernest Hemingway also were present)

13 April   "A Day in Spain" appeared in New Republic (Walter Winchell had requested her piece on Spain for his column, but William Randolph Hearst refused to permit King features to syndicate the article; served on the Executive Board of the Motion Picture Guild; prepared for rehearsals for The Little Foxes

1939   one of the sponsors of the Hollywood Theater Alliance

9 January   rehearsals began for The Little Foxes

2 February   The Little Foxes, dedicated to Arthur Kober and Louis Kronenberger, directed by Herman Shumlin, opened in Baltimore at the Ford Theatre (Lillian Hellman, Max Hellman, Hammet, Dorothy Parker and Alan Campbell, Sara and Gerald Murphy, Will and John Bankhead attended the opening)

15 February   The Little Foxes opened in New York at the National Theatre for 410 performances; attended dinner given by Mr. and Mrs. Henry Luce, which Dorothy Thompson also attended

March   went to Havana for rest

May   moderated a discussion of contemporary issues and the problems of the dramatist as part of the New School's Third American Writers' Congress

June   bought Hardscrabble Farm (the Lederer Estate), Westchester County, her home until 1952; The Little Foxes considered for the New York Drama Critics' Circle Award

1940
10 January   joined Lin Yutang and Edna Ferber as one of the speakers at the Book and Author Luncheon at the Hotel Astor: "I am a writer and also

a Jew. I want to be sure I can continue to say what I wish without being branded by the malice of people making a living by that malice"; began analysis with Gregory Zilboorg

19 January   refused to let The Little Foxes be staged as benefit for Finnish Relief

3 February   The Little Foxes closed in New York and went on national tour

14 February   Dorothy Thompson's New York Herald Tribune column identified LH with the left-wing

June   went to Philadelphia to cover the Republican National Convention for PM

25 June   "The Little Men in Philadelphia" appeared in PM; worked on screenplay The Little Foxes

1941
1 April   Watch on the Rhine, dedicated to Herman Shumlin, directed by Herman Shumlin, opened in New York at the Martin Beck Theatre for 378 performances

27 April   awarded the New York Drama Critics' Circle Award for Watch on the Rhine, at a dinner at the Algonquin Hotel: "To Lillian Hellman for Watch on the Rhine, a vital, eloquent and compassionate play about an American family suddenly awakened to the danger threatening its liberty."

15 June   awarded honorary Master of Arts degree, Tufts University: "The student of mankind may learn much concerning the inner life of each cycle of civilization by a study of the living theater of the period. Lillian Hellman, you have demonstrated unusual ability as an author in transforming the permanent and the transient in the spirit of our times into enduring and coherent drama which will record for future generations much that is both good and bad in the psyche of our age"; appealed for funds to aid wounded veterans of the Abraham Lincoln Brigade in the Spanish Civil War

21 August   the film <u>The Little Foxes,</u> directed by William
                 Wyler for Sam Goldwyn, opened at Radio City
                 Music Hall; was matron of honor at Arthur
                 Kober's re-marriage; lived at 5 East 83rd
                 Street after <u>Watch on the Rhine</u> until summer
                 of 1943

<u>1942</u>   Random House published <u>Four Plays</u> (<u>The
                 Children's Hour, Days to Come, The Little
                 Foxes, Watch on the Rhine</u>), with an intro-
                 duction by Miss Hellman; agreed with William
                 Wyler, under contract to Sam Goldwyn, to
                 make a documentary film of the war in Russia;
                 went to Washington, D. C. with Wyler to see
                 Ambassador Maxim Litvinov about going to
                 Russia to do <u>The North Star</u>

23 February   <u>Watch on the Rhine</u> went on the road, opening
                 in Philadelphia

spring   edited Hammett's film version of <u>Watch on the
                 Rhine</u>

March   participated in dinner honoring Paul Robeson

April   <u>Watch on the Rhine,</u> directed by Emlyn Wil-
                 liams, opened in London

22 June   matinee of <u>Watch on the Rhine</u> held to aid
                 Actors' Orphanage, London

3 August   illustrated, limited edition of 349 copies of
                 <u>Watch on the Rhine,</u> with a special forward
                 by Dorothy Parker, privately published by the
                 Joint Anti-Fascist Refugee Committee for the
                 general relief; Rockwell Kent, 11 other artists,
                 and Dorothy Parker donated their services

October   <u>The Little Foxes,</u> directed by Emlyn Williams,
                 opened at Piccadilly Theatre, London

9 October   co-chairman with Ernest Hemingway of dinner
                 at Biltmore Hotel "Europe Today" held to
                 raise money for the release and transport of
                 noted anti-fascists from French internment
                 camps to Mexico; saw Guthrie McClintic's
                 <u>Three Sisters</u> at the Ethel Barrymore Theatre

1943   bought 63 East 82nd Street and lived there
                       until 1969

27 August   Warner Brothers' <u>Watch on the Rhine</u> opened
                       at the Rialto Theater, New York

4 November   film <u>The North Star</u> premiered in two Broad-
                       way theaters simultaneously; donated typescript
                       of <u>The North Star</u> as part of the war effort;
                       it was auctioned off in Toledo, to the organi-
                       zation selling the greatest number of war bonds

1944
February   <u>The Searching Wind</u> in rehearsal

12 April   <u>The Searching Wind</u>, dedicated to Dorothy
                       Parker, directed by Herman Shumlin, opened
                       at the Fulton Theatre, for 318 performances

September   left from Fairbanks, Alaska, on a cultural
                       mission to Moscow; lived at Spasso House,
                       Ambassador Harriman's residence in Moscow;
                       had almost daily tea with Sergei Eisenstein,
                       who was cutting the first part of <u>Ivan the Ter-
                       rible</u>; attended Ambassador Harriman's Christ-
                       mas party; attended rehearsals of <u>The Little
                       Foxes</u> and <u>Watch on the Rhine</u> in Moscow;
                       met Prokofiev; visited hospitals for the severe-
                       ly wounded

27 December   left by train with guide-translator Raya Leiber-
                       sohn from Kiev for the Polish Front

1945
January   spent two weeks with the First White Russian
                       Army on the Warsaw Front; stayed at the
                       quarters of Marshall Zhukov, the Commander
                       of the First and Second White Russian Armies
                       fighting the Germans across the Vistula; in-
                       vited by General Chernov to remain with the
                       Armies for the march on Berlin, but returned
                       to Moscow to return to New York

27 February   returned to New York from Russia via Cairo
                       and a month in England

August   finished the movie script for <u>The Searching
                       Wind</u>

1946   joined Independent Citizens Committee of the
                Arts, Sciences and Professions with Jo David-
                son and Franklin Delano Roosevelt, Jr.

17 May   inducted into the National Institute of Arts and
                Letters with Wallace Stevens, Robert P. Tris-
                tram Coffin, Franklin P. Adams, Simon Strun-
                sky

26 June   film The Searching Wind shown at the Para-
                mount Theater, New York

20 November   Another Part of the Forest, dedicated to
                Gregory Zilboorg, produced by Kermit Bloom-
                garden and directed by Lillian Hellman, opened
                at the Fulton Theatre for 191 performances

1947
26 April   Another Part of the Forest closed; placed
                third in New York Drama Critics' Circle bal-
                loting; vacationed abroad; met in Paris with
                representatives from 15 countries for sessions
                of the International Theatre Institute

1948   father died; went to Hollywood for two weeks
                to prepare the presentation of Streetcar Named
                Desire for submission to the Breen Office;
                William Wyler proposed to do a film based on
                Theodore Dreiser's Sister Carrie and asked
                Paramount to hire Miss Hellman. Wyler was
                told she could not be hired because her name
                was on the secret blacklist; talked with Norman
                Mailer about dramatizing The Naked and the
                Dead, plans she put aside after seeing Mont-
                serrat and after she met Emmanuel Roblès
                (introduced to by the poet Phillipe Soupault)

18 May   film Another Part of the Forest, adapted by
                Vladimir Posner, released

summer   taught week course in playwriting at the Indi-
                ana University Writers' Conference, Bloom-
                ington; spoke publicly on Henry Wallace, the
                poverty of the contemporary theater (ashamed
                because it refused to deal seriously with a
                serious world), and the promise of Tennessee
                Williams

July   became actively involved in Henry Wallace's
                campaign for the Presidency, 1948-49; helped
                write platform for Progressive Party and at-
                tended the Convention

October   flew to Prague, Belgrade, Paris, principally
                to interview Marshall Tito for PM's successor,
                the New York Star; saw performance of The
                Little Foxes in Belgrade

1949
January   manuscript of Montserrat ready for Kermit
                Bloomgarden

25-27 March   a principal speaker at the Cultural and Scien-
                tific Congress for World Peace, sponsored
                by the National Council of the Arts, Sciences
                and Professions, at the Waldorf-Astoria Hotel,
                New York

8 June   named, with Pearl Buck, Charlie Chaplin, Le-
                na Horne, Hammett, Katharine Hepburn, Danny
                Kaye, Dorothy Parker among others, by Sena-
                tor Jack B. Tenney as "having followed or ap-
                peased some of the Communist party-line pro-
                grams"

October   Another Part of the Forest done by the Moscow
                Drama Theatre under the title Ladies and Gen-
                tlemen

29 October   Montserrat, adapted from the French play by
                Emmanuel Roblès, directed by Lillian Hellman
                and then by Harold Clurman, opened at the
                Fulton Theatre for 65 performances; received
                the Vernon Rice Award for direction

31 October   Regina, the musical version of The Little
                Little Foxes, with the libretto and music of
                Marc Blitzstein, directed by Robert Lewis,
                opened at the Forty-Sixth Street Theatre for
                56 performances

1950   visited a month in New Orleans with aunts

April   began writing first attempt at The Autumn
                Garden; abandoned first version after Hammett's

criticism; went to New York to start what became the final version of her favorite play

1951
7 March   The Autumn Garden, "For Dash, " directed by
                 Harold Clurman, opened at the Coronet Thea-
                 tre for 102 performances

April   Federal Judge Sylvester Ryan held Hammett
                 in contempt of court and sentenced him to six
                 months in jail (Hammett had refused to name
                 the persons who had contributed to the bail-
                 bond fund of the Civil Rights Congress); went
                 to Europe while Hammett was in jail

19 September   screenwriter Martin Berkeley testified before
                 HUAC

1952
May   Montserrat opened in London after playing in
                 Hammersmith; subpoened to appear before
                 HUAC

19 May   sent letter to Committee Chairman John S.
                 Wood stating the conditions under which she
                 would testify and not take the Fifth

20 May   reply from Representative Wood telling her
                 the "Committee cannot permit witnesses to
                 set forth the terms under which they will tes-
                 tify. "

21 May   Lillian Hellman and her counsel Joseph L.
                 Rauh, Jr. met with subcommittee, Represen-
                 tatives John S. Wood and Francis E. Walter
                 and their counsel, Frank S. Tavenner, Jr.,
                 in Room 226 of the Old House Office Building,
                 Washington, D. C., ; dismissed without charges;
                 sold Hardscrabble Farm; was persuaded by
                 Kermit Bloomgarden to revive The Children's
                 Hour; blacklisted by Hollywood

18 December   The Children's Hour, directed by Lillian Hell-
                 man, re-opened on Broadway at the Coronet
                 Theatre for 189 performances

1953
26 March   Hammett appeared before the Permanent Sub-

committee on Investigations of the Committee on Government Operations (before Senators Joseph R. McCarthy and John L. McClennan, and Roy Cohn and David Schine; Senators Dirksen, Mundt, Potter, and Symington were absent); Louis Kronenberger invited her to edit the Chekhov letters; went to Rome to do a movie for Alexander Korda, but the plans did not materialize; met Theodore Roethke in Rome; Hammett returned to teaching at the Jefferson School

1954
spring   finished work on the Chekhov letters; advance selection published in July Partisan Review; Kermit Bloomgarden asked her to adapt Jean Anouilh's L'Alouette for Broadway

May   went to London to see Christopher Fry's adaptation of L'Alouette, directed by Peter Brook

1955   Farrar, Straus and Company published The Selected Letters of Anton Chekhov, edited by and with an introduction by Lillian Hellman, translated by Sidonie K. Lederer; bought house at Vineyard Haven, Martha's Vineyard

17 November The Lark, adapted from the French play by Jean Anouilh, directed by Joseph Anthony, opened at the Longacre Theatre for 229 performances

1956
1 December Candide, A Comic Operetta Based Upon Voltaire's Satire, adapted by Lillian Hellman into a libretto for the score by and with Leonard Bernstein, Richard Wilbur, John Latouche, and Dorothy Parker, directed by Tyrone Guthrie, opened at the Martin Beck Theatre for 73 performances

1957
2 February Candide closed; began work on Toys in the Attic

fall   went abroad; visited London and Paris; Autumn Garden produced for MHAT'S 1957-58 season, Moscow

1958
February   returned to New York

May   lectured at the University of Chicago

June   completed full first draft of Toys in the Attic

1959
30 April   Candide produced in London

December   Kermit Bloomgarden, Howard Bay, and Arthur
                     Penn began preparing Toys in the Attic for
                     production

1960
25 February   Toys in the Attic, dedicated to Richard Wilbur,
                     directed by Arthur Penn, opened at the Hud-
                     son Theatre for 556 performances

May   elected to American Academy of Arts and
                     Sciences

19 May   received New York Drama Critics' Circle
                     Award for Toys in the Attic; went to England
                     to supervise the London production of Toys
                     in the Attic, which opened in November

1961
1 January   Hammett hospitalized

10 January   Dashiell Hammett died, Lenox Hill Hospital;
                     ("my closest, my most beloved friend")

12 January   memorial service for Hammett (Quentin Rey-
                     nolds, Bennett Cerf, Dorothy Parker, Leonard
                     Bernstein, Arthur Kober, Louis Kronenberger,
                     Patricia Neal, Diana and Lionel Trilling, Phil-
                     ip Rahv, Richard Maney were among those
                     present.)

13 January   Lillian Hellman, Kermit Bloomgarden, and
                     Howard Bay accompanied Hammett to Wash-
                     ington for interment in Arlington National
                     Cemetery

spring   visiting lecturer in English at Harvard, where
                     she became fascinated by Burt Blechman's

novel <u>How Much?</u>; lived with her friend and cook Helen Jackson at Leverett Towers

April   received the women's division of Albert Einstein College of Medicine of Yeshiva University Achievement Award. *

4 June   awarded honorary Litt. D. by Wheaton College (Norton, Massachusetts): "Because you are a penetrating observer of human behavior as well as a superb architect of dramatic structure, your plays for over twenty-five years have continued to delight us with their skillful teaching. Deeply concerned with the problems of justice and injustice, with good and evil-- the problems which are the source of all enduring literature--you have always had something valuable to say and have said it well, speaking freely through the exacting demands of realistic drama. Not only have you dramatized great issues but you have also found material in the quiet dilemmas from which no man is free. Your concern for truth, your gifts for characterization and for craftsmanship, place you among the most distinguished playwrights of our time. "

10 June awarded the Brandeis University Creative Arts Medal in Theatre for Distinguished Contribution to the American Theatre, presented by Leonard Bernstein: (to) "Lillian Hellman, playwright, who has added depth and luster to the American Theatre; whose incisive portrayals of character demonstrate true understanding of human strengths and frailties; who from her first play <u>The Children's Hour</u> has been a dominant figure in the contemporary theatre world; hailed by critics, respected by actors, and beloved by audiences; her reputation will endure so long as the theatre remains a mirror of our culture"; Theodore Roethke's book of children's poems <u>I Am! Says the Lamb</u> dedicated to Lillian Hellman

---

* The files "on the event" were "totally inaccessible, " so the citation is not included.

__1962__
13 February   elected vice-president of the National Institute
                  of Arts and Letters

14 March   film version of The Children's Hour, written
                  chiefly by John Michael Hayes, directed by
                  William Wyler, opened in New York, re-filmed
                  under the title The Loudest Whisper

summer   built new and smaller house on Martha's
                  Vineyard

5 December   elected to American Academy of Arts and
                  Letters to replace Robinson Jeffers; Simone
                  Signoret's adaptation of The Little Foxes open-
                  ed at Sarah Bernhardt Theater, Paris

__1963__
21 March   My Mother, My Father and Me, based upon
                  the novel How Much? by Burt Blechman, dedi-
                  cated to Blair, directed by Gower Champion
                  and then by Arthur Penn, opened at the Ply-
                  mouth Theatre for 17 performances

22 May   inducted as member of the American Academy
                  of Arts and Letters

5 June   awarded honorary Litt. D. by Douglass College,
                  the women's division of Rutgers--The State
                  University (New Brunswick, New Jersey):
                  "As the watchman, as the searching wind, as
                  the guardian of our most precious fruits of
                  humanity and liberty, you have spoken drama-
                  tically and commanded us to be your attentive
                  and applauding audience. "

31 July   film Toys in the Attic released

summer   attended the Edinburgh Festival and the concur-
                  rent sessions of the International Drama Con-
                  ference

August   went to Washington to cover the Civil Rights
                  March; talked with Bayard Rustin and heard
                  Martin Luther King

__1964__   went to Israel to cover Pope Paul's visit

19 April   narrator for the Marc Blitzstein Memorial
                  Concert in New York

20 May   awarded the National Institute of Arts and
                  Letters Gold Medal for Drama for extraordi-
                  nary distinction in the arts (given only every
                  five years) presented by Louis Kronenberger:
                  "One thinks, happily, of many reasons for the
                  Institute to bestow its highest honor on Lillian
                  Hellman.   Conceivably the least of these is
                  not altogether the least interesting--that she
                  is the most distinguished woman playwright of
                  our time.   That, in a way, only makes more
                  notable an almost opposite form of homage--
                  that she is one of the most powerful play-
                  wrights of our time, the vigor of whose con-
                  ceptions, the brilliance of whose characteriza-
                  tions, the trenchancy of whose writing have
                  left a vivid imprint on the theatre.   Miss
                  Hellman's success, in the 1930's, with her
                  first play, The Children's Hour, was both
                  immediate and authoritative.   Indeed, no play-
                  wright of our time has struck more ringing
                  opening chords.   Miss Hellman's eminent
                  career since then is not least impressive for
                  the range of her work.   A play like The Au-
                  tumn Garden might indeed be called a rever-
                  sal of her method.   For here a playwright
                  celebrated for portraying psychological tensions
                  and for coming to grips with social forces
                  has written, with great understanding, of
                  rather lost and unfulfilled human beings.
                  Again, amid much range of mood in Lillian
                  Hellman's work, we must not lose sight of
                  her humor, which, it it can be harsh and
                  sardonic, can also be gay and delightfully
                  sassy...."

1965   Sam Spiegel invited her to adapt Horton Foote's
                  novel The Chase

13 June   awarded honorary Doctor of Humane Letters
                  by Brandeis University: "Playwright of the
                  dark forest of human emotions, twice receiv-
                  ing the New York Drama Critics' Circle Award
                  for works of caustic power and searing cathar-
                  sis; editor of Chekhov's letters; author and
                  adapter of notable motion picture scripts.

From The Children's Hour through Toys in
the Attic, she anatomizes evil at its heart
and excises the pathology of sins against
the spirit.   Yet her memorable Watch on the
Rhine acclaims and celebrates singular courage.
Her impeccable discernment identifies every
production, bearing out Edward Fitzgerald's
observation that 'Taste is the feminine of ge-
nius' "; worked on memoirs An Unfinished
Woman

7 December   joined in letter (with Edward Albee, Hannah
                  Arendt, Reinhold Niebuhr, Michael Harrington,
                  Lewis Mumford, William Styron) to Premier
                  Aleksei N. Kosygin protesting arrest of Soviet
                  writers

1966
February   conducted a seminar in literature and writing
                  for group of Yale freshmen at the invitation
                  of John Hersey, then Master of Pierson Col-
                  lege

18 February   film The Chase opened at the Sutton and Vic-
                  toria, New York; edited a collection of Ham-
                  mett's stories for Random House: The Big
                  Knockover: Stories and Short Novels by Da-
                  shiell Hammett; visited the Soviet Union and
                  old friends; met Alexander Solzhenitsyn at the
                  apartment of Lev and Raya Leibersohn Kopelev
                  in Moscow; met and talked with Tallulah Bank-
                  head at Truman Capote's black and white ball

6 November   awarded honorary Doctor of Fine Arts at
                  Founder's Day Ceremony by Mount Holyoke
                  College   (South Hadley, Massachusetts):
                  "America's most distinguished woman play-
                  wright, you have already received Broadway's
                  highest accolades by achieving boxoffice suc-
                  cesses with your plays with remarkable and
                  enviable regularity.   What makes yours the
                  greater triumph is that you do not write to
                  entertain a jaded audience.   To the contrary,
                  your powerful characterizations present human
                  weakness and human strength in great variety
                  and the dramatic conflicts which these plays
                  depict are an unflinching and disquieting exam-
                  ination of our public and private morality. "

1967
April-May   visited France and Budapest; attended reception
                     for President of PEN in Budapest; saw acquain-
                     tances of Edmund Wilson

May   visited the Soviet Union; housed in Pekin Hotel
                     in Moscow; visited the poet Olga Bergholz
                     and then Leningrad with Raya Kopelev

22 May   attended the opening session of the Fourth
                     National Congress of the Union of Writers as
                     their guest; left the same day to return to
                     New York to work with Mike Nichols casting
                     The Little Foxes

7 June   Dorothy Parker died

9 June   memorial service held for Dorothy Parker;
                     Zero Mostel gave opening tribute, and Lillian
                     Hellman spoke

23 September   CBS showed old MGM film of The Little Foxes

October-
November   visited Moscow, stayed at National Hotel;
                     visited London and Paris

26 October   all star revival of The Little Foxes, directed
                     by Mike Nichols, opened at the Vivian Beau-
                     mont Theatre at Lincoln Center for 60 per-
                     formances before moving on to the Ethel Barry-
                     more Theatre for 40 additional performances

1968   invited to give seminar at Harvard by Reuben
spring   Brower, Master of Adams House; shared time
                     with M. I. T. students

                     received first Jackson Award of Distinction of
11 April   Jackson College, the women's division of Tufts
                     University, for "significant contributions to
                     her field" and cited as "one of the finest
                     craftsmen of the American theater" by Elliot
                     Norton who presented the Award; Jackson Col-
                     lege students endowed a Chair in Lillian Hell-
                     man's name at the Elma Lewis School of Fine
                     Arts in Roxbury, Mass.; appeared with Eugene
                     McCarthy at his Madison Square Garden Rally

summer   completed final revision of An Unfinished Wo-
                    man at the Vineyard

1-5 December   joined "100 Notables" (including John Galbraith,
                    Elizabeth Hardwick, Andreas Papandreou, Henry
                    Kissinger, George Kennan, Arthur Schlessinger,
                    Jr., Jean Jacques Servan-Schreiber) for a
                    seminar at Princeton, sponsored by the Insti-
                    tue for Advanced Study and the Paris-based
                    International Association for Cultural Freedom
                    for Intellectuals to share their views on "The
                    United States, Its Problems, Impact and Image
                    in the World"

1969
26 June   Little, Brown published An Unfinished Woman
                    and launched it at dinner at the Four Seasons,
                    New York; Helen Jackson died

1970
4 March   awarded National Book Award for An Unfinished
                    Woman at Carnegie Hall

April   appeared on panel with Professor John Fair-
                    banks of Harvard at the Association for Asian
                    Studies, San Francisco

spring   Regents Professor, University of California,
                    Berkeley; founded Committee for Public Justice;
                    sold house on 82nd Street and moved into Park
                    Avenue apartment

1971
February   taught month's writing seminar at University
                    of California, Berkeley

spring   taught for month at M. I. T.

1972   Little, Brown published The Collected Plays

15 June   attended Edmund Wilson's funeral on Cape Cod

26 September   named Distinguished Professor, Hunter College
                    (New York); Richard Moody's Lillian Hellman,
                    Playwright, the first critical biography, was
                    published

<u>1973</u>	Little, Brown published <u>Pentimento, A Book of Portraits</u>
19 November	named to Theater Hall of Fame
7 December	honored by first Woman of the Year Award by New York University Alumnae Club
<u>1974</u>	awarded honorary Doctor of Letters by Smith College with the citation: "The temptation to dwell on the paradoxes in your life and achievement is irresistible, especially since you have exposed so much of it yourself in your two unforgettable volumes of autobiography. You describe yourself as a stranger in the world of theatre yet <u>The Little Foxes</u> (1939), The <u>Children's Hour</u> (1934), and the <u>Watch on the Rhine</u> (1944) demonstrate a sense of craft that amounts to genius. You hold causes in suspicion lest they become diversionary; yet no stronger voice than yours has ever been raised against Fascism, the black comedy of the McCarthy period, or the frightening horror of Watergate and after. Neither sentimental nor romantic but realistic to the end you see, in your words, 'the world divided into those who get so much for giving nothing and those who get nothing and give so much.' You once thought you would like to attend Smith and it is an honor and a privilege now for this College to make you one ot its own"; awarded honorary Doctor of Letters by Yale University: "All who care about dramatic and literary quality will long honor your artistry as a writer. Generations will find their spines a little stiffer, their courage stouter, because of your defense of freedom and character against the harassment of coercive philistines. Everyone who has felt your influence is held to a higher honesty. For your integrity, your candor, your literary perception of the glories and foibles of humanity, Yale takes delight in conferring upon you the degree of Doctor of Letters"; named Lucy Martin Donnelly Fellow in Creative Writing at Bryn Mawr
29 October	spoke at Bryn Mawr College

11 November   spoke at Smithsonian's Baird Auditorium

1975   joined the editorial board of The American
                  Scholar, through April 1978

13 November   lectured at Boston College; honored at Circle
                  in the Square celebration to benefit the Com-
                  mittee for Public Justice "for her contribution
                  to the theater, to literature and to the pro-
                  tection of civil liberties."

1976   Little, Brown published Scoundrel Time, with
                  an introduction by Garry Wills

                  The Autumn Garden revived at Long Wharf
                  Theater, New Haven

12 May   awarded honorary Doctor of Letters by Colum-
                  bia University: "Illustrious woman of letters,
                  born in New Orleans, educated at New York
                  and Columbia Universities, you endowed the
                  American theatre of the 1930's and 1940's
                  with a civilized conscience. Whether depicting
                  the devastating effects of slander in The Child-
                  ren's Hour, the rapacity of economic predators
                  in The Little Foxes or the quiet resolution of
                  an anti-fascist underground in Watch on the
                  Rhine, you repeatedly dramatized decency de-
                  fending itself against the ruthless and the heart-
                  less. When civil liberties and freedom of in-
                  quiry were attacked in the 1950's, you followed
                  in your own life the remarkable example set
                  in your plays.
                      During the last decade you have extended
                  your influence through sensitive, candid, finely
                  written memoirs. You have set a very high
                  standard, by living in pursuit of civil liberties
                  instead of simply extolling them in your writing.
                  For your unselfish and courageous literary and
                  personal achievements...."

26 May   addressed luncheon meeting of the Council of
                  New York Law Associates at the Association
                  of the Bar of the City of New York

30 May   Commencement speaker, Mount Holyoke College

15 August   received the Edward MacDowell Medal for
                 contribution to literature

8 October   received Actors' Equity Association third annu-
                 al Paul Robeson Award

1977
2 October   film Julia, for which she had declined to do
                 the filmscript, opened at Cinema 1 (New York)

10 November   received the Lord and Taylor Award

1978
April   participated in the Rutgers' Conference on
                 "Women and the Arts in the 1920's in Paris
                 and New York"

August   attended Leonard Bernstein's Sixtieth Birthday
                 Party celebration; consultant for the authorized
                 biography of Dashiell Hammett being written
                 by Diane Johnson for Random House.

A

PLAYS AND ADAPTATIONS

Arranged Chronologically
by Production Date

A1   THE CHILDREN'S HOUR   1934
Lillian Hellman, The Children's Hour.   New York: Alfred
A. Knopf.   115 p.   19½ cm.

A2   DAYS TO COME   1936
Days to Come, by Lillian Hellman.   New York: Alfred A.
Knopf.   105 p.   19½ cm.

A3   THE LITTLE FOXES   1939
The Little Foxes, A play in three acts by Lillian Hellman.
New York: Random House.   159 p.   21½ cm.

A4   WATCH ON THE RHINE   1941
Watch on the Rhine, A play in three acts by Lillian Hellman.
New York: Random House.   170 p.   illus.   21 cm.

Note: A limited edition of 349 numbered copies was published
in cooperation with Random House by the Joint Anti-Fascist
Committee, August 3, 1942.   Copies #1-50 were leather
bound.   The illustrations were by Rockwell Kent, Hans Muel-
ler, Philip Reisman, Benjamin Kopman, Donald Gelb, William Gropper, Lawrence Beall Smith, Don Freeman, William
Sharp, Luis Quintanilla, Fritz Eichenberg.

Watch on the Rhine, A play in three acts by Lillian Hellman,
with a special forward by Dorothy Parker.   New York: Privately published.   175 p.   plates   31 cm.

A5   THE SEARCHING WIND   1944
The Searching Wind, A Play in Two Acts by Lillian Hellman.
New York: The Viking Press.   96 p.   21 cm.

A6   ANOTHER PART OF THE FOREST   1947
Another Part of the Forest, A Play in Three Acts by Lillian
Hellman.   New York: The Viking Press.   134 p.   illus.
19½ cm.

A7   MONTSERRAT   1949
Montserrat, Play in Two Acts.   An adaptation by Lillian
Hellman, From the French play by Emmanuel Roblès.   New
York: Dramatists Play Service, Inc.   76 p.   illus.   19 cm.

A8   THE AUTUMN GARDEN   1951
The Autumn Garden, A Play in Three Acts by Lillian Hellman.   Boston: Little, Brown and Company.   139 p.   20 cm.

A9   THE LARK   1956

The Lark, by Jean Anouilh, Adapted by Lillian Hellman.
New York: Random House. 144 p.   illus.   21 cm.

A10   CANDIDE   1957
Candide, A Comic Operetta Based on Voltaire's Satire.   Book
by Lillian Hellman, Score by Leonard Bernstein, Lyrics by
Richard Wilbur, Other lyrics by John Latouche and Dorothy
Parker.   New York: Random House.   143 p.   illus.   21 cm.

A11   TOYS IN THE ATTIC   1960
Toys in the Attic, A new play by Lillian Hellman.   New
York: Random House.   116 p.   illus.   21 cm.

A12   MY MOTHER, MY FATHER AND ME   1963
My Mother, My Father and Me by Lillian Hellman.   Based
on Burt Blechman's novel How Much?   New York: Random
House.   98 p.   illus.   22 cm.

A13   THE COLLECTED PLAYS   1972
The Collected Plays, Lillian Hellman.   Boston-Toronto: Little,   Brown and Company.   815 p.   25 cm.

Note: Two earlier editions of Miss Hellman's plays were
published with an introduction by her in which she comments
on her approach to re-examining the plays, the themes of,
the shortcomings of the plays, on melodrama, and on herself
as a "moral writer."   This preface was not included in The
Collected Plays, which the publisher notes: "brings together
for the first time all of Lillian Hellman's work for the theatre, and supersedes any previous collections and editions.
For this edition Miss Hellman has made numerous small revisions and emendations in each of the plays: the texts as
given here are henceforth to be regarded as definitive."
          Because of Miss Hellman's introduction, these earlier
editions are noteworthy, however:

Four Plays by Lillian Hellman.   1942
(The Children's Hour, Days to Come, The Little Foxes,
Watch on the Rhine) With an introduction by the author.
New York: Random House.   intro. vii-xiv; 330 p.   21 cm.

Six Plays By Lillian Hellman   1960
(The Children's Hour, Days to Come, The Little Foxes,
Watch on the Rhine, Another Part of the Forest, The Au-
tumn Garden) with an introduction by the author.   New York:
The Modern Library.   intro. vii-xiv; 546 p.   19 cm.

See also: F94.

B

SCREENPLAYS BY LILLIAN HELLMAN, BY LILLIAN HELLMAN
WITH ANOTHER AUTHOR, AND BASED ON HER WORKS

Arranged Chronologically by Release Date

B1   THE DARK ANGEL   1935
The Dark Angel, written with Mordaunt Shairp, founded on
play by G. Bolton, directed by George Fitzmaurice for United Artists.

B2   THESE THREE   1936
These Three, an adaptation of The Children's Hour for William Wyler's direction for Goldwyn-United Artists.

A shooting script of this is in the Harvard Theatre Collection,
Harvard College Library.   A filmscript is at the University of
Texas, Austin, as well as earlier stages of the final version.

B3   DEAD END   1937
Dead End, written by Lillian Hellman, based on the Sidney
Kingsley play, directed by William Wyler for Samuel Gold-
wyn and United Artists.

A shooting script of this is in the Harvard Theatre Collection,
Harvard College Library.

B4   THE SPANISH EARTH   1937
The Spanish Earth: The story for this documentary was written by Archibald MacLeish and Lillian Hellman; Ernest Hemingway wrote the spoken commentary for Joris Ivens who was
to direct the film.   Issued by Prometheus Pictures.

B5   THE LITTLE FOXES   1941
The Little Foxes, an adaptation of the play, directed by William Wyler for Goldwyn and RKO.

A motion picture script is at the University of Texas, Austin.

B6   WATCH ON THE RHINE   1943
Watch on the Rhine, an adaptation of the play, directed by
Herman Shumlin for Warner Brothers.   The screenplay was
written by Dashiell Hammett, with additional scenes and dialogue by Lillian Hellman.

Manuscripts and motion picture scripts are in the University
of Texas Hellman Collection, including the screenplay with
Hellman's name crossed out and Hammett's name pencilled
in.   Movie pressbook for the film starring Bette Davis and
Paul Lukas is in the Lilly Library, Indiana University.

B7   THE NORTH STAR   1943
The North Star, written by Lillian Hellman, directed by Lewis
Milestone for Crescent-RKO.

A typescript of this is in the University of Toledo Library.
Movie pressbook for the film starring Dana Andrews and Anne
Baxter is at the Lilly Library, Indiana University.

The "master script" was published:
The North Star, A Motion Picture About Some Russian People.
New York: The Viking Press, 1943.   118 p.   21 cm.

This edition contains an introduction by Louis Kronenberger
in which he comments on the merits of the filmscript, the
adjustments a reader must make in reading a moviescript,
Miss Hellman's sharpness and clarity of description, the dy-
namic narrative, and the telling economy of her script and
her command of highly expressive detail.   The author's note
identifies the text as a master script and defines the technical terms used in the script that a reader might not be familiar with.

B8   THE NEGRO SOLDIER   1944
The Negro Soldier in World War II is an unpublished script,
but the Lillian Hellman story for the Stuart Heisler documentary is in the Stuart Heisler Papers in the library of the University of California, Los Angeles.

B9   THE SEARCHING WIND   1946
The Searching Wind, an adaptation of the play, directed by
William Dierle for Hal Wallis Productions-Paramount Pic-
tures.

Motion picture scripts are at the University of Texas.

B10   ANOTHER PART OF THE FOREST   1948
Another Part of the Forest, adapted chiefly by Vladimir Pos-
ner, directed by Michael Gordon, for Universal Motion Pictures.

B11   THE CHILDREN'S HOUR   1961
      re-released as THE LOUDEST WHISPER   1962
The Children's Hour, adapted by Lillian Hellman, written
chiefly by John Michael Hayes, directed by William Wyler for
United Artists.

Mimeographed filmscripts, "Cutting Continuity" and "Dialogue
Continuity, " are in the Lilly Library, Indiana University. A
first draft of Hayes' script with Lillian Hellman's emendations
and notes is at the University of Texas.

B12   TOYS IN THE ATTIC   1963

Toys in the Attic, an adaptation of the play, directed by George Roy Hill for United Artists.

Mimeographed filmscript, "Dialogue Continuity, " is in the Lilly Library, Indiana University.

B13 THE CHASE   1966
The Chase, an adaptation of Horton Foote's novel and play, directed by Arthur Penn for United Artists.

Various drafts and scripts with revisions and notes are held in the Hellman Collection at the University of Texas, Austin.

B14 JULIA   1976
Julia, screenplay by Alvin Sargent, directed by Fred Zinne-mann for Twentieth Century Fox.

C

BOOKS BY OR EDITED BY LILLIAN HELLMAN

Arranged Chronologically

C1 THE SELECTED LETTERS OF ANTON CHEKHOV 1955
The Selected Letters of Anton Chekhov, Edited by Lillian Hellman, Translated by Sidonie K. Lederer. (with an introduction by Lillian Hellman) New York: Farrar, Straus and Company. intro. ix-xxvii; 331 p. 22cm.

Biographical notes and a translator's note are also included.
The letters are divided into three periods: 1885-1890, 1890-
1897, 1897-1904. A group of 10 letters from The Selected
Letters was published in the July 1954 issue of Partisan Review.

C2 THE BIG KNOCKOVER 1966
The Big Knockover: Selected Stories and Short Novels of
Dashiell Hammett, Edited and with an introduction by Lillian
Hellman. New York: Random House. intro. v-xxi; 355 p.
22 cm.

Contents: "The Cutting of Couffignal, " "Fly Paper, " "The
Scorched Face, " "This Kind of Business, " "The Gatewood
Caper, " "Dead Yellow Women, " "Corkscrew, " "Tulip, " "The
Big Knockover, " "$106, 000 Blood Money. " Most of the sto-
ries originally appeared in Black Mask magazine between 1924-
29.

C3 AN UNFINISHED WOMAN 1969
An Unfinished Woman--a memoir by Lillian Hellman.
Boston-Toronto: Little, Brown and Company. 280 p. por-
traits. 25 cm.

Chapters 1-13 are headed with only the number of the chapter;
Chapter 14 carries the sub-heading "Dorothy Parker"; Chapter 15, "Helen"; Chapter 16, "Dashiell Hammett. " An illustrated excerpt "An Unfinished Woman" was published in Atlantic Monthly, April 1969. Chapter 10 was published as
"Metropole Hotel" in Partisan Review, 36, #2, 1969. "Dashiell Hammett" was published originally as a memoir in The
New York Review of Books, November 25, 1965, and later
as the "Introduction" to The Big Knockover.

C4 PENTIMENTO 1973
Pentimento, A Book of Portraits by Lillian Hellman.
Boston-Toronto: Little, Brown and Company. 297 p. 25 cm.

Contents: "Berthe, " "Willy, " "Julia, " "Theatre, " "Arthur W.
A. Cowan, " " 'Turtle, ' " "Pentimento. "

"Julia" was pre-published in Esquire, July 1973; "Theatre" appeared as "Theatre Pictures" in Esquire, August 1973. The "Arthur W. A. Cowan" piece was published under the title "A Man of Unnecessary Things" in Atlantic Monthly, June 1973. " 'Turtle' " appeared in Esquire, June 1973. An excerpt from "Pentimento" was published under the title "Death Ain't What You Think" in the London Times, April 6, 1974.

C5   SCOUNDREL TIME   1976
Scoundrel Time by Lillian Hellman, Introduction by Garry Wills.   Boston-Toronto: Little, Brown and Company.   intro. 3-34; 155 p. photographs.   24 cm.

Note: An edition was also published in England in 1976: Scoundrel Time by Lillian Hellman, Introduction by James Cameron, Commentary by Garry Wills.   London: The Macmillan Company.   intro. 13-21; text 25-143; commentary 147-172; 172 p. photographs.   23 cm.

D

CONTRIBUTIONS TO NEWSPAPERS AND PERIODICALS

Arranged Chronologically

D1 "Fictionalized Science for Lay Readers." New York
    Herald Tribune Books, Sept. 26, 1926, p. 21.
    A review of Our Doctors by Maurice Duplay.

D2 "A Strange Power." New York Herald Tribune Books,
    Sept. 26, 1926, p. 26.
    A review of The Unearthly by Robert Hickens.

D3 "Five Generations." New York Herald Tribune Books,
    Oct. 24, 1926, p. 22.
    A review of Sweepings by Lester Cohen.

D4 "Light Reading Good of Its Kind." New York Herald
    Tribune Books, Nov. 28, 1926, p. 14.
    A review of Summer Bachelors by Warner Fabian.

D5 "Futile Souls Adrift on a Yacht." New York Herald
    Tribune Books, June 19, 1927, p. 9.
    A review of Mosquitoes by William Faulkner.

D6 "Simple Worldliness." New York Herald Tribune Books,
    Oct. 23, 1927, p. 22.
    A review of This Way Up by Solita Solano.

D7 "A Moral Immorality." New York Herald Tribune Books,
    Dec. 4, 1927, p. 40.
    A review of Face Value by J. L. Campbell.

D8 "Desolation that Man Calls Peace." New York Herald
    Tribune Books, Dec. 11, 1927, p. 16.
    A review of Angel's Flight by Don Ryan.

D9 "Feminist." New York Herald Tribune Books, Feb. 24,
    1929, p. 27.
    A review of Her Son by Margaret Fuller.

D10 "Over Hurdles." New York Herald Tribune Books, June
    2, 1929, p. 12.
    A review of Labyrinth by Gertrude Diamant.

D11 "I Call Her Mama Now." American Spectator, I, 11
    (Sept., 1933), 2.
    A short story written by Lillian Hellman Kober.

D12 "Perberty in Los Angeles." American Spectator, II, 15
    (Jan., 1934), 4.
    A short story written by Lillian Hellman Kober.

D13 "The Theatre: Barchester Towers (adapted by Thomas
      Job). " Time, 30 (Dec. 13, 1937), 57.
      An unsigned review of the revival produced by Guthrie
      McClintic.

D14 "A Day in Spain. " New Republic, 94 (Apr. 13, 1938),
      297-98.
      Describes her October day in Valencia and in Madrid
      and the shelling of Madrid, with a headnote explaining
      that W. R. Hearst would not permit the article to be
      distributed to papers carrying Walter Winchell's column.
      A copy of this appears in Curt Riess, ed. , They Were
      There: The Story of World War II and How It Came
      About (Garden City, New York: Garden City Publishing
      Company, Inc. , 1944).

D15 "Back of Those Foxes. " New York Times, Feb. 26,
      1939, 9, pp. 1, 2.
      Tells of when she first thought of doing the play, of
      how she feels now that it is on stage, of melodrama,
      of Hammett and Shumlin's first reactions.

D16 "Valley Town: A New Documentary About Labor's Old-
      est Lament. " PM, June 14, 1940, the preview edition,
      p. 14. illus.
      In "History of PM" (PM, Aug. 16, 1946, p. 3C), the
      author of the supplement--probably Ralph Ingersoll--
      claims that LH did a movie review for the first edition
      of the paper for which she had suggested the name.
      Since the review in the first issue is signed by another,
      it is presumed that the one LH did is this unsigned
      commentary for Valley Town that appeared in the pre-
      view edition.

D17 "The Little Men of Philadelphia. " PM (New York),
      June 25, 1940, p. 6.
      An article about her grief that the workingmen she in-
      terviewed would not speak freely about politics because
      they were too tired and frightened.

D18 "They Fought for Spain: Lion Feuchtwanger and Lillian
      Hellman Ask Your Aid for the Real Defenders of Demo-
      cracy. " New Masses, 37 (Dec. 10, 1940), 11.
      Appeals for funds and gives the background of the Span-
      ish Civil War. "We, the ordinary people of America,
      must save these extraordinary ordinary people. "

D19 "Preface and Postscript: Miss Hellman Casts a Glance
Backward to Four of Her Plays. " New York Times,
Feb. 22, 1942, 8, pp. 1, 3.
From the preface to Four Plays published by Random
House (A13).

D20 "I Meet the Front Line Russians. " Collier's, 115
(Mar. 31, 1945), 11, 68-71.
An account of her trip to the Russian Front.

D21 "Author Jabs the Critic. " New York Times, Dec. 15,
1946, 2, pp. 3, 4.
An article/letter in response to the frowns of the New
York Times' drama critic Brooks Atkinson.

D22 "The Judas Goats. " The Screen Writer, 3 (Dec. , 1947),
7.
An editorial in the Screen Writers' Guild magazine stating strong opposition to the HUAC activities.   It is reprinted in Stefan Kanfer's A Journal of the Plague Years
(F106).

D23 "One Good Exception. " New York Star, July 1, 1948,
p. 19.
This is a letter signed LH and is presumed to be by
Lillian Hellman, not by Leicester Hemingway who wrote
for PM.   The letter asks why "they" did not "face facts
and honestly come out for Wallace, the only real liberal. "

D24 "Reports on Yugoslavia. " New York Star (successor to
PM), Nov. 4, 1948, p. 13; Nov. 5, p. 9; Nov. 7, p. 8;
Nov. 8, pp. 1, 9; Nov. 9, p. 6: Nov. 10, p. 11.
Six reports of her interview with Tito, her trip and at-
tempt to understand the people, and on Czechoslovakia.

D25 "Anton Chekhov, Letters about Writers and Writing. "
Partisan Review, 21 (July, 1954), 371-86.
A pre-publication of 10 letters to Gorki, Suvorin, Ples-
chcheyev, Menshikov, Shavrova, Leontief from The Selected Letters of Anton Chekhov (C1).

D26 "Scotch on the Rocks. " The New York Review of Books,
1 (Oct. 17, 1963), 6.
An account of the 1963 International Drama Conference
in Edinburgh. See also: "The Beautiful City of Edinburgh"
(E3).

D27 "Sophronia's Grandson Goes to Washington. " <u>Ladies'</u>
<u>Home Journal</u>, 80 (Dec., 1963), 78-80, 82; 81 (Mar.,
1964), 82.
Writes of the March on Washington, of her interview
with Bayard Rustin who engineered the March, and of
her walk through the crowd gathered to hear Dr. King
in search of Sophronia's grandson to whom she had sent
money to go to Washington from Alabama.

D28 "Marc Blitzstein Remembered. " <u>New York Times</u>, Feb.
2, 1964, 2, p. 3.

D29 "Lillian Hellman Makes the Following Statement. <u>Ladies'</u>
<u>Home Journal</u>, 81 (Mar., 1964), 82.
A refusal of Mr. McCord's request for a retraction of
portions of "Sophronia's Grandson Goes to Washington"
(G124).

D30 "Land that Holds the Legend of Our Lives. " <u>Ladies'</u>
<u>Home Journal</u>, 81 (Apr., 1964), 56-57+, 122-24. illus.
Writes of the difficulties getting into Jordan to cover
Pope Paul's visit, of her visits to the holy places, of
her own first religious experience as a child, focuses
on the lives of the religious on the periphery of it all.
<u>See also</u>: E4.

D31 "Lillian Hellman Asks a Little Respect for Her Agony,
An Eminent Playwright Hallucinates after a Fall Brought
on by a Current Dramatic Hit. " <u>Show</u>, LV (May, 1964),
12-13.
Parodies Arthur Miller and <u>After the Fall</u> because he
dropped the fictional shield to write about Marilyn Mon-
roe and himself.

D32 "Dashiell Hammett, a Memoir. " <u>The New York Review</u>
<u>of Books</u>, 5 (Nov. 25, 1965), 16-23.
<u>See</u>: C3 and G16.

D33 "Dear Mr. Kosygin. " <u>New Republic</u>, 154 (Jan. 1, 1966),
36+.
A letter written with Edward Albee, W. H. Auden, Hannah Arendt, Robert Lowell, John Hersey, Lionel Trilling,
Philip Roth, Robert Penn Warren and others asking Kosygin to review the case of Andrei Sinyavsky and Yuli Daniel awaiting trial for having published abroad.

D34 "The Time of the <u>Foxes</u>. " <u>New York Times</u>, Oct. 22,

1967, 2, p. 1. illus.
Talks of the opening in Baltimore and of the 1967 revival of The Little Foxes. See: D15.

D35 "Interlude in Budapest. " Holiday, 42 (Nov., 1967), 60-
61.
Impressions of her 1966 trip and of the Hungarians, of
the young and the old.

D36 "An Unfinished Woman. " Atlantic Monthly, 223 (Apr.,
1969), 90-122+. illus.
An excerpt from the book. See: C3.

D37 "Metropole Hotel. " Partisan Review, 36, 2 (1969), 179-
88.
From her Moscow 1944 diary. See also: C3.

D38 "The Baggage of a Political Exile. " New York Times,
Aug. 23, 1969, p. 26.
Protests the easy acceptance of any political refugee,
such as Soviet novelist Anatoly V. Kuznetsov, who saved
only himslef and did not speak out. See: G58.

D39 "Living with Dash. " Observer (London), Oct. 12, 1969,
p. 29.
An excerpt from Unfinished Woman with photos of both.

D40 "My Friend Dottie. " Observer (London), Oct. 19, 1969,
p. 29.
An excerpt from Unfinished Woman with photos of Alan
Campbell, Dorothy Parker, LH, and Hammett.

D41 "And Now--An Evening with Nichols and Hellman. "
New York Times, Aug. 9, 1970, p. 9.
A conversation between the two on art, work, Catch-22.

D42 "Visas for the Treppers. " New York Times, Jan. 13,
1972, p. 40.
A letter signed by LH, John Hersey, E. Y. Harburg,
Hiram Haydn, Millen Brand, Frederic Ewen, Yuri Suhl
appealing that the Polish authorities permit the Leopold
Treppers to go to Israel for the remainder of their lives.

D43 "Baby-Cries. " New York Times, Jan. 21, 1973, 2,
p. 18.
A letter praising Barbara Harris' courtesy and restraint
after leaving Arthur Miller's play.

D44 "A Man of Unnecessary Things. " Atlantic Monthly, 231
(June, 1973), 56-62, 64-68.
See: C4.

D45 "Turtle. " Esquire, 79 (June, 1973), 146-48, 232-34.
A remembrance of Dashiell Hammett. See: C4.

D46 "Julia. " Esquire, 80 (July, 1973), 95-101, 144+. illus.
See: C4.

D47 "Theatre Pictures. " Esquire, 80 (Aug. , 1973), 64-68,
142+. illus.
Excerpts from a theatrical journal. See: C4.

D47a "Martinique, Pearl of the Antilles. " Travel and
Leisure, 4 (Jan. , 1974), 27-28, 47-48. photographs
by Slim Aarons.
A personal essay of her remembrances of Martinique,
with historical background and commentary on the people.

D48 "Death Ain't What You Think. " Times (London), Apr.
6, 1974, p. 9. illus.
An excerpt about Helen and Jimsie from Pentimento
(C4).

D49 "H. G. Wells and Rebecca West. " New York Times,
Oct. 13, 1974, 7, pp. 4-5. illus.
A review of Gordon N. Ray's book of the same name.
See also: G86 and G172.

D50 "Wells and West. " New York Times, Nov. 17, 1974,
7, p. 56.
A letter in reply to Frederick Hilles and Christina Robb
(G86 and G172).

D51 "A Scene from an Unfinished Play; Text. " New Republic, 171 (Nov. 30, 1974), 35-39.
Dr. Campion returns from Africa to sort his papers.

D52 "On Jumping into Life. " Mademoiselle, 81 (Aug. , 1975),
166-67.
A re-print of the commencement address LH gave at
Barnard, May 14, 1975.

D53 "For Truth, Justice and the American Way. " New York
Times, June 4, 1975, p. 39.
The text of the commencement address at Barnard.
See also: G103.

D54 "On Truth, Justice and the American Way. " Encore,
     4 (Sept. 8, 1975), 6.

D55 "On Henry Wallace. " New York Times, Apr. 11, 1976,
     7, pp. 27-28. illus.

D56 "Plain Speaking with Mrs. Carter. " Rolling Stone, Nov.
     18, 1976, pp. 43-45.   illus.

D57 "Forward" to To Be Preserved Forever, by Lev Kope-
     lev.   (Philadelphia: J. B. Lippincott Company, 1977)
     Notes on her friendship with Raya and Lev Kopelev; tells
     of her intention to show respect for Lev by writing the
     forward.

E

MISCELLANEA

Unpublished Works of Lillian Hellman

Index of Letters and Manuscripts held in
Special Collections

Recordings

Unpublished Works by Lillian Hellman

E1   Dear Queen, an unproduced play written with Louis
      Kronenberger, copyrighted in 1932.

E2   "Richard Harding Davis, 1938, " a short story.   A manu-
      script is in the Kriendler Collection at Rutgers Univer-
      sity; a xerox copy of the story is in the Hellman Collec-
      tion at the University of Texas.

E3   "The Beautiful City of Edinburgh, " an account of the
      1963 Drama Conference at which a number of the atten-
      dees appeared rather foolish.   At the University of Tex-
      as.

E4   Untitled articles regarding her trip to Jordan and Israel
      are at the University of Texas.

E5   The Blessing, an adaptation of Nancy Mitford's novel.
      A "first script" is at the University of Texas.

Index of Letters and Manuscripts in Special Collections

E6   Archives of American Art in the Stephen Greene Papers,
      3 letters LH to SG (1957 and n. d.).

E7   Academy of Motion Picture Arts and Sciences, 8949
      Wilshire Boulevard, Beverly Hills, California, 90211,
      has an extensive biography file on LH which contains
      clippings and studio biographical material.

E8   Boston Public Library has notes by LH typed and signed
      to Louisa Sohier Metcalf (1945) and to Edwin O'Connor
      (1966).

E9   Boston University has notes and letters from LH to
      Mildred Buchanan Flagg (1961), Blair Fuller (1964), 2
      to Edmund Fuller (1938), 4 to Roddy McDowell (1965,
      1966), and Marjorie Osterman (1962).

E10   Columbia University has letters or notes to Donald S.
      Klopfer (1959), 2 to Max Lincoln Schuster (1951), 10 to

Leah Salisbury (1960-1970), 2 to Cass Canfield, Jr.
(1960), Erik Wensberg (1960), Berenice Hoffman (1960),
Helen (Mrs. Isidor) Schneider (n. d.), 42 to Random
House (1938-1967), Bishop Francis J. McConnell (1939),
Gladys Cooper (1939), Herman F. Reissig (1939), Mr.
and Mrs. Isidor Schneider (1941), Jaffray Cuyler (1969),
Charlotte Mayerson (1971), Francis Steegmuller (1961),
Joseph M. Fox (1961), Eric P. Swenson (1963), Bennett
A. Cerf (1964), Allan Nevins (1966), Manuel Komroff
(1969); and 2 photocopies, one signed, of LH's reminiscences of Hammett which appeared in the posthumous
publication of The Big Knockover (C2).   Corrections in
the hand of LH.   The original of this piece is in Houghton Library at Harvard.

E11   The Ford Foundation, 320 East 43rd Street, New York,
       10017, has 2 letters from LH to McGeorge Bundy (1972).

E12   Harvard Theatre Collection, Harvard College Library,
       has shooting scripts of Dead End (B3) and These Three
       (B2).

E13   Houghton Library, Harvard University, has letters to
       Alexander Woollcott (1942), Stephen M. Savage (1965),
       and Robert Lowell (1958) and a telegram to Edward
       Estlin Cummings (n. d.); and, the original typed manu-
       script, with hand written revisions, of the Hammett
       composition which was originally published in The New
       York Review of Books and later in The Big Knockover
       (C3).

E14   Diane Johnson, University of California, Department of
       English, Davis, California, 95616, has letters regarding
       Hammett from LH.

E15   The Lilly Library, Indiana University, Bloomington,
       74701, in the Richard Albert Cordell Manuscripts Collec-
       tion, has 2 letters to Cordell (1946, 1957).   It also
       has mimeographed film scripts titled "Cutting Continuity"
       and "Dialogue Continuity" for The Children's Hour and
       Toys; a mimeographed playscript of The Lark and of
       My Mother, My Father and Me; a movie pressbook for
       The North Star; one of the Dorothy Parker special edi-
       tions of Watch on the Rhine (A4), and a copy of the
       special edition limited to friends of the author and of
       Little, Brown of Unfinished Woman (mention of this is
       not made in Section A because the substance of the work
       is the same; the color of the boards is different).

E16   The Milton S. Eisenhower Library of Johns Hopkins
       University has 1 letter to Professor Raymond Dexter
       Havens (1941).

E17   Library of Congress lists 40 items in the American
       Academy of Arts and Letters Library, 633 West 155th
       Street, New York, 10032. Papers of living members
       are not released without their written permission to do
       so; however, a letter to LH will be forwarded by the
       Academy. The Library of Congress, Manuscript Divi-
       sion, Washington, D. C., holds letters to Archibald
       MacLeish (1944), Solita Solano (1969, 1973), and pro-
       bably others in the many unindexed collections of papers
       of her contemporaries. It also has a typescript of
       Autumn Garden (A8).

E18   Metro-Goldwyn-Mayer, Inc., 10202 West Washington
       Blvd., Culver City, California, 90230, has some cor-
       respondence from LH in her capacity as Executrix of
       the Estate of Dashiell Hammett, but nothing else.

E19   Minnesota Historical Society, 1500 Mississippi Street,
       St. Paul, 55101, has 1 letter from LH to James Gray
       in the James Gray and Family Papers (1947).

E20   The Berg Collection of the New York Public Library,
       Fifth Avenue and 42nd Street, New York, 10018, has
       8 folders from the files of the American Play Company
       of agreements, correspondence, forms, statements from
       various theatrical agencies concerning LH and 1 folder
       referring to her translation of Montserrat (n. d.), but
       no other correspondence. It also has a mimeograph of
       Autumn Garden and of Children's Hour ("Property of
       Kermit Bloomgarden") and a carbon typescript of Regina.

E21   The Newberry Library, 60 West Walton Street, Chicago,
       60610, has 3 letters from LH to Malcolm Cowley in its
       Cowley Collection (1948, 1949, n. d.).

E22   Pack Memorial Public Library, Ashville, North Carolina,
       28801, has a note from LH to Carl Sandburg (1950).

E23   Southern Illinois University at Carbondale, Carbondale,
       92901, has 2 letters to James K. Feibleman (1949, 1955)
       and 1 letter to Mr. and Mrs. James K. (Shirley and
       Jim) Feibleman (incomplete date).

E24   Bancroft Library, University of California, Berkeley,
       94720, lists a 2 page memo to Sidney Howard (1938),
       one of her jokes, in the Sidney Coe Howard Papers.

E25   University of California, Los Angeles, 90024, holds
       LH's screenplay for The Negro Soldier in the Stuart
       Heisler papers.

E26   University of Michigan, Ann Arbor, 48109, has 6 pieces
       of correspondence from LH to Professor Roy William
       Cowden (1950, 1951), Director of the annual Avery Hop-
       wood and Jule Hopwood Award Contests in Creative Writ-
       ing.

E27   The Charles Patterson Van Pelt Library of the Univer-
       sity of Pennsylvania, Philadelphia, 19104, has 15 notes
       or letters from LH to Van Wyck Brooks (1946-1961).
       Many of the Horace Liveright papers are also housed
       in the library.

E28   University of Texas, Austin, 78712, has the major in-
       stitutional collection of manuscript material in the Lil-
       lian Hellman Collection. Various versions of all the
       plays, typescripts, notebooks that document the exhaus-
       tive research LH usually does for a play, adaptations
       and filmscripts. Letters include 2 to Maxwell Ander-
       son (1936), 1 to Kermit Bloomgarden (3 small pages
       bearing notes on the production of Foxes, 1938), 1 to
       W. G. Hayter (1943), 2 telegrams to Edith Kean (1946),
       1 note to Marc Blitzstein (4 pages of yellow paper with
       notes criticizing his operatic version of Foxes, 1949),
       1 to Lucy Kroll (1956), 1 to E. W. Tedlock (1957), 1
       to Harper's regarding Alfred Hayes (1957), 1 to Carson
       McCullers (1953), 11 to Jerome Weidman (and several
       addressed to Peggy Weidman) (1944-1947). The Collec-
       tion also includes letters to LH from Hammett. Man-
       fred Triesch's descriptive catalogue of the Collection
       supplies a list of what is available (F195).

E29   University of Toledo, 2801 West Bancroft Street, Tole-
       do, 43606, has a typescript of The North Star.

E30   University of Washington, Seattle, 98195, has 11 Hell-
       man letters: 9 to Theodore (1954, 1958, 1960, 1962)
       and 2 to Beatrice Roethke (1969).

E31   The Viking Press, 626 Madison Avenue, New York,

10022, has 3 letters to Pascal Covici (1946, 1947, 1948), 1 to Marjorie Griesser (1947), and 1 to Robert Hatch (1943).

E32   Washington University Library, St. Louis, 63130, has a note written by LH to Isabella Gardner (1956).

E33   YIVO Institute for Jewish Research, 1048 Fifth Avenue, New York, 10028, has 3 letters from LH on behalf of the Dinner Forum on "Europe Today" (as well as news clippings on the controversy surrounding the event) in the Horace M. Kallen Papers (1941).

Recordings

E34   "A Profile of Lillian Hellman, " interviewed by Dan Rather, from the CBS News Broadcast Who's Who, March 8, 1977.   Visual History Cassettes-Encyclopedia Americana/CBS News Audio Resource Library: Cassette #2 for March, 1977.   Side A. Code: 03772.   15 minutes.   LH discusses blacklisting, Stalinism, women's liberation, freedom, her vanity and the Blackgama coat ad, Julia and Scoundrel Time ("I wasn't out to write history ... in my memoirs. ") William Wyler and Jane Fonda also are heard on the tape.

E35   "An Interview with Lillian Hellman. " Sound recording, #23059.   New York: J. Norton Publishers, 1974.   Originally recorded in 1969 and issued by McGraw-Hill, New York, as #75598, in series Sound Seminars.   46 minutes.   LH discusses her plays and other writings and reminisces with Fred Gardner.

E35a   "Fear of Involvement: The Legacy of the 50's. " #BB2458.   Pacifica Tape Library, 5316 Venice Boulevard, Los Angeles, 90019.   53 minutes.   "The legacy of fear and ignorance" addressed by a panel at the 1970 Concerned Asian Scholars' Conference.   LH speaks of those who "turned their heads away" during the McCarthy days.

E36   "Interview with Lillian Hellman, " by Richard G. Stern. Tape is in the Modern Poetry Collection, University of Chicago Library.   (A portion of this interview is printed in Contact, #3 (1959), 113-119; See: G199.   LH tells of the ideas out of which Toys came, of how she feels about the women in Foxes, of the play she has in mind but for which she lacks a plot.

E37 "Lillian Hellman: The Great Playwright Candidly Re-
     flects on a Long, Rich Life, " an interview with Bill
     Moyers. Esteemed Women Series: Audio-Text Cas-
     sette, # 36648, released by the Center for Cassette Stu-
     dies, Inc. , 8110 Webb Avenue, North Hollywood, 91605;
     c1974. 57 minutes. Talks of Hemingway, Thurber,
     Roosevelt, heroes and heroism, her temper, success,
     herself as a moral writer, The Little Foxes, the thea-
     ter, women's liberation, Hammett, life; tells the story
     of the fig tree.

E38 "Pentimento: Memory as Distilled by Time, a Reading
     of Julia by Lillian Hellman. " # 35989.   Center for Cas-
     sette Studies, Inc. , 8110 Webb Avenue, North Hollywood,
     91650. 25 minutes. Tells meaning of pentimento and
     the special risks she ran in 1937 Germany, what Child-
     ren's Hour is, what Dashiell Hammett was.

E38a "Sweetest Smelling Baby in New Orleans. " Cassette.
     Los Angeles: Pacifica Foundation Tape Library, 5316
     Venice Boulevard, Los Angeles, 90019. 1975. An
     interview, with excerpts from her works.

E39 A tape of the ceremony at which LH was awarded the
     first Jackson Award of Distinction, April 11, 1968, is
     held in the Archives, University Library, Tufts Univer-
     sity, Medford, Massachusetts, 02155.

E40 "The Works of Lillian Hellman, " a lecture by Kimball
     King. # 903, Southern American Writers Series.   C.
     Hugh Holman, General Editor.   Everett/Edwards, Inc. ,
     P. O. Box 1060, Deland, Florida, 32720. 26 minutes.
     An effectively compressed comprehensive over-view of
     her major plays; uses Foxes to exemplify the Ibsen type
     play; speaks of her major themes and her contribution
     to drama, her craftsmanship and significance.

E41 "Women Writers: The Twentieth Century--Part II. "
     Learning Seed Company, 145 Brentwood Drive, Palatine,
     Illinois, 60067. 17 minutes. A filmstrip that includes
     only a brief mention of LH as part of that continuing
     contribution to literature made by women.

F

BOOKS ABOUT AND REFERENCES IN BOOKS TO LILLIAN
HELLMAN, DISSERTATIONS AND THESES

Arranged by Author

Page references are supplied when an index is not found in
the text, for full length works other than dissertations and
theses, and for articles or passages of some length and,
therefore, of interest. Not every book with a one page reference to Lillian Hellman in circulation is included in this
section, but some are. Selection was made of those that
added bits of biographical or critical information not supplied
in longer works listed and when the source was particularly
helpful or valuable in coming to an appreciation of Miss Hellman professionally or personally.

F1   Aaron, Daniel. Writers on the Left, Episodes in Ameri-
      can Literary Communism. New York: Harcourt,
      Brace, World, Inc. , 1961.

      LH mentioned in passing in connection with Watch
      in a discussion of "art is a weapon".

F2   Ackley, Meredith E. The Plays of Lillian Hellman.
      Ph. D. dissertation. University of Pennsylvania,
      1969.

F3   Adler, Jacob H. Lillian Hellman. Southern Writers
      Series, No. 4. Austin, Texas: Steck-Vaughn Com-
      pany, 1969. 42 p.

      Adler writes as one who has a hold of a perspective
      about LH's works, of her as an American writer.
      He seems closest to her own thinking with regard to
      the issues of melodrama and the well-made play so
      often brought out in discussion of her plays. His
      expanded distinction between melodrama as play and
      melodramatic devices is informing especially because
      his thinking concurs with Miss Hellman's use of the
      terms in the introduction to Four Plays (A13). His
      study deals with her virtues as a playwright, accounts
      for her failings, discusses her use of dialogue and
      of characterization and the believability of her char-
      acters, and allows for the complexities of the plays
      the critics have sometimes over-looked. She is "the
      single most important American Ibsenian outside of
      Arthur Miller, " and at good length Adler establishes
      the basis for his judgment. He also writes of her
      shift in allegiance from Ibsen to Chekhov in Autumn
      Garden.
          Adler notes that Hellman inevitably suffers by the

comparison with Williams their plays invite, yet in his, Hellman seems to come off the stronger of the two playwrights.

He writes of the definite presence of compassion, love, wit, humor in her plays. He pursues Hellman's themes of good and evil and concludes that the critics have concentrated on the presence of evil instead of noting adequately her strong interest in goodness. Adler's examination of evil and villainy in her plays includes references to earlier playwrights from the tradition that precedes her as well as to those of her contemporaries who are initiating the new.

The study includes discussions of the adaptations as well as of the major works and a bit of comment concerning the productions; Adler is, however, chiefly interested in Lillian Hellman's quality, craftsmanship, themes, realism, and stature.

This short work is very readable, and one does not mind not having an index. Two pages of selected bibliography are included.

F4   _____. "The Rose and the Fox: Notes on the Southern Drama, " in Louis D. Rubin, Jr. and Robert D. Jacobs, eds. , South: Modern Southern Literature in its Cultural Setting. Garden City, New York: Dolphin Books, Doubleday and Company, Inc. , 1961, pp. 349-375.

In the chapter devoted chiefly to Tennessee Williams, Paul Green, and Lillian Hellman, Adler writes of the greater range of LH, her rigorously high standards of dramaturgy, her commercial successes, her identification with the South because of Foxes, Another Part of the Forest, Autumn Garden, Toys. He concludes LH deserves second place to Williams and compares their respective views of the South. LH uses straightforward realism to the extent that she wants her characters in Foxes to be representatives of something beyond themselves (which Adler does not believe she achieves). He concludes she does not truly make her themes Southern; in Autumn Garden, for instance, Adler writes, LH had Chekhov in mind.

F5   Anger, Kenneth. Hollywood Babylon. New York: A Delta Special, Dell Publishing Company, 1975.

Pictures from her films.

F6   Angermeier, Brother Carrol. <u>Moral and Social Protest</u>
      <u>in the Plays of Lillian Hellman</u>. Ph. D. dissertation.
      University of Texas at Austin, 1970.

F7   Atkinson, Brooks. <u>Broadway</u>. New York: The Mac-
      millan Company, 1970.

F8   _____ and Albert Hirschfeld. <u>The Lively Years</u>,
      <u>1920-1973</u>. New York: Association Press, 1973.

F9   Axelrod, Steven Gould. <u>Robert Lowell, Life and Art</u>.
      Princeton, New Jersey: Princeton University Press,
      1978.

      Listed with the 20 who endorsed Lowell's refusal to
      attend President Johnson's Festival of the Arts.

F10   Balio, Tino, ed. <u>The American Film Industry</u>. Madi-
      son, Wisconsin: University of Wisconsin Press,
      1976.

      Includes in his chapter of "The Mass Hearings" a
      chapter from John Cogley's <u>Report on Blacklisting</u>,
      <u>I: The Movies</u> (F55).

F11   Bankhead, Tallulah. <u>Tallulah, My Autobiography</u>. New
      York: Harper and Brothers Publishers, 1952.

      Writes of her dealings with LH during the time of
      the <u>Foxes</u> and thereafter and of her great admiration
      for Hellman.

F12   Baxter, John. <u>The Hollywood Exiles</u>. New York: Tap-
      linger Publishing Company, 1976.

      LH's remark about Otto Kahn and mention of her
      $400 loan to Mrs. Patrick (Stella) Campbell.

F13   Behlmer, Rudy, ed. <u>Memo from David O. Selznick</u>.
      Introduction by S. N. Behrman. New York: The
      Viking Press, 1972.

      Note of Hitchcock's cable asking LH to do <u>Rebecca</u>;
      Selznick had LH give detailed criticisms of the new
      lines for <u>Tender Is the Night</u>.

F14   Belfrage, Cedric. <u>The American Inquisition, 1945-1960</u>.

Indianapolis: The Bobbs-Merrill Company, Inc., 1973.

Regarding the Waldorf Conference.

F15 Benjamin, Madeline L. The Social and Historical Vision of Lillian Hellman. M. A. thesis. Ohio State
University, 1967.

F16 Bentley, Eric. Are You Now or Have You Ever Been?
The Investigation of Show Business by the Un-Ameri-
can Activities Committee, 1947-1958. New York:
Harper-Colophon Books, 1972, pp. 109-113.

Bentley's play that includes LH's letter to Congressman Wood and a photo of Martin Berkeley and of
LH at the time.

F17 _____. In Search of Theater. New York: Alfred
A. Knopf, 1953.

Passing references.

F18 _____. "Lillian Hellman's Indignation, " The Dramatic Event: An American Chronicle. New York:
Horizon Press, 1953.

F19 _____. The Theatre of War, Comments on 32
Occasions. New York: The Viking Press, 1972.

On LH's appearance before the 1952 HUAC Hearing.

F20 _____. The Life of the Drama. New York: Atheneum, 1964.

F21 _____. What Is Theatre? New York: Atheneum,
1968.

"Lillian Hellman's Indignation" and other references.

F21a _____, ed. Thirty Years of Treason, Excerpts from
Hearings before the House Committee on Un-Ameri-
can Activities, 1938-1968. New York: The Viking
Press, 1971.

Unindexed pp. 532-43 and 949 include a copy of LH's
testimony before the Committee, an excerpt of related
material from Unfinished Woman, and commentary on
LH's significant approach to her questioners.

F22   Bernstein, Burton. <u>Thurber, A Biography.</u> Illustrated
      with drawings by James Thurber. New York: Dodd,
      Mead and Company, 1975.

      Records the regulars of Tony's, the whiskey throw-
      ing incident, that they spent time together in Paris
      in 1937, that he very much admired LH for her
      stance during the McCarthy days.

F23   Biascoechea, Rosario. <u>Three Plays by Lillian Hellman,</u>
      <u>A Study in Modern American Melodrama.</u> Ph. D.
      dissertation. Catholic University, 1962.

F24   Bigsby, C. W. E. <u>Confrontation and Commitment, A</u>
      <u>Study of Contemporary American Drama, 1959-1966.</u>
      Columbia, Mo. : University of Missouri Press, 1969.

      LH's status comes from her commercial success.

F25   Birmingham, Stephen. <u>The Late John Marquand.</u> Phila-
      delphia: J. B. Lippincott Company, 1972.

      Describes LH's visit to Marquand in Cambridge.

F26   Bladel, Roderick. <u>Walter Kerr, An Analysis of His</u>
      <u>Criticism.</u> Metuchen, New Jersey: The Scarecrow
      Press, 1976.

      Kerr in relation to his reviews of <u>Children's Hour,</u>
      <u>Foxes,</u> and <u>My Mother, My Father and Me.</u>

F27   Blitgen, Sister Carol. <u>The Overlooked Hellman.</u> Ph. D.
      dissertation. University of California, Santa Barbara,
      1972.

F28   Bloom, Lynn Z. "Promises Fulfilled: Positive Images
      of Women in Twentieth-Century Autobiography, " in
      Cheryl L. Brown and Karen Olson, eds. , <u>Feminist</u>
      <u>Criticism: Essays on Theory, Poetry and Prose.</u>
      Metuchen, New Jersey: The Scarecrow Press, 1978.

      A paper first presented at the "Women and Literature"
      section of the mid-West MLA meeting, Chicago, 1975,
      and about Hellman as revealed in <u>Unfinished Woman.</u>

F29   Blotner, Joseph. <u>Faulkner: A Biography.</u> Volume I
      and II. New York: Random House, 1974.

LH's reading of Mosquitoes, of their friendship in and New York, of Hammett and Nathanael West, of their meeting in May 1957 and in May 1962, of how their friendship had changed because Faulkner had not spoken out about the jailing of Hammett.

F30 Blum, Daniel. A Pictorial History of the American Theatre, 1860-1976. New York: Crown Publishers, 1977.

F31 Bonin, Jane F. Prize-winning American Drama, a Bibliographical and Descriptive Guide. Metuchen, New Jersey: The Scarecrow Press, 1973.

Comments about the controversy of not awarding Children's Hour the Pulitzer Prize.

F32 _____. Major Themes in Prize-Winning American Drama. Preface by Paul T. Nolan. Metuchen, New Jersey: The Scarecrow Press, 1975.

F33 Bosworth, Patricia. Montgomery Clift, A Biography. New York: Harcourt, Brace, Jovanovich, 1978.

F34 Boyd, Alice K. Interchange of Plays between London and New York, 1910-1939: A Study in Relative Audience Response. New York: King's Crown Press, 1948.

F35 Bradbury, John M. Renaissance in the South. Chapel Hill: University of North Carolina Press, 1963.

General background.

F36 Bradbury, Malcolm, Eric Maltram and Jean Franco, eds. The Penguin Companion to American Literature. New York: McGraw-Hill Company, 1971.

Biographical information and general concerns of the 8 plays and Unfinished Woman.

F37 Breault, Sister Mary Amata, O. P. A Comparative Analysis of the Structure of Selected Plays by Lillian Hellman and Willian Inge. M. A. thesis. Siena Heights College, 1963.

F38 _____. A Comparative Analysis of the Structure of

Selected Plays by Lillian Hellman and William Inge.
Ph. D. dissertation.   Catholic University, 1963.

F39   Brockington, John.   A Critical Analysis of the Plays of
      Lillian Hellman.   Ph. D. dissertation.   Yale Univer-
      sity, 1962.

F40   Brooks, Van Wyck.   An Autobiography.   New York:
      E. P. Dutton and Company, Inc. , 1965.

      Comments on Hammett and LH and on LH's reading
      Autumn Garden to Brooks.

F41   Brown, John Mason.   Dramatis Personae, A Retrospec-
      tive Show.   New York: The Viking Press, 1963.

F42   Brown, Kent R.   Lillian Hellman and Her Critics.
      M. A. thesis.   University of California, Santa Bar-
      bara, 1967.

F43   Bruccoli, Matthew J. , ed.   Selected Letters of John
      O'Hara.   New York: Random House, 1978.

      Of O'Hara's disregard for LH and her group.

F44   _____ and C. E. Frazer Clark, Jr. , eds.   First
      Printings of American Authors, Contributing Toward
      Descriptive Checklists.   Volume II.   Detroit: Gale
      Research Company, 1978.

F45   Buckley, William F. , Jr.   A Hymnal.   New York:
      G. P. Putnam's Sons, 1978.
      "The Long War Against McCarthyism: Lillian Hell-
      man: Who is the ugliest of them All. "

F46   _____ and the editors of National Review.   The Com-
      mittee and Its Critics, A Calm Review of the House
      Committee on Un-American Activities.   New York:
      G. P. Putnam's Sons, 1962.

F46a Cameron, James.   "Introduction" to Scoundrel Time, by
      Lillian Hellman.   London: The Macmillan Company,
      1976.   (C5)

      An essay in judgment of the times and in praise of
      LH.

F47   Carlson, Eugene T. Lillian Hellman's Plays as a Re-
      flection of the Southern Mind. Ph. D. dissertation.
      University of Southern California, 1975.

F48   Carr, Virginia Spencer. The Lonely Hunter: A Bio-
      graphy of Carson McCullers. Garden City, New
      York: Doubleday and Company, 1975.

F49   Caute, David. The Great Fear, The Anti-Communist
      Purges Under Truman and Eisenhower. New York:
      Simon and Schuster, 1978.

      Cites LH as saying Hammett did not know who the
      contributors to the Bail Fund were, among other
      references.

F50   Cerf, Bennett. At Random, The Reminiscences of
      Bennett Cerf. New York: Random House, 1977.

F51   Clark, Barrett H. , and George Freedley, eds. A
      History of Modern Drama. New York: Appleton-
      Century-Crofts, Inc. , 1947.

F52   Clurman, Harold. All People Are Famous (instead of
      an autobiography). New York: Harcourt, Brace,
      Jovanovich, 1974.

F53   _____. The Fervent Years. New York: Hill and
      Wang, 1957.

F54   _____. The Naked Image: Observations on the
      Modern Theatre. New York: The Macmillan Com-
      pany, 1966.

      The first two books cited include casual references
      to LH; the last tells of the Paris production of Foxes
      and of LH's reactions to the Edinburgh Drama Con-
      ference in 1963.

F55   Cogley, John. Report on Blacklisting, I: Movies.
      New York: The Fund for the Republic, Inc. , 1956.

      LH's letter to Congressman Wood, background of
      her appearance before the Committee, asserts LH
      indicated her membership in the CP was before 1949.

F56   Crane, Joshua. A Comparison of G. B. Shaw's "Saint

Joan" and Lillian Hellman's Adaptation of "The Lark"
by Jean Anouilh. M. A. thesis. University of Florida, 1961.

F57 Curley, Dorothy Nyren, Maurice Kramer, Elaine Fialka
      Kramer, eds. A Library of Literary Criticism.
      Volume II, 4th enlarged edition. New York: Freder-
      ick Ungar Publishing Company, 1976. See also: F163.

      Four pages of excerpts from articles appearing in
      American publications and books since 1936.

F58 Davis, Mac. Jews at a Glance. New York: Hebrew
      Publishing Company, 1956.

      A portrait.

F59 Dessler, Harold. Lillian Hellman: An Evaluation.
      M. A. thesis. University of North Carolina at Chapel
      Hill, 1948.

F60 Dillon, Ann and Cynthia Bix. Contributions of Women:
      Theater. Minneapolis: Dillon Press, Inc. , 1978.
      pp. 76-99.

F61 Downer, Alan S. The American Theater Today. New
      York: Basic Books, Inc. , Publishers, 1967.

F62 Easton, Carol. The Search for Sam Goldwyn. New
      York: William Morrow and Company, Inc. , 1976.

F63 Edmiston, Susan, and Linda D. Cirino. Literary New
      New York, A History and Guide. Boston: Houghton
      Mifflin Company, 1976. illus.

      Addresses at which LH has lived.

F64 Engel, Lehman. The Critics. New York: The Mac-
      millan Publishing Company, 1976.

      How various critics have treated LH.

F65 Estrin, Mark W. An Evil World Well-Made: The
      Plays of Lillian Hellman. M. A. thesis. Columbia
      University, 1961.

F66 Falk, Doris V. Lillian Hellman. New York: Frederick
      Ungar Publishing Company, 1978. 180 p.

All the while concentrating on LH's process of discovery and creative consciousness throughout this
most recent of full length critical studies of LH,
Doris Falk keeps separated the woman from the works
and so produces a book that presents an understanding and appreciation of both. She discusses from
several perspectives the plays, the memoirs, and the
edited works. "Hellman in Her Time: A Biographical Preface" is followed by a chapter in which Falk
examines melodrama and the well-made play, but
passes to consider LH's belief "The Theatre Is a
Trick" as the principle for appreciating her plays.
She divides the plays into two opposite groups of
people: The Despoilers (Foxes, Another Part of the
Forest, Watch) and the Bystanders (Searching Wind,
Autumn Garden, Toys) and considers ultimately the
memoirs for the "Form and Theme" of Hellman's
life and work. She writes of the presence of Mel-
ville, Hawthorne, Henry James, Ibsen, Chekhov in
Hellman's work. Her discussion of Gregory Zilboorg
and his interest in religion and psychoanalysis as
two different but equally necessary systems is infor-
mative and in the context of her explication of the
religious streak in LH. She extracts Hellman's value
system, points to her criteria for good and evil,
comments on her temperament.

Falk supplies information, interprets, suggests,
illuminates by the cross-referencing of memoirs and
plays, always aware of the deeper dimension of the
plays and the author. She writes with a view of the
whole and does not neglect detail.

The bibliography and chapter notes are ample and
helpful.

F67   Fisher, Lois H.   A Critical Analysis and Evaluation of
      Lillian Hellman's Dramatic Works.   M. A. thesis.
      University of Pittsburgh, 1960.

F68   Flexnor, Eleanor.   American Playwrights, 1718-1938,
      The Theatre Retreats from Reality.   Preface by
      John Gassner.   New York: Simon and Schuster,
      1938.

F69   French, Warren, ed.   The Thirties, Fiction, Poetry,
      Drama.   2nd rev. edition.   DeLand, Fla.:   Everett/
      Edwards, Inc., 1976.

F70   Friedman, Sharon P.   <u>Feminist Concerns in the Works</u>
      <u>of Four Twentieth-Century American Women Drama</u>-
      <u>tists: Susan Glaspell, Rachel Crothers, Lillian Hell</u>-
      <u>man, and Lorraine Hansberry</u>.   Ph. D.   dissertation.
      New York University, 1977.

F71   Fryer, Jonathon.   <u>Isherwood</u>.   Garden City, New York:
      Doubleday and Company, Inc. , 1978.

F72   Furhammar, Leif, and Folke Isaksson.   <u>Politics and</u>
      <u>Film.</u>   Trans.   Korsti French.   New York: Praeger
      Publishers, 1971.

      Re blacklisting.

F73   Furnas, J. C.   <u>Stormy Weather, Crosslights on the</u>
      <u>Nineteen Thirties, An Informal Concise History of</u>
      <u>the U. S. , 1929-41</u>.   New York: G. P. Putnam's Sons,
      1977.

      Quotes the remark from <u>Unfinished Woman</u> that never
      before in her lifetime had liberals, radicals, intel-
      lectuals, middle-class educated come together as a
      single force the way they had against Fascism in
      their support of Loyalist Spain; mentions her pilgrim-
      mage to Spain during the Civil War and that Hearst
      had killed the Winchell column (F207).

F74   Gascoigne, Bamber.   <u>Twentieth-Century Drama</u>.   Lon-
      don: Hutchinson University Library, 1962.

      Arthur Miller develops an American tradition which
      he derives directly from Clifford Odets and LH.

F75   Gassner, John.   <u>The Theatre in Our Times, A Survey</u>
      <u>of the Men, Materials and Movements in the Modern</u>
      <u>Theatre</u>.   New York: Crown Publishers, Inc. , 1954.

F76   Geisinger, Marion.   <u>Plays, Players, and Playwrights.</u>
      Updated by Peggy Marks.   New York: Hart Publish-
      ing Company, 1975.

F77   Gill, Brendan.   <u>Tallulah</u>.   New York: Holt, Rinehart
      and Winston, 1972.

F78   Goldstein, Malcolm.   "The Playwright of the 1930's"
      in Alan S. Downer, ed. , <u>The American Theatre Today</u>.
      New York: Basic Books, Inc. , 1967.   p. 39.

F79   _____. The Political Stage: American Drama and
           Theater of the Great Depression. New York: Ox-
           ford University Press, 1974.

           LH's black characters possess dignity; she analyzes
           social forces that created anti-social beings. Dis-
           cusses her contributions to the theater and the de-
           velopment of her reputation.

F80   Goldstone, Richard H. Thornton Wilder, An Intimate
           Portrait. New York: E. P. Dutton Company, 1975.

           In connection with Contemporary Historians.

F81   Goodman, Walter. The Committee, The Extraordinary
           Career of the House Committee on Un-American Ac-
           tivities. New York: Farrar, Straus and Giroux,
           1968.

           LH's connections with the Committee.

F82   Gottfried, Martin. Opening Nights, Theater Criticism
           of the Sixties. New York: G. P. Putnam's Sons,
           1969.

           "Where Have All the Heroes Gone?" (originally in
           Women's Wear Daily, March 25, 1966) and "The
           Taste but not the Craft" (April 21, 1967). LH has
           abandoned the theater after developing a fine, intel-
           ligent style for realistic writing. Comments on the
           1967 revival of Foxes.

F83   Gould, Jean. "Lillian Hellman, " Modern American
           Playwrights. Illustrated with photographs. New
           York: Dodd, Mead and Company, 1966, pp. 168-
           186.

           In her warm portrait of LH, Gould establishes Hell-
           man's genius in the theater, her strength and deter-
           mination, her integrity and the power of her ideas,
           her relationship to her plays, and the contexts out
           of which they arose for LH. She writes of Hammett,
           Dorothy Parker, William Wyler, the Federal Theater
           Project, LH's travels and assesses her writing gener-
           ally.

F84   Gross, Theodore L. , ed. The Literature of American

<u>Jews</u>. New York: The Free Press, The Macmillan
Publishing Company, Inc., 1973.

F85   Guernsey, Otis L.   <u>Directory of the American Theater,
      1894-1971, Index to the Complete Series of Best Plays
      Theater Yearbooks</u>.   New York: Dodd, Mead and
      Company, 1972.

F86   Guernsey, Otis L., Jr.   <u>The Best Plays of 1977-1978</u>.
      New York: Dodd, Mead and Company, 1978.

      Regarding the Dramatists' Guild open letter concern-
      ing Phillip Hayes Dean's play <u>Paul Robeson</u>.

F87   Guernsey, Otis L., Jr., ed.   "Lillian Hellman Reflects
      on Her Own Reputation," <u>Playwrights, Lyricists,
      Composers on Theater</u>.   New York: Dodd, Mead and
      Company, 1974, pp. 250-257.

      An edited transcript of a discussion with LH and
      Jerome Weidman and other Dramatists' Guild mem-
      bers.

F88   Gurko, Leo.   <u>The Angry Decade, American Literature
      and Thought from 1929 to Pearl Harbor</u>.   New York:
      Harper-Colophon Books, 1967.

      The decade produced no poet of the proportions of
      LH in drama.   Writes of the political influence of
      <u>Watch</u>, of <u>Foxes</u> as a "superb illustration of FDR's
      oft repeated thesis that property rights must not be
      put above human rights."

F89   Guthrie, Tyrone.   <u>A Life in the Theatre</u>.   New York:
      McGraw-Hill, Inc., 1959.

F90   Hall, Donald.   <u>Remembering Poets, Reminiscences and
      Opinions, Dylan Thomas, Robert Frost, T. S. Eliot,
      Ezra Pound</u>.   New York: Harper and Row, Publish-
      ers, 1978.

      LH was on the Academy of Arts and Sciences' com-
      mittee that nominated Ezra Pound for the Emerson-
      Thoreau Medal although she did not vote.

F91   Haller, Charles D.   <u>The Concept of Moral Failure in
      the Eight Original Plays of Lillian Hellman</u>.   Ph. D.
      dissertation.   Tulane University, 1967.

E92 Hartnoll, Phyllis, ed. The Oxford Companion to the
     Theatre. 3rd ed. London: Oxford University Press,
     1967.

     John Gassner's entry of 5 inches mentions plays and
     gives the gist of what they are about in addition to
     an evaluation of her work generally.

F93 Hasbany, Richard. Rituals of Reassurance: Studies in
     World War II American Drama. (M. Anderson, Sher-
     wood, Hellman, Wilder) Ph. D. dissertation. Michi-
     gan State, 1973.

F94 Hellman, Lillian. "An Introduction to Four Plays, "
     in George Oppenheimer, ed. The Passionate Play-
     goer, A Personal Scrapbook. New York: The Viking
     Press, 1963, pp. 294-301. See: A13.

     LH looks at her original 4 plays and sees their
     shortcomings, but also explains the type of writer
     she is. She discusses melodrama and melodramatic
     techniques.

F95 Herbert, Ian, et al., eds. Who's Who in the Theatre,
     A Biographical Record of the Contemporary Stage.
     16th ed. Pitman, London: Gale Research, Detroit,
     1977.

     An over-view of her professional life.

F96 Heymann, C. David. Ezra Pound: The Last Rower,
     A Political Profile. New York: The Viking Press,
     1976.

F97 Higham, Charles. Warner Brothers, A History of the
     Studio: Its Pictures, Stars, and Personalities. New
     York: Chas. Scribner's Sons, 1975.

F98 Holmin, Lorena Ross. The Dramatic Works of Lillian
     Hellman. (Studia Anglistica Upsaliensia: No. 10)
     Stockholm: Almquist and Wiksell (distr.), 1973.
     Austin, Texas: The Humanities Press. 178 p.

     Ms. Holmin's study surveys the major eight plays
     and is concerned with Lillian Hellman's application
     of dramatic devices as used to structure and to char-
     acterize, especially with her use of dialogue as a

means of characterization. Ms. Holmin notes trends
in development in the plays, comments on the oft-
cited "melodrama" and "well-made play" discussion,
the influences of Ibsen, Chekhov, Faulkner. She
gives plot summaries, provides analyses of the plays,
notes progress in the development of Miss Hellman's
craft, comments on the themes in the plays. She
discusses the poignant use of children in Autumn
Garden, the uses of pantomime in Autumn Garden
and Foxes, and her belief that LH idealizes Europeans. Probably the most attractive chapter is
Holmin's treatment of Toys.
      The study also includes information about the
production of plays by LH in the Nordic Countries
and a very helpful, lengthy bibliography, pp. 172-178.
      Although the book lacks an index, a quick skim
through will be enough to finger the references wanted.

F99 Howard, Maureen, ed.   Seven American Women Writers
     of the Twentieth-Century, An Introduction.   Minnea-
     polis: University of Minnesota Press, 1977.

F100 Hynes, Carolyn.   An Analysis of Nine Tragedies by
     American Playwrights: Eugene O'Neill, Maxwell
     Anderson and Lillian Hellman.   M. A. thesis.   Univer-
     sity of Houston, Texas, 1954.

F101 Israel, Lee.   Miss Tallulah Bankhead.   New York:
     G. P. Putnam's Sons, 1972.

     Chapter 17 of this biography is "The Little Foxes".

F102 Jelinek, Estelle C.   The Tradition of Women's Auto-
     biographies (Hellman, Millett, Stein, Elizabeth Stan-
     ton).   Ph. D. dissertation.   State University of New
     York, Buffalo, 1977.

F103 Johnson, Annette Bergmann.   A Study of Recurrent
     Character Types in the Plays of Lillian Hellman.
     Ph. D. dissertation.   University of Massachusetts,
     1971.

F104 Kahn, Albert E.   High Treason, The Plot Against the
     People.   New York: The Hour Publishers, 1950.

F105 Kalaher, Lucille F.   The Theme of Evasive Idealism in
     the Plays of Lillian Hellman.   M. A. thesis.   Univer-
     sity of Wyoming, 1964.

F106 Kanfer, Stefan. <u>A Journal of the Plague Years, A
Devastating Chronicle of the Era of the Blacklist</u>.
New York: Atheneum, 1973.

Numerous references to LH and to Cogley's <u>Report</u>
are found in the index. Includes an excerpt of the
LH letter to Chairman Wood [a copy of the entire
letter is found in the Moody biography (F152) and
in Cogley (F55)] and an account of Wood's reply;
the statement that LH was never a Communist, an
account of Wyler's discovery that she was on the
blacklist, of the 1952 meeting with Elia Kazan at
the Plaza, and LH's characterization of the entire
period.

F107 Kanin, Garson. <u>Hollywood: Stars and Starlets, Ty-
coons and Flesh-Peddlars, Moviemakers and Money-
makers, Frauds and Geniuses, Hopefuls and Has-
Beens, Great Lovers and Sex Symbols</u>. New York:
The Viking Press, 1974.

Reminiscences of their Hollywood days, LH's understanding of Goldwyn.

F108 Kaufmann, Stanley. <u>Persons of the Drama, Theater
Criticisms and Comment</u>. New York: Harper and
Row, Publishers, 1976.

F109 Kay, Karyn. <u>Myrna Loy</u>. New York: Pyramid Publi-
cations, 1977.

On the <u>Thin Man.</u>

F110 Kazin, Alfred. <u>New York Jew</u>. New York: Alfred A.
Knopf, 1978.

F111 Keats, John. <u>You Might as Well Live, The Life and
Times of Dorothy Parker.</u> New York: Simon and
Schuster, 1970.

The author's note includes a passage explaining LH
chose not to be involved in this biography in any
way. Keats writes of the friendship between LH and
Miss Parker, of their differences, of LH asking
Parker to work on <u>Candide,</u> of Parker's appraisal of
LH as a playwright.

F112 Keller, Alvin J.   Form and Content in the Plays of
      Lillian Hellman: A Structural Analysis.   Ph. D.
      dissertation.   Stanford University, 1965.

F113 Kempton, Murray.   Part of Our Time, Some Ruins and
      Monuments of the Thirties.   New York: Simon and
      Schuster, 1955, p. 195.

F114 Kenny, Arthur F.   Dorothy Parker.   Boston: Twayne
      Publishers--G. K. Hall and Company, 1978.

F115 Kerr, Walter.   The Theater in Spite of Itself.   New
      York: Simon and Schuster, 1963.

      A fine appreciation of LH's talent; to be read also
      with Foxes (H).

F116 Kramer, Dale.   Ross and "The New Yorker".   Garden
      City, New York: Doubleday and Company, Inc.,
      1951.

      Passing references; a picture of Arthur Kober after
      p. 180.

F117 Kronenberger, Louis.   No Whippings, No Gold Watches,
      The Saga of a Writer and His Jobs.   Boston: Little,
      Brown and Company, 1970.

      Writes of knowing LH as a very young woman at
      Liveright, of her influencing him to go to Time, her
      personality.

F118 Landman, Isaac, ed.   The Universal Jewish Encyclo-
      pedia.   New York: The Universal Jewish Encyclo-
      pedia, Inc., 1941.

      Helpful biographical entry and photo.

F119 Lardner, Ring, Jr.   The Lardners, My Family Remem-
      bered.   New York: Harper and Row, 1977.

      LH on Dorothy Parker and on her feelings about the
      Spanish Civil War.

F120 Larimer, Cynthia Diane Miller.   A Study of Female
      Characters in the Eight Plays of Lillian Hellman.
      Ph. D. dissertation.   Purdue University, 1970.

F121 Lederer, Katherine G. The Critical Reaction to the
      Dramatic Works of Lillian Hellman. Ph. D. disser-
      tation. University of Arkansas, 1967.

F122 Lewis, Allan. "The Survivors of the Depression--Hell-
      man, Odets, Shaw, " American Plays and Playwrights
      of the Contemporary Theatre. New York: Crown
      Publishers, Inc. , 1965, pp. 99-115. (The revised
      edition, 1970, carries the same entries.)

      Writes of the Hellman parody of Arthur Miller's
      After the Fall and cites excerpt of "Buy My Guilt"
      (D31) in addition to his discussion of LH as one of
      the committed writers concerned with the fight for
      social justice and critical of complacency producing
      myths abundant in society.   Allows that LH's strength
      lies in the dramatic power she extracts "from the
      realistic form. " He tells of LH's resilliency, of
      her concern that greed and avarice have eroded love;
      he concludes that LH has best withstood the test of
      time. Use especially with Candide, My Mother ...,
      Toys.

F123 _____. The Contemporary Theatre, The Significant
      Playwrights of Our Time. Forward by John Gassner.
      rev. ed. New York: Crown Publishers, Inc. , 1971.

F124 Lewis, Peter. The Fifties. New York: J. B. Lippin-
      cott Company, 1978.

F125 Lindsay, Howard. "Some Notes on Playwriting, " in
      Rosamond Gilder, ed. , The Theatre Arts Anthology.
      New York: Theatre Arts Books, 1950, p. 124.

F126 Logan, Joshua. Movie Stars, Real People, and Me.
      New York: Delacorte Press, 1978.

F127 Long, Norma Rae. Creative Autonomy of The Literary
      Woman: Case of Lillian Hellman. Ph. D. disserta-
      tion. University of Maryland, 1977.

F128 Lumley, Frederick. Trends in Twentieth-Century Drama,
      A Survey Since Ibsen and Shaw. rev. ed. Fair Lawn,
      New Jersey: Essential Books, 1960.

F129 McCarthy, Mary. Sights and Spectacles, 1937-1956.
      New York: Farrar, Straus and Cudahy, 1956.

F130 McClintic, Guthrie. Me and Kit. Boston: Little,
      Brown and Company, 1955.

      Of LH's approval of his direction of The Three Sis-
      ters.

F131 McGraw-Hill Encyclopedia of World Drama. Volume II.
      New York: McGraw-Hill Company, 1972.

      Photographs and brief biography, mentions most im-
      portant plays, play dates and publication dates, cri-
      ticism; mentions that she became prey for the HUAC
      because of her efforts on behalf of Hammett.

F132 McPherson, Michael L. Lillian Hellman and Her Cri-
      tics. Ph. D. dissertation. University of Denver,
      1976.

F133 Madsen, Axel. John Huston. Garden City, New York:
      Doubleday and Company, Inc. , 1978.

F134 _____ . William Wyler, The Authorized Biography.
      New York: Thomas Y. Crowell Company, 1973.

      Numerous anecdotes and references to her Hollywood
      days and contacts, her influence on Wyler, her in-
      tegrity and devotion to her work.   Comments on LH's
      insights and influence on Wyler in directing Children's
      Hour and Foxes; cites Bette Davis' account of work-
      ing on Foxes and Pauline Kael's devastating review of
      the 1962 version of Children's Hour (H615).
          A 1969 photo of LH and William Wyler comes be-
      fore p. 379.

F135 Maltaw, Myron. Modern World Drama, An Encyclopedia.
      New York: E. P. Dutton and Company, 1972.

      A full page of comprehensive biography, thematic
      concerns of plays, stature, relating plays to Becque
      and Ibsen.

F136 Maney, Richard. Fanfare, Confessions of a Press A-
      gent. New York: Harper and Brothers, Publishers,
      1957.

      On Lillian and Arthur Kober.

F137 Mantle, Burns. Contemporary American Playwrights.
      New York: Dodd, Mead and Company, 1938.

      Two pages on LH and her work.

F138 _____, ed. The Best Plays of 1934-35. New York:
      Dodd, Mead and Company, 1935.

      Volumes appropriate for the dates of LH's plays pro-
      vide history, production information, comment, and
      evaluation of the plays.

F139 Martin, Boyd. Modern American Drama and Stage.
      London: The Pilot Press, 1943, pp. 54-56.

F140 Martin, Jay. Always Merry and Bright, The Life of
      Henry Miller. Santa Barbara, California: Capra
      Press, 1978.

F141 _____. Nathanael West, The Art of His Life. New
      York: Farrar, Straus and Giroux, 1970.

      Of their friendship in Hollywood and in New York.

F142 Martin, Robert A. , ed. The Theater Essays of Arthur
      Miller. Foreword by Arthur Miller. New York: The
      Viking Press, 1978.

F143 Marx, Arthur. Goldwyn, A Biography of the Man Behind
      the Myth. New York: W. W. Norton and Company,
      1976.

F144 Mellow, James R. Charmed Circle, Gertrude Stein
      and Company. New York: Praeger Publishers,
      1974.

      An account of the Ehrman dinner with Hammett and
      LH.

F145 Meredith, Claire. The Decline of the Southern Aristo-
      cratic Tradition in American Drama: Paul Green,
      Lillian Hellman, Tennessee Williams, and Joshua
      Logan. M. A. thesis. Columbia University, 1962.

F146 Mersand, Joseph. The American Drama Since 1930,
      Essays on Playwrights and Plays. New York: Mod-
      ern Chapbooks Press, 1949.

F147 _____. Traditions in American Literature, A Study
      of Jewish Characters and Authors. Port Washington,
      New York: Kennikat Press, Inc., c. 1939 (1968 re-
      print).

F148 Meserve, Walter J. An Outline History of American
      Drama. Totowa, New Jersey: Littlefield, Adams
      and Company, 1965.

F149 Miller, J. William. Modern Playwrights at Work.
      Volume I. London: Samuel French, Inc., 1965.

F150 Miller, Wayne Charles. A Handbook of American Mi-
      norities. New York: New York University Press,
      1976.

      Mentioned as an important American Jewish play-
      wright.

F151 Moers, Ellen. Literary Women. Garden City, New
      York: Doubleday and Company, Inc., 1976.

      Discussion of women and money, the need of and
      rarity of.

F152 Moody, Richard. Lillian Hellman, Playwright. New
      York: Pegasus American Authors, The Bobbs-Mer-
      rill Company, Inc., 1972. 373 p.

      Harold Clurman's introduction, xi-xv, to the first
      critical biography to appear is a very warm tribute
      to Lillian Hellman and her achievement. Moody's
      book is thoroughly researched, sympathetic but schol-
      arly. He uses biographical context when available
      for Hellman's writing; he is perceptive and insight-
      ful. He provides a plot summary of each of her
      plays and of Unfinished Woman, giving his own in-
      terpretations in his sensible blend of research and
      review of the critical material concerning Hellman's
      work.
          Moody's book provides an appreciation for LH and
      for her achievement as an artist. He supplies con-
      siderable personal information that supplements Miss
      Hellman's memoirs. A selected bibliography is in-
      cluded.

F153 Morehouse, Ward. Matinee Tomorrow, Fifty Years of
      Our Theater. New York: Whittlesley House, McGraw-
      Hill Book Company, Inc., 1949.

Tells LH finished Children's Hour in Florida,
how pleased John Mason Brown was with Foxes, Zoe
Atkins' high regard for LH, and Kronenberger's appraisal.   Some background on the Pulitzer Prize not
going to Children's Hour.

F154 Morella, Joe and Edward Z. Epstein.   Brando, An Un-
authorized Biography.   New York: Crown Publishers,
Inc. , 1973.

F155 Mosel, Tad, with Gertrude Macy.   Leading Lady, The
World and Theatre of Katharine Cornell.   Foreword
by Martha Graham.   Boston: An Atlantic Monthly
Book, Little, Brown and Company, 1978.

F156 Nannes, Caspar H.   Politics in the American Drama.
Washington, D. C. :   Catholic University of America
Press, 1961.

On the place of The Searching Wind and Watch.

F157 _____.   Politics in the American Drama as Revealed
by Plays Produced on the New York Stage, 1890-1945.
Ph. D. dissertation.   University of Pennsylvania, 1950.

F158 Nathan, George Jean.   Encyclopedia of the Theatre.
New York: Alfred A. Knopf, 1940.

F159 _____.   "The Status of the Finale Playwrights, "
The Entertainment of a Nation, or Three Sheets to
the Wind.   New York: Alfred A. Knopf, 1942, pp.
34-38.

"My first guess is that a woman dramatist seldom
succeeds in mastering an economy of the emotions. "

F160 The New York Critics' Theatre Reviews.   New York:
Critics' Theatre Reviews, Inc. , 1940.

Major New York newspaper reviews of premières
of plays and adaptations by Lillian Hellman are found
in the volume appropriate to the year of the production for each of the plays.

F161 The New York Times Directory of the Theater.   Introduction by Clive Barnes.   New York: Arno Press,
1973.

Chronological ordering of New York Times reviews
of LH's plays from Children's Hour, 1934, to Foxes,
1968. Contains an appendix and index to the Times
reviews 1920-1970.

F161a Nolan, William F. Dashiell Hammett, A Casebook.
Introduction by Philip Durham. Santa Barbara, California: McNally and Loftin Publishers, 1969.

Numerous Hellman references.

F162 Notable Names in the American Theatre. Clifton, New
Jersey: James T. White and Company, 1976.

F163 Nyren, Dorothy, Maurice Kramer, Elaine Fialka, com-
pilers and editors. A Library of Literary Criticism,
Modern American Literature. Volume IV, Supplement to the fourth edition. New York: Frederick
Ungar Publishing Company, 1976.

Evaluative commentary excerpted on Unfinished Woman and Pentimento. See also: F57.

F164 O'Hara, Frank Hurburt. Today in American Drama.
Chicago: University of Chicago Press, 1939.

F165 _____ and Marguerite Harmon Bro. Invitation to the
Theater. New York: Harper and Brothers Publishers, 1951.

F166 Olsen, Tillie. Silences. New York: Delacorte Press,
1978.

F167 Oppenheimer, George. The View from the Sixties.
New York: David McKay, 1966.

F168 Parrish, James A. A Study of the Plays of Lillian
Hellman. M. A. thesis. University of Florida,
1949.

F169 Partnow, Elaine, compiler and ed. The Quotable Woman, 1800-1975. Los Angeles: Corvin Books, 1977.

Pages of quotes from her plays, memoirs, and The
North Star.

F170 Patraka, Vivian Mary. Lillian Hellman, Dramatist of
the Second Sex. Ph. D. dissertation. University of
Michigan, 1977.

F171 Peary, Gerald, and Roger Shotzkin, eds. The Modern American Novel and the Movies. New York: Frederick Ungar Publishing Company, 1978.

As a friend of Nathanael West.

F172 Rahv, Philip. Essays on Literature and Politics, 1932-1972. Boston: Houghton Mifflin Company, 1977.

F173 Reed, Rex. "Lillian Hellman," Valentines and Vitriol. New York: Delacorte Press, 1977.

F174 Rhode, Eric. A History of the Cinema from Its Origins to 1970. New York: Hill and Wang, 1976.

Background of The Spanish Earth (H), writes about William Wyler and Foxes (H) and about The Chase (H).

F175 Rice, Elmer. The Living Theatre. New York: Harper and Brothers, Publishers, 1959.

Brief references but interesting judgments of LH's stature and place. Rice believes she owes her fame to her commercial success, for instance.

F176 Robertson, Helen E. Lillian Hellman and the Psychology of Evil. M. A. thesis. University of Texas at Austin, 1964.

F177 Scanlan, Tom. Family, Drama, and American Dreams. Contributions in American Studies, #35. Westport, Conn.: Greenwood Press, 1978.

A discussion of LH's treatment of the family in her plays.

F178 Schemerhorn, Leora H. Lillian Hellman: Craftsman, Moralist, Thinker. M. A. thesis. Stetson University, 1966.

F179 Seager, Allan. The Glass House, The Life of Theodore Roethke. New York: McGraw-Hill Book Company, 1968.

Of their continuing friendship, of his fascination because she wrote plays, of his projected musical Me and Hellman.

F180 Sexton, Linda Gray, and Lori Ames, eds.   Anne Sexton,
      A Self-Portrait in Letters.   Boston: Houghton Mif-
      flin Company, 1977.

F181 Sheaffer, Louis.   O'Neill, Son and Artist.   Boston:
      Little, Brown and Company, 1973.

      Excerpts of his letter to the New York Drama Cri-
      tics' Circle stating his displeasure that The Chil-
      dren's Hour was not awarded the Pulitzer Prize.

F182 Shropshire, Anne W.   The Plays of Lillian Hellman:
      A Study of Contemporary Drama.   M. A. thesis.
      University of Kentucky, 1946.

F183 Sievers, S. David.   "Freudian Fraternity of the Thir-
      ties, " Freud on Broadway: A History of Psychoanaly-
      sis and the American Drama.   New York: Cooper
      Square Publishers, Inc. , 1970, pp. 279-289.

      Sievers gives plot summaries and thematic summaries
      of LH's plays written through 1951 (Autumn Garden)
      in the light of psychoanalytic interpretation.   Speaks
      of LH's "special genius for exploring the dark world
      of human sadism. "   Speaks of her restraint and suc-
      cess as a playwright.

F184 Signoret, Simone.   Nostalgia Isn't What It Used to Be.
      New York: Harper and Row, Publishers, 1978.

      Of her 1962 Paris adaptation of Foxes.

F185 Simon, Linda.   The Biography of Alice B. Toklas.
      Garden City, New York: Doubleday and Company,
      Inc. , 1977.

      Mentions Carl Van Vechten's friend's party at which
      Toklas met LH.

F186 Sobol, Louis.   The Longest Street.   New York: Crown
      Publishers, 1968.

      A glimpse at the Kober marriage.

F187 Spacks, Patricia M.   The Female Imagination.   New
      York: Alfred A. Knopf, 1975.

      Notes the similarities and dissimilarities to Isak
      Dinesen.

F188 Stevens, George. <u>Speak for Yourself, John: The Life</u>
<u>of John Mason Brown</u>. New York: The Viking Press,
1974.

F189 Stine, Whitney. <u>Mother Goddam: The Story of the</u>
<u>Career of Bette Davis.</u> With running commentary
by Bette Davis. New York: Hawthorn Books, Inc.,
1974.

Her account of making <u>The Little Foxes</u> in 1941,
about Wyler, Hammett, LH, Dorothy Parker.

F190 Styron, William. "Lillian Hellman, Definition and a
Fragment of a Dialogue," in Roddy McDowall, <u>Dou-</u>
<u>ble Exposure.</u> New York: Delacorte Press, 1966,
pp. 190-193.

Styron's text and McDowall's photograph.

F191 Sullivan, Victoria, and James Hatch. <u>Plays by and</u>
<u>about Women</u>. New York: Random House, 1973.

On the type of woman LH is.

F192 Teichmann, Howard. <u>George S. Kaufman, An Intimate</u>
<u>Portrait</u>. New York: Atheneum, 1972.

F193 "Testimony of Miss Lillian Hellman, Accompanied by
her Counsel Joseph L. Rauh, Jr." in "Communist
Infiltration of the Hollywood Motion Picture Industry--
Part 8, Wednesday, May 21, 1952." <u>Hearings Be-</u>
<u>fore the Committee on Un-American Activities, House</u>
<u>of Representatives, Eighty-Second Congress, Second</u>
<u>Session.</u> Washington, D.C.: U.S. Government Print-
ing Office, 1952.

F194 Thorp, Willard. <u>American Writing in the Twentieth</u>
<u>Century</u>. The Library of Congress Series in Ameri-
can Civilization. Ralph Henry Gabriel, ed. Cambridge, Massachusetts: Harvard University Press,
1963.

F195 Triesch, Manfred, compiler. <u>The Lillian Hellman Col-</u>
<u>lection at the University of Texas.</u> Austin, Texas:
(The Humanities Research Center) The University of
Texas Press, 1966. 167 p.

The value of this descriptive catalogue is not only

for its listing of the vast collection of manuscript
material, but for what it reveals about LH's method
of composition, her sources, the development of each
play.   The materials for <u>Candide</u> represent the lar-
gest portion in the collection; and, Triesch accounts
for its size because of LH's method of writing and
revising each scene rather than waiting to revise
after each draft.   He notes that the <u>Candide</u> materials
provide the best example to which a person who wishes
to learn about her method of writing can turn for
illumination.
　　His short comment with each play entry points to
the particular problems which have concerned the
critics and which in some cases are resolved by a
study of the manuscripts and the typescripts.   These
remarks also include production information.   LH's
own quotes from her notes and the different versions
are most helpful and further provide the personality
sketch of Miss Hellman that emerges from this bibliography.
　　The bibliography also lists reviews of the opening night performances and secondary sources as
well.   It gives a chronological listing of the plays,
a list of reviews of the first performances, contributions and letters, manuscripts, and in an appendix
provides scenes and additions in LH's hand.

F196 Trilling, Diana.   <u>We Must March My Darlings</u>.   New
　　　York and London: Harcourt, Brace, Jovanovich,
　　　1977.   pp. 41-66.

　　　The 4 page head-note to "Two Symposiums" is a
　　　response to <u>Scoundrel Time</u> and LH's perceptions
　　　of the times and a personal statement responding to
　　　Miss Hellman's mention of the Trillings in <u>Scoundrel
　　　Time</u>.   Further, she gives her account of the Little,
　　　Brown refusal to publish the book unless she deleted
　　　remarks about LH.

F197 Vaughn, Robert.   <u>Only Victims, A Study of Show Busi-
　　　ness Blacklisting.</u>   Foreword by Senator George Mc-
　　　Govern.   New York: G. P. Putnam's Sons, 1972.

　　　LH's letter to Congressman Wood.

F198 Vinson, James, ed.   <u>Contemporary Dramatists.</u>   Pre-
　　　face by Ruby Cohn.   London, St. James' Press; New
　　　York, St. Martin's Press, 1973.

A biographical account, Clurman's introduction to
Richard Moody's biography (F152), a list of screenplays and productions, a bibliography, her theatrical
activities comprise this 3 page entry.

F199 Waldau, Roy S. Vintage Years of the Theatre Guild,
      1928-1939. Cleveland, Ohio: Case Western Reserve
      Press, 1972.

F200 Walton, Richard J. Henry Wallace, Harry Truman and
      the Cold War. New York: The Viking Press, 1976.

F201 Weales, Gerald. The Jumping-Off Place, American
      Drama in the 1960's. London: Collier-Macmillan,
      Ltd. , 1969.

      Mike Nichols' killing effect on LH's best effects.

F202 _____. "The Playwright of the Twenties and Thir-
      ties, " American Drama Since World War II. New
      York: Harcourt, Brace and World, Inc. , 1962.

      On her thematic concerns.

F203 Weinstein, Allen. Perjury, The Hiss-Chambers Case.
      New York: Alfred A. Knopf, 1978.

F204 Whitesides, Glenn E. Lillian Hellman: A Biographical
      and Critical Study. Ph. D. dissertation. The Flori-
      da State University, 1968.

F204a Wills, Garry. "Commentary" in Scoundrel Time, by
      Lillian Hellman. London: The Macmillan Company,
      1976. (C5)

      The "Introduction" to the Little, Brown edition with
      some new material.

F205 _____. "Introduction" to Scoundrel Time, by Lillian
      Hellman. Boston: Little, Brown and Company, 1976.
      See: C5.

      A biographical portrait of LH.

F206 Wilson, Garff B. Three Hundred Years of American
      Drama and Theatre: From Ye Care and Ye Cubb to
      Hair. Englewood Cliffs, New Jersey: Prentice-Hall,
      1973.

F207 Winchell, Walter. Winchell Exclusive: "Things That
      Happened to Me--and Me to Them. " Introduction
      by Ernest Cuneo.   Englewood Cliffs, New Jersey:
      Prentice-Hall, 1975.

      Of Winchell's almost daily contact with Lillian and
      Arthur Kober and their talk.

F208 Woodress, James, ed.   American Literary Scholarship,
      An Annual/1973.   Durham, North Carolina: Duke
      University Press, 1975.

      Comment on the critical attention given the dramatists
      who emerged between the 2 world wars, gives the
      essence of the criticism published.

F209 Yee, Carole Zonis.   Lillian Hellman, Her Attitude
      about Self and Identity.   Paper presented at the PMLA
      meeting, New York, December 1974.

F210 Zolotow, Maurice.   Billy Wilder in Hollywood.   New
      York: G. P. Putnam's Sons, 1977.

F211 Zwick, Edward Mitchell.   Life in Art, a Study of Lillian
      Hellman and "Watch on the Rhine".   Honors thesis.
      Harvard University, 1974.

G

ARTICLES AND LETTERS ABOUT LILLIAN HELLMAN IN NEWSPAPERS AND PERIODICALS

Arranged by Author

G1   "A Hit and Myth Gathering of Intellectuals. " New York
     Times, Dec. 8, 1968, 4, p. 2.   illus.

     Hellman's praise and criticism of George Kennan.

G2   "A New Lillian Hellman Looks at Yesterday and Today. "
     New York Times, July 1, 1969, p. 33.   illus.

     Talks of Hollywood, Hammett, Parker in the context
     of trying to understand the students who disrupted
     the Harvard campus in 1968.

G3   "Academy Elects 116, 37 Foreigners Also Honored by
     Arts and Sciences Institute. " New York Times, May
     12, 1960, p. 22.

G4   "ACLU Honors 4 in North Brunswick. " New York Times,
     Oct. 29, 1973, p. 74.

G5   "Actors Widen Split on Finn Benefits. " New York Times,
     Jan. 20, 1940, p. 17.

     Bankhead questions sincerity of LH and Herman Shum-
     lin in refusing to give Foxes as benefit; charges pro-
     Soviet bias. See also: G184.

G6   Adler, Jacob. "Miss Hellman's Two Sisters, " Educa-
     tional Theatre Journal, 15 (May, 1963), 112-17.

     Her debt to Ibsen and Chekhov.

G7   _____ H.   "Professor Moody's Miss Hellman, "
     Southern Library Journal, 5 (Spring, 1973), 131-40.

     A review of Richard Moody's biography (F152).

G8   "American Scholar Forum: Women on Women, " Ameri-
     can Scholar, 41 (Autumn, 1972), 599-627.

     LH was moderator of the discussion which Hiram
     Haydn began with the question: "If we win, what
     will we lose?" See: Patricia McLaughlin (G126).

G9   Arman, Fran. "Speaking of People. " National Obser-
     ver, Oct. 9, 1976, p. 6. illus.

     An account of the LH-Trilling affair.

G10   Arnold, Martin. "Lillian Hellman Says She Found Fer-
      ment Among Soviet Writers, Author Reports a De-
      termined Drive for Greater Freedom of Literary
      Expression. " New York Times, May 31, 1967, p. 11.

G11   "Arts and Letters Institute Names 13. " New York Times,
      Feb. 13, 1962, p. 40.

      Cites election of LH as vice-president.

G12   "Arts Medal Goes to Miss Hellman, Playwright Named
      Winner of Brandeis Award. " New York Times, Mar.
      11, 1961, p. 15. illus.

G13   "Awards Made for Arts, Brandeis Cites Playwright
      Composer, Poet and Artist. " New York Times,
      Mar. 30, 1961, p. 21.

G14   Bachrach, Judy. "A Tribute to the Old Lillian Hellman,
      the Real Lillian Hellman, Hellman au gratin. " Wash-
      ington Post, Nov. 11, 1975, B. p. 7+. illus.

      Tells of herself on the occasion of the celebration
      of the fifth anniversary of the Committee for Public
      Justice at Gallagher's.

G15   _____. "Lillian Hellman on the Trilling Controversy. "
      Washington Post, Sept. 30, 1976, B, p. 4.

G16   Baker, Carlos. "Dashiell Hammett. " The New York
      Review of Books, 6 (Mar. 3, 1966), 30.

      A letter praising LH's memoir as the best portrait
      of Hammett he knows. The essay appeared in an
      earlier edition of The Review, 5 (Nov. 25, 1965),
      16-23.

G17   Baker, John F. "PW Interviews: Lillian Hellman. "
      Publishers' Weekly, 209 (Apr. 26, 1976), 6-7.

      Talking with her is "very much like reading her ... "

G18   Balfour, Katharine. "Lillian Hellman. " Family Circle,
      88 (Apr. , 1976), 24-27. illus.

G19   Barber, John. "One Woman and Her Fears. " Daily
      Telegraph (London), Oct. 2, 1972, p. 9. illus.

G20   Barnes, H. D.   "Buckley's Attack on Lillian Hellman. "
      Los Angeles Times, Apr. 15, 1977, 2, p. 6.

      A letter supportive of William F. Buckley's criticism
      of LH in "Down with Hellman!" in the Los Angeles
      Times, Apr. 10, 1977 (G34).

G21   Bellow, Saul.   "My Man Bummidge, He's Lost in a
      World Based on Metaphors. "   New York Times, Sept.
      27, 1964, 2, pp. 1, 5.

      On LH's advice to Bellow to write plays.

G22   "Benefits for Finns Stirs Theatre Row, Several Stage
      Folk Refuse to Take Part, Demanding Help for Needy
      Actors, Chided by Helen Hayes. "   New York Times,
      Jan. 19, 1940, p. 21.   See: G5, G184.

G23   Bennetts, Leslie.   "Lillian Hellman Gives a Vivid Read-
      ing Here, " in Barbara Nykoruk, ed. , Authors in the
      News.   Volume I.   Detroit: Gale Research Company,
      1976, p. 219.   illus.

      A reprint of the article that originally appeared in
      the Philadelphia Bulletin, Oct. 30, 1974, as a report
      of LH's presentation at Bryn Mawr in connection with
      the Lucy Martin Donnelly Fellowship in Creative Wri-
      ting she held.

G24   _____.   "Creative Women of the 20's Who Helped to
      Pave the Way. "   New York Times, Apr. 10, 1978,
      1, p. 20.   illus.

      On the Rutgers' three day conference on "Women
      and the Arts in the 1920's in Paris and New York. "

G25   Brady, Kathleen.   "Lillian Hellman's Hour. "   Village
      Voice, Jan. 13, 1975, pp. 35-36.   illus.

      A congenial interview in which Hellman talks of life,
      movies she has liked, the past.

G26   "Brandeis U. Honors 9 in Creative Arts. "   New York
      Times, June 11, 1961, p. 63.

      The Theatre Arts Medal.

G27   Brandon, Henry.   "A Conversation with Arthur Miller. "
       World Theatre, 11 (Autumn, 1962), 229-40.

       In this interview that was originally published as
       "The Man Who Had All the Luck, " in the Sunday
       Times (London), Mar. 20, 1960, p. 69, Miller says
       LH dated quickly.

G28   Braun, Devra.   "Lillian Hellman's Continuing Moral
       Battle. "   Massachusetts Studies in English (Univer-
       sity of Massachusetts, Amherst), 5, iv (1978), 1-6.

G29   Bridges, Katherine.   "Some Representative Louisiana
       Writers. "   Catholic Library World, 40 (Feb. , 1969),
       352-55.

G30   "Briefs on the Arts: 15 from Stage in Hall of Fame. "
       New York Times, Nov. 20, 1973, p. 30.

G31   "Broadway Report. " New York Star, July 1, 1948, p. 24.

       An announcement that LH was working on a drama-
       tization of Norman Mailer's The Naked and the Dead
       to be produced sometime in late November under her
       direction.

G32   Browda, Clara.   "Buckley's Attack of Lillian Hellman. "
       Los Angeles Times, Apr. 15, 1977, 2, p. 6.

       A letter supporting LH.   See: G34.

G33   Brustein, Robert.   "Why American Plays Are not Litera-
       ture. "   Harper's, 219 (Oct. , 1959), 167-72.   Found
       also in John Fischer and Robert B. Silvers, eds. ,
       Writing in America.   New Brunswick, New Jersey:
       Rutgers University Press, 1960.

       Laments the decline and loss of the intellectual fer-
       ment provided by O'Neill, Odets, and LH in the past;
       says there is yet hope and LH's encouragement of
       Bellow, Gold, and Purdy to write plays is significant.

G34   Buckley, William F.   "Down with Hellman!" Los Ange-
       les Times, Apr. 10, 1977, 6, p. 6.

       After reviewing Scoundrel Time, Buckley equates LH
       in the last analysis with Albert Speer.   See: G20, G32,
       G72, G95, G162, G174, G194.

G35   Burton, Humphrey.   "Salute to a New Breed of Hero:
      Bernstein's Sixtieth Birthday Concert." Times
      (London), Aug. 28, 1978, p. 7.

      An account of LH's tribute to Bernstein and to the
      memory of his wife.

G36   Bush, Alfred L.   "Literary Landmarks of Princeton."
      Princeton University Library Chronicle, 28 (Spring,
      1967), 1-90.

      LH is listed in the Catalogue of an exhibition of
      imaginative writing done at Princeton.

G37   Carmody, Deirdre.   "Trilling Case Sparks Publisher-
      Loyalty Debate." New York Times, Sept. 30, 1976,
      p. 34.

      Includes LH's response after hearing of the passage
      that was to be deleted.   See: F196, G155.

G38   Chusmir, Janet.   "Rasping Recollections, No Regrets."
      Chicago Tribune, Mar. 31, 1974, 6, pp. 18-19.
      illus.

      An interview in which LH speaks of how critical she
      is of herself and of the world, of her view of life.

G39   Clark, Barrett H.   "Lillian Hellman." College English,
      6 (Dec., 1944), 127-33.   Published also in English
      Journal, 33 (Dec., 1944), 519-25.

      One of the earliest longer pieces about her work;
      discusses her work as that of an idealist and a phil-
      osopher; discusses the plays and her quality as a
      playwright.

G40   Clemons, Walter.   "Natural-Born Gumshoe." Newsweek,
      84 (Nov. 25, 1974), 116.   illus.

      A review of Hammett's The Continental Op in which
      Hellman is mentioned.

G41   Clives, Francis X.   "FBI Head Scored by Ramsey Clark,
      Hoover Held Ideological--Justice Committee Formed."
      New York Times, Nov. 18, 1970, p. 48.

      LH on Executive Council of Com. for Public Justice.

G42   Coe, Richard L.   "The Importance of Being Lillian:
       A Hellman Mini-Festival. "   Washington Post, Feb.
       20, 1977, K, p. 3 illus.

       The staging of three plays at Baltimore's Center
       Stage.

G43   Cook, Joan.   "Furniture Collection That Charts Lillian
       Hellman's Career. "   New York Times, Nov. 14, 1967,
       p. 40. illus.

G44   Cryer, Gretchen.   "Where Are the Women Playwrights? "
       New York Times, May 20, 1973, 2, pp. 1, 3.   illus.

       LH responds to the Times' inquiry.

G45   Cummings, Judith.   "Columbia Grants Degrees to 6,
       700, 9, Including Carey, Receive Honorary Awards,
       as 40 Hold Protest Walk. "   New York Times, May
       13, 1976, p. 19.

G46   "Curtis Publishing Is Named in a $3 Million Libel Suit. "
       New York Times, Feb. 27, 1964, p. 39.

       Suit filed by Sheriff of Etowah County, Alabama, over
       material in "Sophronia's Grandson Goes to Washing-
       ton. "   See: D27 and G124.

G47   "Dashiell Hammett, Author, Dies; Created Hard-Boiled
       Detectives. "   New York Times, Jan. 11, 1961, p.
       47.

G48   de Pue, Stephanie.   "Lillian Hellman, Interview, " in
       Biography News.   Detroit: Gale Research Company,
       2 (Sept. /Oct. , 1975), 1021-22.   illus.

       A reprint of an article originally in the Miami Herald,
       Sept. 7, 1975.

G49   _____.   "Lillian Hellman, She Never Turns Down an
       Adventure, " in Barbara Nykoruk, ed. , Authors in the
       News.   Volume II.   Detroit: Gale Research Com-
       pany, 1976, pp. 142-43.   illus.

       An interview that appeared originally in the Cleveland
       Plain Dealer, Dec. 28, 1975, in which LH talks of her
       work, villains, relativistic morality, human relations.

G50 "Dorothy Parker Recalled as Wit, Mostel and Lillian
        Hellman Deliver Brief Eulogies. " New York Times,
        June 10, 1967, p. 33.

G51 Doudna, Christine. "A Still Unfinished Woman. " Rolling
        Stone, Feb. 24, 1977, pp. 52-57.

G52 "Doughty Dramatist. " MD Medical Newsmagazine, March,
        1974, p. 159.

        A feature personality article.

G53 "Drama Still Alive Stage Experts Say, Four Tell Har-
        vard Law Forum Serious Works Have Not Given Up
        to Musicals. " New York Times, Dec. 2, 1951, 1,
        p. 85.

G54 Drutman, Irving. "Hellman: A Stranger in the Theater. "
        New York Times, Feb. 27, 1966, 2, pp. 1, 5. illus.

        Speaks of her disaffection for and of the barrier be-
        tween her and the theater, about playwriting as a
        "peculiar form"; tells what she said during her term
        at Yale.

G54a Eichelbaum, Stanley. "Teaching Writers How to Steal. "
        San Francisco Examiner, Feb. 10, 1971, p. 22.
        illus.

        An interview while in San Francisco for her seminar
        at the University of California, Berkeley.

G55 "Eight 'Women of the Year' Honored by Magazine. " New
        York Times, Apr. 20, 1975, p. 16.

        The Ladies' Home Journal Award.

G56 Emerson, Gloria. "Lillian Hellman: At 66, She's
        Still Restless. " New York Times, Sept. 7, 1973,
        p. 24. illus. Found also in The New York Times
        Biographical Edition for that year, pp. 1481-82.

        This interview at Martha's Vineyard covers her lack
        of patience with the theater, her lack of energy to
        have her temper any longer, her surprise at the stu-
        dent unrest of the sixties in that there is not a his-
        tory of student dissent in the U. S. , her thinking that

the dullest of all the generations was that of the thirties and the early forties, that since we have no national memory, we will forget the Watergate business after a year.

G57 Ephron, Nora. "Lillian Hellman, Walking, Cooking, Writing, Talking. " New York Times, Sept. 23, 1973, 7, pp. 2, 51. illus.

LH talks about getting older, taking a year to write Pentimento, the friendship of Parker, being shocked by people who took no stand at all during the McCarthy years, how hard some women have made it for other women.

G58 Ezergailis, A. "Kuznetsov's Exile. " New York Times, Aug. 30, 1969, p. 20.

A letter defending Kuznetsov against Hellman's attack (D38).

G59 Ferrell, Tom. "Ideas and Trends: In Summary, McCarthy Era Revisited. " New York Times, Oct. 3, 1976, 4, p. 8.

An account of the Little, Brown and Company cancellation of the Trilling book because it was critical of LH in part. See also: G61.

G60 "50 Women Named Most Influential in U. S. " Chicago Tribune, Aug. 17, 1975, p. 5.

G61 Firth, John. "Talking with Diana Trilling. " Saturday Review, 4 (May 28, 1977), 22-23.

DT speaks of not hearing any protest about the censorship from LH; talks of LH in conjunction with the section on her in We Must March My Darlings.

G62 Flander, Judy. "Hellman: Doling Out the Tidbits, " in Barbara Nykoruk, ed. , Authors in the News. Volume I. Detroit: Gale Research Company, 1976, p. 219.

Concerning Hellman's speech at Smithsonian's Baird Auditorium, a report that was published originally in the Washington Star-News, Nov. 11, 1974.

G63 "Footnotes on Headliners: Applause. " <u>New York Times,</u>
     Apr. 23, 1939, 4, p. 2.

     About the Drama Critics' inability to decide on a
     1939 prize winning play.

G64 "400 Writers Hold First U. S. Meeting, Authors and
     Dramatists Take Up Contract Flaws and Trend to
     Conformity. " <u>New York Times,</u> May 7, 1957, p.
     29.

     LH's comment to panel on the "Emotional Problems
     of Writers. "

G65 Fraser, C. Gerald.   "33 Playwrights Protest 'Censure'
     of <u>Robeson</u>. " <u>New York Times</u>, May 18, 1978, 3,
     p. 20.

G66 Fremont-Smith, Eliot. "Lillian Hellman: Portrait of
     a Lady. " <u>New York Magazine</u>, Sept. 17, 1973, p.
     82.

G67 Friedman, Mickey.   "Book Scene. " <u>San Francisco
     Examiner</u>, Nov. 27, 1978, p. 20.

     Announces that LH is working in cooperation with
     Diane Johnson on the Random House Hammett bio-
     graphy.

G68 Fussell, B. H.   "On the Trail of the Lonesome Drama-
     turge. " <u>Hudson Review</u>, 26 (Winter, 1973-74), 753-
     62.

     Picks up with LH's comment that theater is boring
     and continues the discussion that "we have always
     opposed art to Nature and wholly sided with Nature"
     (G132).

G69 Gehman, Richard B.   "The Critics. " <u>Theatre Arts,</u>
     35 (Sept. , 1951), 10+.

     Background of and pictures of many of the critics
     who reviewed LH's work; an account of the formation
     of the New York Drama Critics' Circle.

G70 Gold, Arthur, and Robert Fizdale.   "Lillian Hellman's
     Creole Cooking, Recipes from an American Woman

Playwright. " Vogue, 163 (June, 1974), pp. 98, 150+. illus.

Talks of life at Hardscrabble Farm and gives recipes for pickled curried eggs, stuffed eggplant, baked fish creole, dirty rich, Bouilli.

G71 Goldstein, Malcolm. "Body and Soul on Broadway. " Modern Drama, 7 (Feb. , 1965), 411-21.

A discussion of the popularity of American psychological drama; LH's concern with people whose worry is the inability to enjoy what they have.

G72 Gomez, Cynthia J.   "Buckley's Attack of Lillian Hellman. " Los Angeles Times, Apr. 15, 1977, 2, p. 6.

A letter supportive of Hellman (G34).

G73 "Governor (Lehman) to Shun 'Communist' Forum, He Rescinds Sponsorship of Dinner for Fascist Victims, Calling Committees Red: Lillian Hellman's Reply. " New York Times, Oct. 4, 1941, p. 34.

LH insists the "Europe Today" dinner forum is solely to raise funds for the 50 anti-Fascists threatened with death in French camps.

G74 Grose, Peter. "Soviet's Writers Given Party Line, Convention Is told to Fight West's 'Dirt and Filth'. " New York Times, May 23, 1967, p. 12.

Report of the Fourth Congress of the Union of Writers in Moscow; states LH left for New York after the opening session May 22.

G75 Gussow, Mel. "For Lillian Hellman, More Honors and a New Book. " New York Times, Nov. 7, 1975, p. 28. illus.

Anticipating the Circle in the Square celebration of LH and benefit for the Committee for Public Justice.

G75a Haber, Joyce. "A Lady Who Believes in Answering Back. " San Francisco Chronicle, Nov. 16, 1969, DATEBK, pp. 9-10. illus.

An interview.

G76   "Hammett Eulogized by Lillian Hellman." New York
      Times, Jan. 13, 1961, p. 29.

      Obituary.

G77   "Hammett's Will Filed, Less than $10,000 in Estate of
      Mystery Story Writer." New York Times, Feb. 7,
      1961, p. 66.

      LH named executrix.

G78   Handler, M.S. "Lillian Hellman Is Among Nine Named
      to City University Chairs." New York Times, Sept.
      26, 1972, p. 38.

      Distinguished Professor in the Romance Language
      Department at Hunter College.

G79   Harriman, Margaret Case. "Miss Lily of New Orleans."
      New Yorker, 17 (Nov. 8, 1941), 22-26, 28-29, 32-
      33+.   Found also in Margaret Case Harriman, Take
      Them Up Tenderly, A Collection of Profiles. New
      York: Alfred A. Knopf, 1944, pp. 94-109.

      A warm appraisal of LH, a biographical and pro-
      fessional portrait.   Harriman gives a physical de-
      scription of LH, writes of Hammett, Parker, the
      Mrs. Luce-Dorothy Thompson-Somerset Maugham
      comment, the subsequent crack of Dorothy Thompson
      in her Valentine Day's column, LH's fierce anti-
      Fascism, her working habits, her friendships, her
      likes and dislikes, her accomplishment as a superb
      dramatist.

G80   "Hellman Returns from Paris." New York Times, Aug.
      26, 1947, p. 26.

      After attending a Unesco meeting; will help prepare
      Another Part of the Forest for the road.

G81   "Hellman Talks about Hellman." Biography News.
      Detroit: Gale Research Company, 1 (Apr., 1974),
      411-12.   illus.

G82   "Hellman Talks about Hellman," in Barbara Nykoruk,
      ed., Authors in the News. Volume I. Detroit: Gale
      Research Company, 1976, pp. 217-18.   illus.

A reprint of an article that was published originally
in the Miami Herald, Mar. 17, 1974, in which Hellman talks about marriage, age, drinking, peace, her
own nature, her life.

G83   Hersey, John.   " 'Anger ... Feeds Her Love of Life.' "
      Los Angeles Times, Sept. 26, 1976, 6, pp. 1, 5.

      Published originally as "Lillian Hellman" in the New
      Republic (G84), this piece was delivered on the oc-
      casion of the MacDowell Prize.   Anger and rebellious-
      ness are at the heart of Hellman's vibrancy, Hersey
      claims.

G84   _____.   "Lillian Hellman."   New Republic, 175
      (Sept. 18, 1976), 25-27.   illus.   Found also in Colony
      Newsletter (The MacDowell Colony, Inc.), 6 (Summer,
      1976), 4-5, with Miss Hellman's response.

      Hersey's homage on the occasion of the MacDowell
      Prize in which he discusses her nature and her very
      self, the complexity of her work and approach to life.

G85   Hill, Gladwin.   "Writer Names 100 as Film Reds After
      Threats Against His Family, Former Party Member
      Gives House Group Long List of His Ex-Comrades."
      New York Times, Sept. 20, 1951, p. 25.

      LH listed in Martin Berkeley's testimony.

G86   Hilles, Frederick W.   "Wells and West."   New York
      Times, Nov. 17, 1974, 7, p. 55+.

      A letter in which Hilles wonders if LH's review is
      a review of "a supplement to" her autobiography.
      See: D49.

G87   "History of PM."   PM, Aug. 16, 1946, p. 3C.

      Presumably this account was written by Ralph Inger-
      soll, the editor of PM.

G88   "Honors Bestowed by Arts Academy."   New York Times,
      May 23, 1963, p. 34.

G89   Hughes, Charlotte.   "Women Playmakers."   New York
      Times, May 4, 1941, 6, pp. 10-11, 27.   illus.

Writes of LH's "masculine mind, " her discipline and
patience while writing.

G90 "Hundreds Named as Red Appeasers: California's Ten-
      ney Committee Lists Actors, Musicians, and Others
      as 'Line' Followers. " New York Times, June 9, 1949,
      p. 5.

G91 "Is the Theatre Worth Saving?" New York Times, June
      7, 1974, p. 20.

G92 Isaacs, Edith J. R. "Lillian Hellman, A Playwright on
      the March. " Theatre Arts, 28 (Jan. , 1944), 19-24.
      Found also in Walter J. Meserve, ed. , Discussions
      of American Drama. Boston: D. C. Heath and Com-
      pany, 1965, pp. 46-51.

      An evaluation of LH's writing progress, claims LH
      lacks faith in the theater as a medium and in the
      audience, so she over-works. Notes that perhaps
      the movies will ultimately remedy the fault of her
      over-writing.

G93 "Jo's Girls: The Literary Women of the '20's. " San
      Francisco Chronicle, Apr. 13, 1978, p. 26.   illus.

      Regarding the "Women and the Arts" Conference at
      Rutgers (G24).

G94 Josephson, Matthew. "Leane Zugsmith: The Social
      Novel of the Thirties. " Southern Review, 2 (1975),
      530-52.

      An over-view of the radical writers of the thirties;
      LH is mentioned briefly.

G95 Judge, John A. "Buckley's Attack on Lillian Hellman. "
      Los Angeles Times, Apr. 15, 1977, 2, p. 6.

      See: G34.

G96 Kaplan, Morris. "Dorothy Parker's Will Leaves Estate
      of $10, 000 to Dr. King. " New York Times, June
      27, 1967, p. 22.

      And LH's response to Parker's bequest.

G97 Kazin, Alfred. "The Legend of Lillian Hellman." Esquire, 88 (Aug., 1977), 28, 30, 34. illus.

Recounts the Trilling-Little, Brown incident regarding
We Must March My Darlings, writes of the power of
LH's personality, that she is easy on herself and on
Hammett.

G98 Kellogg, Mary Alice. "Newsmakers." Newsweek, 88
(Oct. 11, 1976), 53.

An account of the Trilling-Little, Brown-LH rift.

G99 "Keenan Analysis Coolly Received, Intellectuals at Princeton Seminar Criticize Speech." New York Times,
Dec. 4, 1968, p. 93.

See also: G163, G185, G186.

G100 "Kennedy Doctor Widens Activity." New York Times,
Apr. 20, 1961, p. 23.

LH received 1 of 6 achievement awards from the
Women's Division of the Albert Einstein College of
Medicine of Yeshiva University.

G101 Kernan, Michael. "Friends and 'Scoundrels': Publishing Fray Centered on the 50's." Washington Post,
Sept. 29, 1976, B, pp. 1, 11. illus.

G102 Klemesrud, Judy. "Lillian Hellman Denies Having Played
a Role in Little Brown's Rejection of Trilling Book."
New York Times, Sept. 29, 1976, p. 28.

Identifies the controversial passage as "Liberal Anti-
Communism Revisited."

G103 Klion, Stanley R. "On Dumping Business." New York
Times, June 21, 1975, p. 26.

A letter in which he states his objection to LH's con-
demnation of the business community in her speech
at Barnard College (D53) as not worthy of LH.

G104 Koch, Beverly. "Through the Years with Lillian Hellman." San Francisco Chronicle, Feb. 11, 1971, p.
38. illus.

G105 Krebs, Albin. "Note on People. " New York Times,
      Dec. 4, 1973, p. 55.

      LH absent from ceremonies inducting new members
      to Hall of Fame.

      Tells of herself, of the month's writing seminar at
      the University of California, Berkeley, of living in
      San Francisco.

G106 _____. "Note on People. " New York Times, June
      30, 1976, p. 34.

      To receive Edward MacDowell Medal, August 15,
      1976.

G107 _____. "Note on People. " New York Times, Oct.
      6, 1976, p. 40.

      Notice that she will be a recipient of the Actors'
      Equity Association third annual Paul Robeson Award,
      October 8, 1976.

G108 _____. "Note on People. " New York Times, Oct.
      9, 1976, p. 25.

      That Harcourt, Brace, Jovanovich will pick up Diana
      Trilling's book without deletion of passage about LH.

G109 "Ladies' Home Journal Women of the Year, 1975. "
      Ladies' Home Journal, 92 (May, 1975), 38.   illus.

G110 Lask, Thomas. "Books of the Time, Many Voices,
      Many Rooms. " New York Times, Nov. 14, 1967,
      p. 45.

      A review of Writers at Work, The Paris Review
      Interviews, Third Series (G157), with comment on the
      Hellman interview.

G111 Laurence, Michael. "Autonomy in Staging. " New York
      Times, Oct. 23, 1949, 2, pp. 1, 2.

      In reaction to LH's discussion of directors, Laurence
      claims in his letter directors usually discard play-
      wrights' stage directions (G182).

G112 Levine, Jo Ann. "Author Lillian Hellman--A Portrait
in Words. " Christian Science Monitor, Dec. 21,
1973, B, p. 2. illus.

A lengthy interview in which LH talks especially of
Dorothy Parker and Arthur Cowan, of friendship.

G113 "Lillian Hellman. " Wilson Bulletin, 13 (May, 1939),
632. illus.

A biographical sketch.

G114 "Lillian Hellman at Mount Holyoke. " Mount Holyoke
Alumnae Quarterly, 60 (Summer, 1976), 16-17. illus.

An outline and summary of her 1976 commencement
speech.

G115 "Lillian Hellman Balks House Unit, Says She Is Not
Red Now, but Won't Disclose if She Was Lest It Hurt
Others. " New York Times, May 22, 1952, p. 15.

Quotes letter to Congressman Wood.

G116 "Lillian Hellman Buys Estate of 130 Acres, Playwright
Gets Property in Westchester. " New York Times,
June 7, 1939, p. 43.

G117 "Lillian Hellman Fails to Bar Her Toys from Opening. "
New York Times, May 12, 1978, 3, p. 13.

Regarding the WPA Theater Production of Toys.

G118 "Lillian Hellman Gets Lord and Taylor Award. " New
York Times, Nov. 10, 1977, 2, p. 16.

" ... whose creative mind has brought new beauty
and deeper understanding to our lives. "

G119 "Lillian Hellman in Moscow. " New York Times, Nov.
6, 1944, p. 25.

G120 "Lillian Hellman to Be Lecturer. " New York Times,
July 31, 1960, 1, p. 48.

Spring term at Harvard.

G121 "Lillian Hellman's Credo." Nation, 174 (May 31, 1952), 518.

An excerpt of her letter to Congressman Wood regarding her appearance before the HUAC.

G122 "Lin Yutang Holds 'Gods' Favor China." New York Times, Jan. 10, 1940, p. 19.

LH also spoke at the Book and Author luncheon: "I am a writer and I am also a Jew...."

G123 Lochte, Dick. "Book Notes: Picking up the Trail of Hammett." Los Angeles Times, Oct. 1, 1978, BKS, p. 2.

Concerning previous denial of access to letters, documents now lifted for the Diane Johnson biography.

G124 McCord, Roy P. "Retraction: We Have Received the Following Letter from Mr. Roy P. McCord of Gadsden, Alabama." Ladies' Home Journal, 81 (Mar., 1964), 82.

Regarding sections of "Sophronia's Grandson" (D27, D29) that falsely accused the Sheriff that McCord wished an apology for.

See also: G46.

G125 McFadden, Robert D. "Diana Trilling Book Is Cancelled, Reply to Lillian Hellman is Cited." New York Times, Sept. 28, 1976, pp. 1, 45. illus.

Account of the Little, Brown refusal.

G126 McLaughlin, Patricia. "Comment." American Scholar, 41 (Fall, 1972), 622-27.

A response to the participants' remarks as a summary of the discussion "Women on Women" (G8). "If you win everything you want ... you can't lose anything you can respect by winning."

G127 Mackay, Barbara. "What Ever Happened to the Ingenue?" Saturday Review, 1 (July 27, 1974), 42.

Brief mention of LH is made in the discussion.

G128 Marcus, Steven. "Dashiell Hammett and the Continental Op. " Partisan Review, 41 (Autumn, 1974), 362-77.

Includes comment on the Hammett-Hellman relation-ship and Hammett's connection with and influence on LH.

G129 Margolis, Jon. " ... or You Can't Tell a Man by the Song He Sings. " Chicago Tribune Book World, Jan. 8, 1978, p. 1.

On the politics of writers: LH "has become some-thing of a cult figure in the last few years. "

G130 Marshall, Thomas F. "Lillian Hellman, Playwright, by Richard Moody. " American Literature, 45 (May, 1973), 312-13.

A review of Moody's book and of Hellman.

G131 Mee, Charles, L. , Jr. "Woman of Courage. " Horizon, 18 (Summer, 1976), 104-05. illus.

A portrait of Hellman and comment on the memoirs.

G132 Meehan, Thomas. "Q: Miss Hellman, What's Wrong with Broadway? A: It's a Bore. " Esquire, 58 (Dec. , 1962), 140-42, 235-36. Found also under the title "An Interview with Lillian Hellman, " in Robert W. Corrigan, The Modern Theatre. New York: The Macmillan Company, 1964.

An interview in which she speaks fully and freely about Broadway, of Beckett, Inge, Albee, Williams, and Miller. Theater is not fun any longer.

G133 "Meeting-goer. " Time, 59 (June 2, 1952), 74. illus.

Regarding her appearance at HUAC.

G134 "Miss Hellman Again. " New York Times, Dec. 13, 1936, 11, p. 4.

A feature article on her career before the opening of Days to Come, which she mulled over for 6 years; a biographical sketch that also deals with the relation-ship between LH and Herman Shumlin.

G135 "Miss Hellman and Shahn Honored. " New York Times,
     Jan 28, 1964, p. 28, illus.

     Concerning the National Institute of Arts and Letters'
     Gold Medal.

G136 "Miss Hellman Wins Award by College. " New York
     Times, Apr. 4, 1968, p. 58.

     The Jackson College Award of Distinction.

G137 Moorehead, Caroline. "A Witch-Hunt Survivor with
     Unfashionable Conscience Still Intact. " Times (Lon-
     don), Dec. 3, 1976, p. 18. illus.

     A warm portrait of LH written by Moorehead after
     a visit together at Claridge's.

G138 Morehouse, Ward. " 'These Full Lean Years'. " Thea-
     tre Arts, 44 (Sept. , 1960), 10, 14+.

     On the '30's.

G139 Morley, Sheridan. "Memoirs of 'an Unfinished Woman'. "
     Times (London), May 1, 1974, p. 11. illus.

G140 Moss, Leonard. "Hammett's Heroic Operative. " New
     Republic, 154 (Jan. 8, 1966), 32-34.

     A review of the volume edited by LH with good men-
     tion of her.

G141 "Mrs. Trilling's Book Killed. " San Francisco Chronicle,
     Sept. 29, 1976, 4, p. 1. illus.

G142 Nemy, Enid. "A Rocky Road to Romance, and a Home
     on Park Avenue. " New York Times, May 12, 1974,
     p. 52.

     LH's home on a house tour to benefit the Industrial
     Home for the Blind.

G143 Nolan, Paul T. "Drama in the Lower Mississippi States. "
     Mississippi Quarterly, 18 (Fall, 1965), 20-28.

     LH as a reminder of plays with a national interest.

G144 "Noting the 'r' in October, Lillian Hellman Hosts a
      Bash at the Oyster Bar. " People, 8 (Oct. 17, 1977),
      44. illus.

G145 Novick, Julius. "Can 'the Facts' Alone Make a Play?"
      New York Times, Dec. 3, 1972, 2, p. 13.

      A review of Are You Now or Have Your Ever Been?
      by Eric Bentley, in which LH's letter to Congress-
      man Wood is part of the drama.

G146 Occhiogrosso, Frank. "Murder in the Dark: Dashiell
      Hammett. " New Republic, 177 (July 30, 1977), 28-
      30.

G147 "On the Current Cinema: The Children's Hour. " Liter-
      ary Digest, 120 (Sept. 14, 1935), 33.

      Mentions the sale of her first piece, "Introspective
      Writing, " was to the Paris Comet; no date is given.

G148 Orth, Maureen. "Hollywood's New Power Elite: The
      Baby Moguls. " New West, June 19, 1978, pp. 20-
      24.

      LH mentioned as a house guest of the Hannah Wein-
      stein family in London, as a model for Paula Wein-
      stein.

G149 "Panel Chooses 50: Most Influential Women Named. "
      Los Angeles Times, Aug. 19, 1975, 4, p. 6.

      Panel named by the Newspaper Enterprise Associa-
      tion to determine which have had most impact on
      American society.

G150 Parke, Richard H. "Our Way Defended to 2, 000 Open-
      ing 'Culture' Meeting: Americans Against Reds, not
      Against Peace, says Norman Cousins at Waldorf
      Session. " New York Times, Mar. 26, 1949, pp. 1,
      3.

      The text of Cousins' speech and LH's response to
      his remarks and criticism of Professor Sidney Hook.

G151 "Peace: Everybody Wars Over It, Lillian Hellman:
      Mastermind. " Newsweek, 33 (Apr. 4, 1949), 20.
      illus.

An account of the Waldorf Conference.

G152 Peck, Seymour. "Lillian Hellman Talks of Love and
    Toys." New York Times, Feb. 21, 1960, 2, p. 3.

    An interview with LH before the opening of Toys in
    which she said it is so important "to live by your
    own standards," even if loneliness and unpopularity
    result.   She does not believe a person always comes
    out lonely living by standards.   Talks of living in
    time of junky "words, junky ideas." Remarks she
    would still like to rewrite the end of Children's Hour.

G153 Penfield, Cornelia.   "Those Obscure Greats--The Screen
    Writers. " Stage, 13 (Sept., 1936), 59.   illus.

G154 "People." Time, 45 (Mar. 12, 1945), 55.   illus.

    Reports recent trip to U. S. S. R.

G155 "People." Time, 108 (Oct. 10, 1976), 62.

    Comments from both women in the Trilling-Hellman-
    Little, Brown affair.

G156 "People Are Talking About ... Lillian Hellman, Distin-
    guished American Playwright. " Vogue, 103 (Apr. 15,
    1944), 98.

G157 Phillips, John, and Anne Hollander.   "The Art of the
    Theater: Lillian Hellman; An Interview. " Paris
    Review, 33 (Winter-Spring, 1965), 64-95.   illus.
    Found also in George Plimpton, ed., with an intro-
    duction by Alfred Kazin, Writers at Work: Third
    Series.   New York: The Viking Press, 1967, pp.
    115-40.

    The attractive resonance and deepness of tone of the
    witty comments that one can hear in the interview
    with Bill Moyers (E37) are found in this with Phillips
    and Hollander, who draw out the complexity of her
    character and her compassion.   LH speaks of her
    marriage to Kober, the warmth and affection for Ham-
    mett, their good times together, about the special
    element of violence in her plays.   She discusses the
    blacklisting, the foolishness and clowning of the people
    of the 30's; she says she has never been interested

in political messages, but writes rather out of the
times in which she lives.   She speaks of her pre-
ference for Autumn Garden, admits to her tiredness
of the people of Foxes, and talks of Brecht's true
talent.

G158 "Portrait. "   Theatre Arts, 33 (Oct. , 1949), 14.   illus.

G159 "Presentation to Lillian Hellman of the Gold Medal for
Drama by Louis Kronenberger of the Institute. "
Proceedings of the American Academy of Arts and
Letters and the National Institute of Arts and Letters.
Second Series, no. 15 (awarded May 20, 1964).

G160 "Private Rites Held for Edmund Wilson. "   New York
Times, June 16, 1972, p. 42.

Attended Wilson's funeral on Cape Cod.

G161 Pryor, Thomas M.   At Peace with the World. "   New
York Times, July 7, 1946, 2, p. 3.

An interview held 4 months before the opening of
Another Part of the Forest in which she talks of how
she conceives of the subject for a play and how she
then goes about the writing of it, of the critics and
their verdicts on The Searching Wind, of William
Wyler as "the best in the business. "

G162 Ranney, Phyllis.   "Buckley's Attack on Lillian Hellman. "
Los Angeles Times, Apr. 15, 1977, 2, p. 6.

A letter in response to Buckley's review (G34).

G163 Raymont, Henry.   "Intellectuals Gather to Discuss Nixon's Problems, Visitors Arriving for Talks at Princeton Reflect a Wide Interest Abroad. "   New York
Times, Dec. 1, 1968, p. 72.

Lists LH and other participants in the sessions (G99,
G185, G186).

G164 _____.   "Winners of 1969 Book Awards Named. "
New York Times, Mar. 3, 1969, p. 34.   illus.

For An Unfinished Woman.

G165 Reed, Edward. "New Faces: 1935." Theatre Arts
     Monthly, 19 (Apr., 1935), 270-71.

G166 Reich, Kenneth. "1,600 at L.A. Rally Hear Call to
     Curtail CIA Power." Los Angeles Times, Apr. 28,
     1975, 2, pp. 3, 18.

     LH set the theme of the 2½ hour meeting.

G167 Reinhold, Robert. "Academy Split Over Plan to Honour
     Ezra Pound." Times (London), July 6, 1972, p. 6.

G168 Rice, Elmer. "Elmer Rice Joins the Disenchanted."
     New York Times, Mar. 13, 1966, 2, pp. 1, 11.

     A letter responding to Irving Drutman's interview of
     LH in which Rice shares Hellman's disenchantment.
     See: G54.

G169 Rice, Robert. "Broadway Report." PM, May 6, 1941,
     p. 23.

     Reports an anecdote involving LH, William Saroyan,
     and a by-stander at Critics' Circle prize dinner.

G170 Ripley, Anthony. "Appeals Court Will Move Quickly on
     Nixon Records." New York Times, Feb. 2, 1975,
     p. 44.

G171 _____. "U.S. Judge Rules Nixon Documents Belong
     to the Nation." New York Times, Feb. 1, 1975,
     pp. 1, 10.

     In response to suit filed by LH and others.

G172 Robb, Christina. "Wells and West." New York Times,
     Nov. 17, 1974, 7, p. 55.

     A letter regarding Hellman's review of Gordon Ray's
     Wells and West (D49).

G173 Robinson, Clarke. "Silhouettes of Celebrities." World
     Digest, 15 (Jan., 1942), 78-83.

G174 Rockman, Alan. "Buckley's Attack on Lillian Hellman."
     Los Angeles Times, Apr. 15, 1977, 2, p. 6.

     See: G34.

G175 Roeder, Bill. "Newsmakers." Newsweek, 88 (Nov. 1, 1976), 61.

An account of the $7,000 Blackglama coat.

G176 "Russia Acclaimed by Miss Hellman: Home, She Says, Soviet Will Deal with Fascism--Hopes We Do the Same in U. S." New York Times, Mar. 2, 1945, p. 5.

Back in the United States as the first foreigner to visit the Russian Army at the Front, LH talks of that and of the Russian people.

G177 "Rutgers Awards Degrees to 2,730, 11 Get Honorary Doctorates." New York Times, June 6, 1963, p. 24.

G178 Sales, Grover. "A Lioness in Our Midst." San Francisco Examiner, Dec. 10, 1978, CAL, pp. 52-53.

In his profile of Diane Johnson, Sales writes of LH and quotes Johnson on Hellman and of her cooperation in the Hammett biography.

G179 Schneider, Alan. "Writers Take Up Issue of Directing Plays." New York Times, Oct. 30, 1949, 2, p. 3.

A letter in reaction to LH's interview on directors and directing (G182).

G180 Schonberg, Harold C. "Music: Marc Blitzstein, Memorial at Philharmonic Hall Attracts Noted Artists and Capacity Audience." New York Times, Apr. 20, 1964, p. 35.

G181 Schrag, Peter. "Lillian Hellman." More, 6 (June, 1976), 3. illus.

G182 Schumach, Murray. "Miss Hellman Discusses Directors." New York Times, Oct. 23, 1949, 2, pp. 1, 3.

An interview a week before the opening of Montserrat in which she spoke of her directing techniques and her approach to directing, of creative directors Elia Kazan, Jed Harris, Herman Shumlin. Explains why she took over staging of her plays.

G183 "Scores Attack on Fund, Lillian Hellman Speaks at Dinner to Aid Anti-Nazis in France. " New York Times,
Oct. 10, 1941, p. 9.

Co-chairman with Ernest Hemingway.   See: G73.

G184 "Sees Finnish Aid Imperiling Peace, Lillian Hellman,
Author, Says Benefit Performances Tend to Fan War
Flames: Reply to Miss Bankhead. " New York Times,
Jan. 21, 1940, p. 27.

See: G5.

G185 "Seminar Studies U. S. Woes. " New York Times, Dec.
3, 1968, pp. 49, 61.   illus.

An account of the "Notables Dinner" (G99, G163).

G186 Shenker, Israel.   "Intellectuals Look at the World, the
U. S. and Themselves and Find All 3 in Trouble. "
New York Times, Dec. 7, 1968, p. 52.

See: G99, G163, G185.

G187 _____.   "Perelman Shaken Up by Florida's Charms. "
New York Times, Apr. 27, 1974, p. 25.

Tells of his visit to Florida with LH, Albert Hackett,
and Frances Goodrich.

G188 _____.   "Rhetoric of Democrats in 1976 Leans Heavi-
ly on Unity and God. " New York Times, July 16,
1976, 1, p. 15.

LH's comment about language of politicians.

G189 _____.   "Those in the New Privileged Class, the
Careless, Don't Miss Their Droshkys. " New York
Times, Jan. 18, 1974, p. 35.

LH on taking cabs instead of using an auto.

G190 Shepard, Richard.   "Lillian Hellman Teaching at Yale,
Playwright Gives a Seminar to Freshman on Writing. "
New York Times, Feb. 1, 1966, p. 28.

See: G54.

G191 Sherwood, Robert E. "Footnote to a Preface." Saturday Review of Literature, 32 (Aug. 6, 1949), 132. illus.

Mentions the rising talent of LH.

G192 "Show People's Campaign: Depict Negro Truthfully, Entertainment Field Urged to 'Treat Problem with Full Seriousness'." PM, May 24, 1944, p. 10. illus.

An account of the adoption of the Declaration of Principles, written by Maxwell Anderson, LH, and Peter Lyon, read by Herman Shumlin at a meeting of the Entertainment Emergency Committee the weekend of May 20.

G193 Sinclair, Dorothy. "Feminist File: The Buyer's Guide to What's Available, What's Worth Your Time, Money, and Respect!" West Coast Review of Books, 3 (Mar., 1977), 53.

Writes of LH, mentions Scoundrel Time.

G194 Smith, Cameron M., Jr. "Buckley's Attack on Lillian Hellman." Los Angeles Times, Apr. 15, 1977, 2, p. 6.

A letter registering disgust with Buckley's comments (G34).

G195 "Some Notables Name Their Best." New York Times, Jan. 6, 1974, 2, p. 9.

Her choice of best films of 1973: The Sorrow and the Pity, Cries and Whispers, and State of Siege.

G196 Spacks, Patricia Meyer. "Free Women." Hudson Review, 24 (Winter, 1971-71), 559-73.

A discussion of what is particularly "feminine" in the autobiographical writing of LH and Anaïs Nin and in the writing of Doris Lessing and Colette and of the difficulties of freedom.

G197 "Special Edition of Hellman Play for Benefit of Refugees." Publishers' Weekly, 142 (July 18, 1942), 170.

The privately published, numbered edition of <u>Watch on the Rhine.</u>

G198 "Sponsors of the World Peace Conference. " <u>New York Times</u>, Mar. 24, 1949, p. 4.

G199 Stern, Richard G. "Lillian Hellman and Her Plays. " <u>Contact</u>, 3 (1959), 113-19.

> Tells of the ideas out of which <u>Toys</u> came, that she is working on a play but at present is blocked.

G200 Strauss, Theodore. "Of Lillian Hellman, A Lady of Principle: The Author of <u>Watch on the Rhine</u> and <u>North Star</u> Stands by Her Guns. " <u>New York Times,</u> Aug. 29, 1943, 2, p. 3.

> Would not be pushed around by Hollywood.

G201 Sullivan, Dan. "Celebrity Toast to Lillian Hellman. " <u>Los Angeles Times,</u> Nov. 14, 1975, 4, pp. 1, 27.

> Tribute at Circle in the Square to her and to raise funds for Committee for Public Justice.

G202 "Summary of Judge's Ruling on the Nixon Document. " <u>New York Times,</u> Feb. 1, 1975, p. 10.

> Text of ruling, cites plaintiffs Hellman, <u>et al.</u> <u>See:</u> G170, G171.

G203 Tanner, Juanita. "They Know Their Heroines. " <u>Independent Woman,</u> 15 (Mar. , 1936), 74.

G204 "The Critics Versus the Playwright. " <u>Life</u>, 21 (Oct. 7, 1946), p. 50. illus.

G205 "The Moscow Trials: A Statement by American Progressives. " <u>New Masses</u>, 27 (May 3, 1938), 19-20.

G206 "The Russians Get a Big Hand from U. S. Friends. " <u>Life,</u> 26 (Apr. 4, 1949), 40, 43. illus.

> Account of the Waldorf Conference (G150).

G207 "The Unpredictable Miss Hellman, No Doctrinaire in Playmaking. " <u>Times</u> (London), Nov. 9, 1960, p. 8. illus.

Speaks of the origin of <u>Candide</u>, of the modish critics, of her approach to writing and working.

G208 "They Stand Out from the Crowd." <u>Literary Digest</u>, 119 (May 4, 1935), 22. illus.

Includes also a physical description.

G209 Thompson, Dorothy. "On the Record: To My Valentines." New York <u>Herald Tribune</u>, Feb. 14, 1940, p. 19.

G210 Thurber, James. "Dark Suspicions, Contemporary Writers Are Handicapped by Current Atmosphere of Distrust." <u>New York Times</u>, July 27, 1952, 2, p. 1.

The effects of the subpoenas of LH and Odets on the theater.

G211 Triesch, Manfred. "The Lillian Hellman Collection." <u>The Library Chronicle of the University of Texas</u>, 8 (Spring, 1965), 16-20. plates.

A ms. of <u>Watch</u> shows her method of developing a subject through insertions and deletions.

G212 _____. "Modern Drama Library Collections." <u>Modern Drama</u>, 7 (Feb., 1965), 374.

G213 Van Gelder, Lawrence. "Notes on People: Honors." <u>New York Times</u>, Dec. 7, 1973, p. 30.

Announcement of LH's receiving the first Woman of the Year Award of the New York University Alumnae Club.

G214 Van Gelder, Robert. "Of Lillian Hellman, Being a Conversation with the Author of <u>Watch on the Rhine</u>." <u>New York Times</u>, Apr. 20, 1941, 9, p. 1.

G215 Vespa, Mary. "It's Hellman's Hour, as Scores of Her Pals Salute a Distinguished Writer." <u>People</u>, 4 (Nov. 24, 1975), 18-20. illus.

Covers the celebration of LH at the Committee for Public Justice fund raiser.

G216 Von Wien, Florence. "Playwrights Who Are Women. "
Independent Woman, 25 (Jan., 1946), 12-14. illus.

G217 Warga, Wayne. "Lillian Hellman's Memory Serves Her
Correctly. " Los Angeles Times, Jan. 13, 1974,
CAL, pp. 1, 48-49. illus.

On her writing and life, on Pentimento.

G218 _____. Writers Write About the Old Hollywood. "
Los Angeles Times, July 28, 1974, CAL, p. 28.
illus.

G219 Whitman, Alden. "Lillian Hellman Gives Her Harvard
Seminar Lesson in Writing for the Screen. " New
York Times, May 10, 1968, p. 54. illus.

G220 Wiesner, Dr. Jerome. "In Celebration of Lillian Hellman: Origins of the CPJ. " Committee for Public
Justice Newsletter, (Spring, 1976), p. 4.

G221 Wills, Garry. "In Response to Murray Kempton. "
New York Review of Books, 23 (June 24, 1976), 40-
42.

A letter in response to Kempton's apparent need for
a history of the Henry Wallace movement after he
reviewed Scoundrel Time (H).

G222 Winter, Ella. "Hollywood Wakes Up. " New Republic,
93 (Jan. 12, 1938), 276-78.

LH a member of the Motion Picture Artists' Committee.

G222a Wood, Jim. "The Unfinished Woman. " San Francisco Chronicle, Dec. 16, 1973, CAL, pp. 12, 14.
illus.

An interview.

G223 "Writer's Writers. " New York Times, Dec. 4, 1977,
7, pp. 3, 58.

LH responds to the Book Reviewer's question: "Who
is the living writer you most admire?" Thomas Pyn-
chon and Christina Stead.

H

ARTICLES AND REFERENCES ABOUT PARTICULAR WORKS

Plays

ANOTHER PART OF THE FOREST

H1   "An Overture to The Little Foxes." Times (London),
      Aug. 31, 1953, p. 3. Regarding the Liverpool pro-
      duction.

H2   "Another Part of the Forest." Life, 21 (Dec. 9, 1946),
      pp. 71-72+. illus. A picture story of the play.

H3   "Another Part of the Forest." New York Times, Feb.
      16, 1947, p. 3. illus. Marks its 100th performance.

H4   "Another Part of the Forest." Booklist, 43 (May 1,
      1947), 269. A very brief review of the published
      edition.

H5   "Applause in December." Harper's Bazaar, 80 (Dec.,
      1946), 220. A brief note on the play.

H6   Atkinson, Brooks. "Eating the Earth: Lillian Hellman
      Tracks Down More 'Foxes'." New York Times, Dec.
      1, 1946, 2, p. 1. A critical review, "a lurid show."

H7   _____. "The Play in Review: Another Part of the
      Forest." New York Times, Nov. 21, 1946, p. 42.
      With comment on LH as director.

H8   Barnes, Howard. "At Home with the Foxes." New
      York Herald Tribune, Nov. 21, 1946, p. 25.

H9   Beyer, William. "The State of the Theatre: Midseason
      Highlights." School and Society, 65 (Apr. 5, 1947),
      251. A critical review; "a jungle of a Deep South
      Buchenwald."

H10   Blum, Daniel, ed. Theatre World Season 1946-1947.
      New York: Stuyvesant Press Corp., 1947. Photos
      of production and cast and credits.

H11   Boucher, Anthony. "The New Books." San Francisco
      Chronicle, July 27, 1947, WOR, p. 12. A brief
      review of the Viking edition.

H12   Brown, John Mason. "Seeing Things: And Cauldron
      Bubble. " Saturday Review of Literature, 29 (Dec.
      14, 1946), 20-23. An extended review.

H13   Calta, Louis. "All My Sons Wins Critics' Laurels. "
      New York Times, Apr. 22, 1947, p. 33. Another
      Part of the Forest listed as considered for the Drama
      Critics' Circle Award.

H14   Collinge, Patricia. "Another Part of the Hubbards, or
      When They Were Younger (with an Awed Bow to Their
      Creator, Lillian Hellman.)" New Yorker, 23 (Mar.
      15, 1947), 29-30. A version of the early family his-
      tory of the Hubbards.

H15   Dusenbury, Winifred L.   The Theme of Loneliness in
      Modern American Drama.   Gainesville, Florida: Uni-
      versity of Florida Press, 1960.   Read also with
      Foxes.

H16   Eaton, Walter Prichard.   "Plays That Can Be Read. "
      New York Herald Tribune Books, May 25, 1947, p.
      27.

H17   "Foxes in the Forest. " Newsweek, 28 (Dec. 2, 1946),
      94. illus.

H18   Freedley, George.   "The Theatre. " Library Journal,
      78 (May 15, 1947), 811. A very brief review and
      recommendation of the Viking edition.

H19   Gassner, John.   "The Theatre Arts. " Forum, 107
      (Jan. , 1947), 81-83. A review of the play: "a joy-
      less comedy, " "Miss Hellman proves again that she
      is a portrait-artist. "

H20   _____.   "The Theatre Arts. " Forum, 107 (Feb. ,
      1947), 175-76. Comment on the play.

H21   Gibbs, Wolcott. "The Theatre: Ladies' Day. " New
      Yorker, 22 (Nov. 30, 1946), 58+. A review.

H22   Gilder, Rosamond. "New Year, New Plays, Broadway
      in Review. " Theatre Arts, 31 (Jan. , 1947), 14, 17.
      illus. A review, with comment on LH's achievement;
      her "characterizations become horribly alive. "

H23 Going, William T.   "The Prestons of Talladega and the
      Hubbards of Bowen: A Dramatic Note, " Essays on
      Alabama Literature. Studies in the Humanities: No. 4.
      Tuscaloosa: University of Alabama Press, 1975.

H24 Herron, Ina Honaker. The Small Town in American
      Drama. Dallas: Southern Methodist University Press,
      1969. Read also with Foxes.

H25 Kronenberger, Louis. "Going to the Theater: Mostly
      to the Ladies. " PM, Dec. 1, 1946, p. 20. A re-
      view and interpretation: "What is significant, too,
      about Miss Hellman's collection of villains is that
      they are not her means of projecting a pessimistic
      or misanthropic view of life.... "

H26 _____. "Lillian Hellman Writes Another Compelling
      Drama. " PM, Nov. 22, 1946, p. 17. A review of
      Forest and an assessment of LH's writing as a whole:
      "beyond the sense of theater and the technical skill
      is a massive force animated by strong personal and
      moral emotion. It never has yet found its exact tra-
      jectory ... when it finds just the right object to be
      exerted upon, it will create something tremendous
      in the theater. "

H27 Krutch, Joseph Wood. "Drama. " Nation, 163 (Dec. 7,
      1946), 671.

H28 Lewis, Theophilus. "Theatre: Another Part of the
      Forest. " America, 76 (Dec. 21, 1946), 333-34.

H29 "Moscow Acclaims a Hellman Play. " New York Times,
      Oct. 18, 1949, p. 34. Played under the title Ladies
      and Gentlemen; enthusiastically received by capacity
      crowds. See also: H36.

H30 "Moscow Likes Hellman Play. " New York Times, Oct.
      17, 1949, p. 19.

H31 Nathan, George Jean. Theater Book of the Year, 1946-
      47. New York: Alfred A. Knopf, 1946. An inter-
      pretation; critical commentary.

H32 O'Connor, John J. "TV Review: Culture a Key to Pub-
      lic Broadcasting. " New York Times, Oct. 3, 1972,
      p. 91. Hollywood Theater's presentation of the play.

H33   Phelan, Kappo.   "The Stage and the Screen. "   <u>Common-weal</u>, 45 (Dec. 6, 1946), 201+.   A critique.

H34   Schneider, Isidor.   "<u>Another Part of the Forest</u>, The Evil Hubbards--Again. "   <u>New Masses</u>, 61 (Dec. 24, 1946), 28-29.   A review: "Miss Hellman brings responsible and progressive social commentary to the stage.... "

H35   Shipley, Joseph T.   "The Meanest Family. "   <u>New Leader</u>, 29 (Dec. 21, 1946), 12.   A review with comment on LH's work.

H36   "Soviet Paper Finds Hellman Play Fails. "   <u>New York Times</u>, Nov. 13, 1949, p. 83.   Fails on the basis of ideas and for treatment of themes.   <u>See also</u>: H29.

H37   Terry, C.V.   "Broadway Bookrack. "   <u>New York Times</u>, Apr. 6, 1947, 6, p. 12.   A review of the published version.

H38   " 'The Little Foxes' as Cubs. "   <u>New York Times</u>, Nov. 17, 1946, 6, pp. 68-69.

H39   "The Liverpool Playhouse: <u>Another Part of the Forest</u>. " <u>Times</u> (London), Sept. 4, 1953, p. 10.   A review of the production.

H40   <u>The New York Critics' Theatre Reviews</u>, 7 (1946), 247-50.

         The reviews are listed in the following order:
         Barnes, Howard.   "At Home with the Foxes. "   New York <u>Herald Tribune</u>, Nov. 21, 1946.
         Kronenberger, Louis.   "Lillian Hellman Writes Another Compelling Drama. "   <u>PM</u>, Nov. 22, 1946.
         Atkinson, Brooks.   "The Play. "   <u>New York Times</u>, Nov. 21, 1946.
         Garland, Robert.   "At Fulton--<u>Another Part of the Forest</u>. "   New York <u>Journal-American</u>, Nov. 21, 1946.
         Chapman, John.   "<u>Another Part of the Forest</u> Makes <u>The Little Foxes</u> a Mere Warmup. "   <u>Daily News</u>, Nov. 21, 1946.
         Hawkins, William.   "<u>The Forest</u>, a Modern Theater Classic. "   New York <u>World-Telegram</u>, Nov. 21, 1946.

Morehouse, Ward. "Hellman's Another Part of the
    Forest is a Fascinating and Powerful Drama. "
    The Sun, Nov. 21, 1946.
Watts, Richard, Jr. "Lillian Hellman's New Play Is
    Fascinating Drama!" New York Post, Nov. 21, 1946.

H41 "The Theater: Big Week in Manhattan. " Time, 48
     (Dec. 2, 1946), 56.

H42 "The Week's Openings. " New York Times, Nov. 17,
     1946, 2, p. 1. illus.

H43 "The Theatrical Week: Ingrid, Ina, Lillian. " PM, Nov.
     17, 1946, pp. 10-11. illus. An announcement of
     the play with production pictures.

H44 Triesch, Manfred. "Hellman's Another Part of the
     Forest. " Explicator, 24 (Oct. , 1965), Item 20.
     On the derivation of the title from Shakespeare's
     stage directions for Act II, sc. iv of Titus Andron-
     icus; parallels the consequences of inhumanity in
     both plays.

H45 Wyatt, Euphemia Van Rensselaer. "The Drama. "
     Catholic World, 164 (Jan. , 1947), 360-61. A re-
     view of the play; discusses the names Hellman used
     from Marquand's Apley novel.

H46 Young, Stark. "Theatre: Ambitious Plays. " New
     Republic, 115 (Dec. 15, 1946), 822.

H47 Zolotow, Sam. "Saturday Closing for Hellman Play,
     Ending of Run at the Fulton of Another Part of the
     Forest. " New York Times, Apr. 23, 1947, p. 32.
     Closing attributed to the Rialto slump.

CANDIDE

H48 Atkinson, Brooks. Broadway. New York: The Mac-
     millan Company, 1970. See also for The Children's
     Hour.

H49 _____. "Musical Candide; Lillian Hellman and Leo-
     nard Bernstein Turn Voltaire Satire into Fine Play. "
     New York Times, Dec. 9, 1956, 2, p. 5. High
     praise for the work that raised to superior the intellec-
     tual and artistic level of musicals.

H50 _____. "No Time for American Drama. " <u>Critic</u>,
25 (Dec., 1966/Jan., 1967), 16-23. illus. Discusses
the decline of American theater, except for <u>Candide</u>.

H51 _____. "The Theatre: <u>Candide</u>. " <u>New York Times</u>,
Dec. 3, 1956, p. 40. illus. A review of this "ad-
mirable version" of the Voltaire satire.

H52 _____. "Writers Wanted: Triumph of Mediocrity
on Musical Stage. " <u>New York Times</u>, Dec. 16, 1956,
2, p. 3.

H53 Bernstein, Leonard. "Colloquy in Boston. " <u>New York
Times</u>, Nov. 18, 1956, 2, pp. 1, 3. Talks of LH
and his work on <u>Candide</u>, that it will be American
because "Miss Hellman is American. "

H54 Blum, Daniel. <u>Theatre World 1957</u>. New York: Greenberg Press, 1957. Photos of productions, cast.
<u>See also</u> for <u>The Lark</u>.

H55 Bordman, Gerald. <u>American Musical Theatre, A Chroni-
cle</u>. New York: Oxford University Press, 1978.
Commentary on and significance of <u>Candide</u>.

H56 "<u>Candide</u>. " <u>Theatre Arts</u>, 41 (Feb., 1957), 17-18.
illus. A critical review, including cast and credits.

H57 "<u>Candide, A Comic Opera</u>. " <u>World Premieres</u>, 8 (Jan.,
1957), 61. On Hellman, Bernstein, and <u>Candide</u>.

H58 "<u>Candide</u> in London: Audience, Critics Divided--Bern-
stein's Music Liked. " <u>New York Times</u>, May 1,
1959, p. 35.

H59 Clurman, Harold. "Theatre. " <u>Nation</u>, 183 (Dec. 15,
1956), 527. A review: "The total effect of the show--
if it can be said to have one--is of an enormous, splen-
did pastry, at the center of which is a hard, bitter pit. "

H60 Driver, Tom F. "On the Run. " <u>The Christian Cen-
tury</u>, 74 (Feb. 6, 1957), 171+. A brief review.

H61 Gassner, John. "Broadway in Review. " <u>Educational
Theatre Journal</u>, 9 (March, 1957), 42+. Comments
on the controversy between the "curiously violent op-
ponents and proponents" of <u>Candide</u> to which he says he
adds nothing.

H62 Gelb, Arthur. "New York Drama Critics' Circle Award,
     Journey Best U. S. Work." New York Times, Apr.
     17, 1957, p. 35. illus. Candide runner-up in best
     musical class.

H63 Gibbs, Wolcott. "Voltaire Today." New Yorker, 32
     (Dec. 15, 1956), 52-54.

H64 Gottfried, Martin. A Theater Divided: The Postwar
     American Stage. Boston: Little, Brown and Com-
     pany, 1967.

H65 Green, Stanley. Encyclopedia of the Musical Theatre.
     New York: Dodd, Mead and Company, 1976. Pic-
     tures of the production as well as information.

H66 Guthrie, Tyrone. A Life in the Theatre. New York:
     McGraw-Hill Book Company, Inc., 1959. Writes
     of the talent and creativity of the genius that put
     Candide together; writes that LH's great "qualities"
     did not show to her advantage; writes of Bernstein's
     brilliance and the production.

H67 Hayes, Richard. "The Stage: Mr. Bernstein Cultivates
     His Garden." Commonweal, 65 (Dec. 28, 1956), 333-
     34. A critical review; Mary McCarthy would have
     been a better choice.

H68 Hewes, Henry. "Broadway Postscript: Free Prose
     and Free Fall." Saturday Review, 34 (Dec. 22,
     1956), 34-35. "A beautiful bore."

H69 Kerr, Walter. "Candide." New York Herald Tribune,
     Dec. 3, 1956, p. 10. A review: "a spectacular
     disaster."

H70 Kolodin, Irving. "Candied Candide." Saturday Review,
     40 (Feb. 23, 1957), 49. Commentary on the play
     and music.

H71 McCarthy, Mary. "The Reform of Dr. Pangloss."
     New Republic, 135 (Dec. 17, 1956), 30-31. Dis-
     cusses where Candide went wrong.

H72 M. [ajeski], F., Jr. "Bernstein Writes Operetta Score."
     Musical America, 76 (Dec. 15, 1956), 26.

H73 Mannes, Marya. "Views and Reviews: New Shows: Three Runs, Three Hits, Whose Error?" The Reporter, 16 (Jan. 24, 1957), 35.

H74 "New Musical Version of Candide." Times (London), Dec. 12, 1956, p. 5.

H75 Prince, Hal. Contradictions, Notes on Twenty-six Years in the Theatre. New York: Dodd, Mead and Company, 1974. About the 1973-74 version and production of Candide; Candide 1956 was Guthrie's mistake, not Hellman's.

H76 Shipley, Joseph T. "Four New Musicals Open on Broadway." New Leader, 40 (Jan. 14, 1957), 21. A review of "the controversial play of the season." LH has not turned "Voltaire's story into a coherent play."

H77 Taubman, Howard. "Broadway and TV, Both Sources Present Music of Stature." New York Times, Dec. 16, 1956, 2, p. 9.

H78 The New York Theatre Critics' Reviews, 17 (1956), 176-80.

The reviews are listed in the following order:
Chapman, John. "Candide an Artistic Triumph; Bernstein's Score Magnificent." Daily News, Dec. 3, 1956.
Donnelly, Tom. "Best Musical News of the Year is Found in New Candide." New York World-Telegram and The Sun, Dec. 3, 1956.
Watts, Richard, Jr. "Voltaire's Candide as an Operetta." New York Post, Dec. 3, 1956.
McClain, John. "Fine, Bright--But Operetta Lacks Spark." Journal-American, Dec. 3, 1956.
Coleman, Robert. "Musical Candide is Distinguished Work, Offering at Martin Beck a Cynical, Colorful Near-Opera Not for Softies." Daily Mirror, Dec. 3, 1956.
Kerr, Walter. "Theater: Candide." New York Herald Tribune, Dec. 3, 1956.
Atkinson, Brooks. "The Theatre: Candide." New York Times, Dec. 3, 1956.

H79 Wyatt, Euphemia Van Rensselaer. "Theater: Candide." Catholic World, 184 (Feb., 1957), 384-85. A review and discussion of the talent involved.

DAYS TO COME

H80   Atkinson, Brooks.   "The Play: Days to Come, or the
      Ethics of Strikebreaking in Lillian Hellman's New
      Drama." New York Times, Dec. 16, 1936, p. 35.
      A luke-warm review; "a bitter play."

H81   Clurman, Harold.   "Days to Come." Nation, 227 (Nov.
      25, 1978), 587-88.

H82   "Come and Gone." Stage, 14 (Jan., 1937), 10.   Brief
      comment on the play after it closed.

H83   "Days to Come: Lillian Hellman's Drama of Labor
      Strife." Springfield Republican, June 16, 1937, p.
      12.   A review of the Knopf edition: "Miss Hellman
      reflects a knowledge of industrial situations.   It is
      a play full of drama--emotion and action combined.
      Moreover, its story has a message for employer and
      employee where dissatisfaction is suspected."

H84   Dexter, Charles E.   "Strikes and Strikebreakers Viewed
      by Lillian Hellman." Daily Worker, Dec. 18, 1936
      p. 7. illus.   LH never gets under the skin of her
      characters.

H85   Eaton, Walter Prichard.   "New Plays to Read." New
      York Herald Tribune Books, June 20, 1937, p. 7.

H86   Himelstein, Morgan Y.   Drama Was a Weapon, The
      Left-Wing Theatre in New York, 1929-1941.   New
      Brunswick, New Jersey: Rutgers University Press,
      1963.   Use also with Watch on the Rhine.

H87   Krutch, Joseph W.   "Plays, Pleasant and Unpleasant."
      Nation, 143 (Dec. 26, 1936), 769-70.

H88   Lawson, John H.   "Lillian Hellman, A Comparative
      Study of The Children's Hour and Days to Come."
      New Theatre, 4 (Mar., 1937), 15-16+.

H89   Nichols, Lewis.   "The Nights Before Christmas, Through
      All the Houses." New York Times, Dec. 20, 1936,
      10, p. 5.   Brief comment and announcement of in-
      tended close.

H90   Shumlin, Herman.   "On 'Billing'." New York Times,

Jan. 3, 1937, 10, p. 3. A letter that the purported advertising and billing arrangements between LH and him are false.

H91 Smiley, Sam. The Drama of Attack. Columbia: University of Missouri Press, 1972.

H92 "Strike-Breakers: New Theme Utilized in Days to Come by Lillian Hellman. " Literary Digest, 122 (Dec. 26, 1936), 22+. A review.

H93 Taylor, Alexander. "Sights and Sounds: Miss Hellman's Noble Experiment. " New Masses, 22 (Dec. 29, 1936), 7. A review with comment on LH's knowledge of the ways of the world.

H94 Vernon, Grenville. "The Play and the Screen: Days to Come. " Commonweal, 25 (Jan. 1, 1937), 276. A review and comment that the play would have been better had LH decided which ideas to let dominate.

H95 Young, Stark. "Social Drama. " New Republic, 89 (Dec. 30, 1936), 274. Not a very impressive drama.

MONTSERRAT

H96 Atkinson, Brooks. "First Night at the Theatre. " New York Times, Oct. 31, 1949, p. 21. illus. A review; direction is "on the monotonous side, " and the play is not impressive.

H97 Balliett, Whitney. "Off Broadway: Martyrs and Misery. " New Yorker, 36 (Jan. 21, 1961), 68-70. A review concluding that the adaptation had not improved since 1947.

H98 Barnes, Howard. "Brilliant Adaptation. " New York Herald Tribune, Oct. 31, 1949, p. 10.

H99 Beyer, William. "The State of the Theatre: The Strindberg Heritage. " School and Society, 71 (Jan. 14, 1950), 25-26.

H100 Blum, Daniel, ed. Theatre World Season 1949-1950. New York: Greenberg Publishers, 1950. Photos of production and cast and credits.

H101 Brown, John Mason. "Seeing Things: With and Without Music." Saturday Review, 32 (Nov. 19, 1949), 53-55. illus.

H102 Clurman, Harold. "Roblès, Hellman, Blitzstein." New Republic, 121 (Dec. 5, 1949), 21-22. A review of Montserrat in which he points up that LH had not done her usual amount of research; she missed the existentialist point of the original.

H103 _____. The Divine Pastime, Theatre Essays. New York: The Macmillan Publishing Company, Inc., 1974. On directing Montserrat.

H104 Darlington, W. A. "London Letter." New York Times, May 11, 1952, 2, p. 3. Arrives in London.

H105 Gassner, John. "The Theatre Arts." Forum, 113 (Oct., 1949), 275-78. Comment on the season, on Montserrat, and on the Moscow production of Ladies and Gentlemen (Forest).

H106 _____. "The Theatre Arts." Forum, 113 (Dec., 1949), 338-39. On Miss Hellman's adaptation and direction.

H107 "George Dillon May End Run." New York Times, Feb. 14, 1961, p. 45. Montserrat withdrawn.

H108 Gibbs, Wolcott. "The Theatre: The End and the Means." New Yorker, 25 (Nov. 5, 1949), 62+.

H109 Gould, Jack. "TV: Of War and Hostages but Lacking Persuasion." New York Times, Mar. 2, 1971, p. 71. A review of the Hollywood Television Theater production of Montserrat.

H110 Kronenberger, Louis, ed. The Best Plays of 1960-1961. New York: Dodd, Mead and Company, 1961. On the off-Broadway revival.

H111 Lewis, Theophilus. "Theatre: Montserrat." America, 82 (Nov. 26, 1949), 262-63. A review; "a psychological horror play."

H112 _____. "Theatre: Montserrat." America, 104 (Jan. 28, 1961), 577.

H113 Marshall, Margaret. "Drama." Nation, 169 (Nov. 12,
      1949), 478. Believes LH and Roblès are not up with
      the times.

H114 "Montserrat." Times (London), Apr. 9, 1952, p. 6.
      A review of the Lyric Theatre, Hammersmith, pro-
      duction.

H115 Nathan, George Jean. Theater Book of the Year, 1949-
      1950. New York: Alfred A. Knopf, 1950. An in-
      terpretation and criticism of the play. See also:
      Regina.

H116 "New Play in Manhattan." Time, 54 (Nov. 7, 1949),
      79+. illus. A brief review.

H117 "New Plays: Montserrat." Newsweek, 34 (Nov. 7,
      1949), 80-81. illus. An "exciting event."

H118 Phelan, Kappo. "The Stage and Screen: Montserrat."
      Commonweal, 51 (Nov. 18, 1949), 179-80.

H119 Shipley, Joseph T. "On Stage." New Leader, 32 (Nov.
      26, 1949), 15. A review of the play.

H120 Simon, J. P. "Lillian Hellman Drama at Barbizon-
      Plaza." New York Times, May 26, 1954, p. 34.

H121 Taubman, Howard. "Theatre: Montserrat, Lillian
      Hellman Play Revived at the Gate." New York Times,
      Jan. 9, 1961, p. 30. "Deserves a rehearing."

H122 "The New Plays: Montserrat." Theatre Arts, 34 (Jan.,
      1950), p. 10. illus. List of credits and the cast
      are included with the critique.

H123 The New York Theatre Critics' Reviews, 10 (1949),
      244-47.

      The reviews are listed in the following order:
      Barnes, Howard. "Brilliant Adaptation." New York
        Herald Tribune, Oct. 31, 1949.
      Chapman, John. "Montserrat a Brutal Melodrama."
        Daily News, Oct. 31, 1949.
      Morehouse, Ward. "Montserrat Disappoints." The
        Sun, Oct. 31, 1949.
      Hawkins, William. "Montserrat Hits Like 'Quake,

Hideous Tension in Hellman Play. " <u>World-Tele-</u>
<u>gram,</u> Oct. 31, 1949.
Garland, Robert. "Grim. " <u>Journal-American,</u> Oct.
31, 1949.
Atkinson, Brooks. "<u>Montserrat</u> Adapted from the
French of Emmanuel Roblès by Lillian Hellman. "
<u>New York Times,</u> Oct. 31, 1949.
Coleman, Robert. "<u>Montserrat</u> Well Acted but Script
is Bumpy. " <u>Daily Mirror,</u> Oct. 30, 1949.
Watts, Richard, Jr. "<u>Montserrat,</u> Tragic Play. "
New York <u>Post,</u> Oct. 31, 1949.

H124 "Venezuelan Venture. " <u>Theatre Arts,</u> 33 (Nov. , 1949),
44-47. illus. A portrait of LH with Irene Sharoff,
costumer for <u>Montserrat.</u>

H125 Wyatt, Euphemia Van Rensselaer. "The Theater:
<u>Montserrat.</u> " <u>Catholic World,</u> 170 (Dec. , 1949),
227-28. The reviewer believes Hellman squandered
her time in adapting Roblès' play.

MY MOTHER, MY FATHER AND ME

H126 Brady, Leo. "<u>My Mother, My Father and Me.</u> " <u>Cri-</u>
<u>tic,</u> 21 (May, 1963), 63. Notes the structural pro-
blems of this bitterly true satire. Accounts for the
audience hating the play because of the truth it tells.

H127 Clurman, Harold. "Theatre. " <u>Nation,</u> 196 (Apr. 20,
1963), 334. Representative of our lop-sided theater.

H128 Cotter, Jerry. "<u>My Mother, My Father and Me.</u> "
<u>Sign,</u> 42 (May, 1963), 38. A review that develops
the faults of the play and relates the weaknesses to
LH's attitudes.

H129 "Family of Gargoyles. " <u>Newsweek,</u> 61 (Apr. 8, 1963),
85. A review.

H130 "Gathering Toadstools. " <u>Time,</u> 81 (Apr. 5, 1963), 56.
Still of the 30's, LH borrows from Albee and the
theater of the absurd for this adaptation.

H131 Hewes, Henry. "Broadway Postscripts: Last Laughs
and Last Tapes. " <u>Saturday Review,</u> 46 (Apr. 27,
1963), 27. A brief review.

H132 Lewis, Emory. Stages, The Fifty-Year Childhood of
the American Theatre. Englewood Cliffs, New Jersey: Prentice-Hall, 1969. Considers the play "a
hilarious satire of uncommon merit. " It failed because the audiences were not up to it.

H133 McCarten, John. "Domestic and Foreign: My Mother,
My Father and Me. " New Yorker, 39 (Mar. 30,
1963), 108+.

H134 Mannes, Marya. "The Half-World of American Drama. "
The Reporter, 28 (Apr. 25, 1963), 48-50.

H135 Pryce-Jones, Alan. "Openings--New York. " Theatre
Arts, 47 (May, 1963), 69-70. LH is not a comedy
writer, inserts commonness in an attempt to reclaim
the failed humor.

H136 Taubman, Howard. The Making of the American Theatre.
New York: Coward McCann, Inc. , 1965.

H137 _____. "Theater: Hellman Satire, Life in Middle-
Class Home Is Mirrored. " New York Times, Mar.
25, 1963, p. 5. Not a tightly made play, but rather
a series of vignettes; "a sardonic hymn of hate. "

H138 The New York Theatre Critics' Reviews, 24 (1963), 302-
04.

Only two complete reviews are listed in this year's
edition:
Coleman, Robert. "Lillian Hellman Play Is Depress-
ing Farce. " New York Mirror, Apr. 1, 1963.
Watts, Richard, Jr. "Angry Comedy by Lillian Hell-
man. " New York Post, Mar. 25, 1963.
A list of critics who reviewed the play is given:
John Chapman, Daily News
Walter Kerr, Herald Tribune
John McClain, Journal-American
Howard Taubman, New York Times
Norman Nadel, World-Telegram and The Sun.

Excerpts headlined with the last name of Taubman,
Nadel, Kerr, and McClain are provided.

THE AUTUMN GARDEN

H139 Atkinson, Brooks. "Autumn Garden: Lillian Hellman
      Puts Emphasis on Characters in a Well-Acted Play. "
      New York Times, Mar. 18, 1951, 2, p. 1.

H140 _____. "The Play: Lillian Hellman Dramatizes
      Middle-Aged People in The Autumn Garden. " New
      York Times, Mar. 8, 1951, p. 36. Believes LH is
      at her peak in this play, a play in the best of the
      Chekhovian tradition.

H141 Blum, Daniel, ed. Theatre World Season 1950-1951.
      New York: Greenberg Publishers, 1951. Photos
      of the production and cast and credits.

H142 _____. Theatre World Season 1951-1952. New
      York: Greenberg Publishers, 1952. Photos of pro-
      duction and cast and credits.

H143 Bowers, Faubion. Broadway, U. S. S. R. Edinburgh:
      Thomas Nelson and Sons, 1959. Regarding MHAT's
      1957-58 production of Autumn Garden in Moscow.

H144 Brown, John Mason. "Seeing Things: A New Miss
      Hellman. " Saturday Review, 34 (Mar. 31, 1951),
      27-29. illus. An extended review that places the
      play in the tradition of Chekhov and Ibsen, one of
      the season's best.

H145 Clurman, Harold. "Director's Explanation. " New
      York Times, Apr. 22, 1951, 2, p. 3. In a letter
      Clurman comments on the character of Sophie and
      on her view of life.

H146 _____. Lies Like Truth. New York: The Mac-
      millan Company, 1958. Discusses the play's ideo-
      logy and content, its significance; believes it is a
      far better play than Children's Hour.

H147 _____. "Lillian Hellman's Garden. " New Republic,
      124 (Mar. 26, 1951), 21-22. Found also in John
      Gassner, ed. , Best American Plays, Third Series,
      1945-1951. New York: Crown Publishers, Inc. ,
      1952. A review that also analyzes LH's relationship
      to character.

H148 _____. On Directing. New York: The Macmillan
         Company, 1972. Director's notes for Autumn Garden.

H149 Coe, Richard L. "Autumn Garden at Arena. " Wash-
         ington Post, Feb. 3, 1977, B, pp. 1, 8. illus. A re-
         view of the play as the most "mellow, " "her finest. "

H150 Darby, Eileen. "The Autumn Garden. " Theatre Arts,
         35 (May, 1951), 18.

H151 Downer, Alan S. Fifty Years of American Drama, 1900-
         1950. Chicago: Henry Regnery Company, 1966.
         Comment and interpretation.

H152 Felheim, Marvin. "The Autumn Garden: Mechanics
         and Dialectics. " Modern Drama, 3 (Sept. , 1960),
         191-95. LH avoids the limitations of her previous
         plays in this most original of all her plays; the most
         completely Chekhovian drama "in the American theater. "

H153 Freedley, George. "The Theatre: The Autumn Garden. "
         Library Journal, 76 (June 15, 1951), 1030. A very
         brief review and recommendation of the Little, Brown
         edition.

H154 Gassner, John. "Entropy in the Drama. " Theatre Arts,
         35 (Sept. , 1951), 16-17+. Writes of LH's philosophy
         and writing in interpreting the play.

H155 _____. Theatre at the Crossroads. New York:
         Holt, Rinehart, Winston, 1960. An appraisal and
         over-view of her significant plays, especially of
         Autumn Garden and The Searching Wind.

H156 Gilroy, Harry. "Lillian Hellman Drama Foregoes a
         Villain. " New York Times, Feb. 25, 1951, 2, pp.
         1, 3. An interview of LH in which she talks of life,
         of emptiness in peoples' lives, about doing something
         with life, about wasting life.

H157 Guernsey, Otis L. , Jr. "The Autumn Garden: Some
         Leaves Are Golden. " New York Herald Tribune,
         Mar. 8, 1951, p. 18.

H158 Gunther, John. Inside Russia Today. New York: Har-
         per and Brothers, 1958. Regarding the success of
         Autumn Garden in Moscow.

H159 Gussow, Mel.   "Dour Autumn Garden at Long Wharf. "
      New York Times, Nov. 16, 1976, p. 52.   A review
      of the Long Wharf revival that "reminds one of Lil-
      lian Hellman's incisiveness and urbanity as a play-
      wright and makes one wish that she were still active
      in the theater. "

H160 Howard, Lewis.   "Writers Express Conflicting Opinions
      on The Autumn Garden. " New York Times, May 13,
      1951, 2, p. 3.   A letter to the drama editor. See:
      H172.

H161 J. , F.   "Among the New Books: The Autumn Garden. "
      San Francisco Chronicle, Sept. 30, 1951, WOR, p.
      25.   A review of the Little, Brown edition.

H162 Kerr, Walter.   "The Stage, The Autumn Garden. "
      Commonweal, 53 (Apr. 6, 1951), 645.   A review.

H163 _____.   "This Garden Is Nearly Perfect. " New
      York Times, Nov. 28, 1976, 2, pp. 3, 42.   illus.
      A review, "an exquisite revival ... one of Miss Hell-
      man's very best.   Fresh recognition of its qualities
      has been overdue for some time ... "

H164 Lardner, John.   "The Theatre: The First Team Takes
      Over. " New Yorker, 27 (Mar. 17, 1951), 52-54.
      A review.

H165 Lewis, Theophilus.   "Theatre: The Autumn Garden. "
      America, 84 (Mar. , 24, 1951), 736.

H166 "March Gets Award of Baxter Theatre, Co-Star of
      Autumn Garden Receives a Virginia Ham and Acre of
      Land as Top Actor. " New York Times, May 16,
      1951, p. 46.

H167 Marshall, Margaret.   "Drama. " Nation, 172 (Mar.
      17, 1951), 237.   A review of Autumn Garden.

H168 Nathan, George Jean.   Theater Book of the Year, 1950-
      1951.   New York: Alfred A. Knopf, 1951.   An in-
      terpretation which pans the play.

H169 "New Plays: The Autumn Garden. " Newsweek, 37
      (Mar. 19, 1951), 84.   A brief review.

H170 "New Plays in Manhattan." _Time_, 57 (Mar. 19, 1951),
      51+. illus. A review

H171 _The New York Theatre Critics' Reviews_, 12 (1951), 325-
      27.

    The reviews are listed in the following order:
McClain, John. "Play at Coronet Beautifully Set."
      Journal-American, Mar. 8, 1951.
Hawkins, William. "_Autumn Garden_ Is Rich and Mel-
      low." _World Telegram and The Sun_, Mar. 8, 1951.
Atkinson, Brooks. "Lillian Hellman Dramatizes
      Middle-Aged People in _Autumn Garden_." _New York
      Times_, Mar. 8, 1951.
Guernsey, Otis L., Jr. "Some Leaves Are Golden."
      New York _Herald Tribune_, Mar. 8, 1951.
Watts, Richard, Jr. "Lillian Hellman's Latest Dra-
      ma." New York _Post_, Mar. 8, 1951.
Coleman, Robert. "_Autumn Garden_ Harps on Depress-
      ing Theme." _Daily Mirror_, Mar. 8, 1951.
Chapman, John. "Hellman's _Autumn Garden_ Meaty
      Comedy Played by Flawless Cast." _Daily News_,
      Mar. 8, 1951.

H172 Schutte, Louis. "Writers Express Conflicting Opinions
      on The Autumn Garden." _New York Times_, May 13,
      1951, 2, p. 3. A letter to the drama editor. _See:_
      H160.

H173 Shanley, J.P. "New York Drama Critics' Circle Award."
      New York Times, Apr. 4, 1951, p. 34. _Autumn
      Garden_ mentioned as one of the nominations.

H174 Shipley, Joseph T. "Hellman Drags, Herbert Soars."
      New Leader, 34 (March 19, 1951), 27. A review:
      "earnest and increasingly boring."

H175 "_The Autumn Garden_." _Booklist_, 47 (June 15, 1951),
      360. A brief review of the published edition, "little
      action, but good dialog."

H176 "The New Plays: _The Autumn Garden_." _Theatre Arts_,
      35 (May, 1951), 18. illus. Criticism that includes
      a list of the cast and the credits; "misses by such
      a slender margin being truly extraordinary."

H177 Wyatt, Euphemia Van Rensselaer. "Theater: _The Autumn
      Garden_." _Catholic World_, 173 (Apr., 1951), 67-68.

THE CHILDREN'S HOUR

H178 "American Play Banned, English Censor Forbids Pre-
      sentation of The Children's Hour. " New York Times,
      Mar. 12, 1935, p. 24.   Banned in London.

H179 Armato, Philip M.   " 'Good and Evil' in Lillian Hell-
      man's The Children's Hour. " Educational Theatre
      Journal, 25 (Dec. , 1973), 443-47.   An interpretation
      of the play with the "good" being mercy and the
      "evil, " cruelty.

H180 Atkinson, Brooks. "At the Theatre. " New York Times,
      Dec. 19, 1952, p. 35.   illus.   Reviewed as still a
      "powerful" play, written "so tersely. "

H181 _____. "Children's Hour. " New York Times, Dec.
      28, 1952, 2, p. 1.   A comment on the revival:
      "with the exception of The Time of the Cuckoo"
      Children's Hour makes all the new plays "seem tri-
      fling and irrelevant. "

H182 _____. "Children's Hour, Circumstantial Tragedy
      Set in a Girls' Boarding School--The Disputed Ending
      to a Swiftly Written Play. " New York Times, Dec.
      2, 1934, 10, p. 1.   A critique of the play that fur-
      ther discusses his point that the ending damages the
      "intensity" of the play in his earlier review (H183).

H183 _____. "The Play: The Children's Hour, Being
      a Tragedy of Life in a Girls' Boarding School. "
      New York Times, Nov. 21, 1934, p. 23.   Found
      also in Bernard Beckerman and Howard Siegman,
      eds. , On Stage, Selected Theater Reviews from The
      New York Times. "   Preface by John Houseman.
      New York: Arno Press, 1973.   See also: Little
      Foxes.   A review.

H184 Benchley, Robert.   "The Theatre: Good News, The
      Children's Hour. " New Yorker, 10 (Dec. 8, 1934),
      34-36+.   A review of the play that gives thorough
      background of "The Great Drumsheugh Case" in re-
      lation to Children's Hour.

H185 Bentley, Eric.   "Hellman's Indignation. " New Republic,
      128 (Jan. 5, 1953), 30-31.   As "drama of indigna-
      tion. "

H186 _____. The Dramatic Event, an American Chronicle.
New York: Horizon Press, 1954. A discussion of
LH and of the play.

H187 _____. The Theatre of Commitment. New York:
Atheneum, 1967. The play represents a kind of
"liberalism that has been dangerous and is now ob-
solescent."

H188 "Beverly Will Bar Out Play, Won't Permit Show Also
Banned in Boston." Boston Post, Dec. 18, 1935,
p. 6.

H189 Beyer, William H. "The State of the Theatre: First
Nights." School and Society, 77 (Feb. 21, 1953),
117-18. A review and commentary on Miss Hellman's
direction.

H190 Block, Anita Cahn. "Contemporary Drama: The In-
dividual in Conflict with Changing Sexual Standards,"
The Changing World in Plays and Theatre. Boston:
Little, Brown and Company, 1939, pp. 122-126.
Commentary on the play.

H191 Bloomgarden, Kermit. "The Pause in the Day's Occu-
pation: Production of Children's Hour." Theatre
Arts, 37 (May, 1953), 33. illus.

H192 Blum, Daniel, ed. Theatre World Season 1952-1953.
New York: Greenberg Publishers, 1953. Photos of
the production and cast and credits.

H193 _____. Theatre World Season 1953-1954. New York:
Greenberg Publishers, 1954. Photos of the production and cast and credits.

H194 "Boston Play Ban Holds, Federal Judge Refuses to For-
bid Action Against Children's Hour." New York
Times, Feb. 25, 1936, p. 22.

H195 "Boston Sued on Play Ban, $250,000 Damages Are Sought
over The Children's Hour." New York Times, Dec.
27, 1935, p. 15.

H196 Bullard, F. Lauriston. "Censor Still Rules Boston
Theatres, The Children's Hour Is Latest Play to
Meet Ban as City's Old Code Persists." New York
Times, Dec. 22, 1935, 4, p. 11.

H197 Burnshaw, Stanley. "Current Theatre." New Masses,
      14 (Jan. 8, 1935), 29. A brief review.

H198 "Censorship Conflict in Theater." Literary Digest, 120
      (Dec. 28, 1935), 20. illus.

H199 "Chicago Sees Children's Hour." New York Times, Nov.
      10, 1953, p. 39.

H200 "Children's Hour Author Doubts Sex Theme Would Shock
      Boston." Boston Herald, Dec. 16, 1935, p. 5.

H201 "Children's Hour Ban Extended." New York Times,
      Dec. 18, 1935, p. 33.   To Beverly, Massachusetts.

H202 "Children's Hour Banned as 'Unfit', Play's Theme Is
      Feared." Boston American, Dec. 15, 1935, p. 3.

H203 "Children's Hour, Banned by Mayor, May Be Produced
      in Nearby City." Boston Herald, Dec. 15, 1935, p. 1.

H204 "Children's Hour Banned in Boston, Mayor Acts After
      Report by City Censor Who Saw Hellman Play Here:
      Private Showing Barred--Mansfield Rejects Manager's
      Offer--Drama was Backed by Guild Affiliate." New
      York Times, Dec. 15, 1935, p. 42.

H205 "Children's Hour Hearing Jan. 29." New York Times,
      Jan. 15, 1936, p. 15.

H206 "Children's Hour Loses Plea." New York Times, Jan.
      14, 1936, p. 24.   Permitting production to be taken
      to Boston.

H207 "Children's Hour Won't Be Seen Here, Mayor Mansfield
      Against Presentation of Play." Boston Evening Globe,
      Dec. 14, 1935, p. 2.

H208 Connelly, Marc. "Laundered for Boston." Stage, 12
      (April, 1935), 39.   A parody of "The Children's Hour
      from the Post Depression Gaieties."

H209 Craven, Thomas. "These American Plays. Are They
      American?" Stage, 12 (Jan., 1935), 14-15.   Does
      not join in the chorus "of enthusiasm for that sen-
      sational play"; "it brings into focus American thought
      on the subject which has been evasive, timorous, ignor-
      ant, and facetious."

H210 "Current Play in New York. Stage, 12 (Jan. , 1935), 3. Brief review: "Miss Hellman has written a magnificently effective and stimulating play. "

H211 Drew, Elizabeth A. Discovering Drama. New York: W. W. Norton Company, 1937. Commentary.

H212 Eaton, Walter Prichard. "New Plays for Reading. " New York Herald Tribune Books, Mar. 10, 1935, p. 20.

H213 "8, 752 Children's Hours, Miss Hellman's Play Passes Its First, or Most Difficult, Year. " New York Times, Nov. 17, 1935, 9, p. 3. A review of the year's production and box office history and Miss Hellman's state in life.

H214 Ernst, Morris L. , and Alexander Lindey. The Censor Marches On, Recent Milestones in the Administration of the Obscenity Law in the U. S. New York: Doubleday and Company, 1940.

H215 "Fight Boston Play Ban, Author of The Children's Hour Calls Mayor Arbitrary. " New York Times, Dec. 16, 1935, p. 22.

H216 Findlater, Richard. Banned! A Review of Theatrical Censorship in Britain. London: MacGibbon and Kee, 1967.

H217 "Flays Hub Ban on Play, Mrs. Roland G. Hopkins Lauds Children's Hour. " Boston Post, Feb. 8, 1936, p. 5.

H218 Gassner, John. "Broadway in Review. " Educational Theatre Journal, 5 (March, 1953), 18-19. A review, with comments on LH's direction of the 1952 production.

H219 Gibbs, Wolcott. "No Pause. " New Yorker, 28 (Jan. 3, 1953), 30. Children's Hour holds up well after 18 years.

H220 Gilder, Rosamond. "Theatre Arts Bookshelf. " Theatre Arts Monthly, 19 (May, 1935), 392. Comment on the Knopf edition of the play; of psychological "rather than social" interest.

H221 Gilroy, Harry. "The Bigger the Lie. " New York
       Times, Dec. 14, 1952, 2, pp. 3, 4. A review of
       the revival.

H222 Gruber, Ide. "The Playbill. " Golden Book, 21 (Feb. ,
       1935), 28.

H223 "Guild May Back Play in Suburb, Ban on Children's
       Hour Stirs Loud Protests. " Boston Globe, Dec. 16,
       1935, p. 4.

H224 Hammond, Percy. "The Children's Hour: A Good Play
       About a Verboten Subject. " New York Herald Trib-
       une, Nov. 21, 1934, p. 16. A review of "a sound
       tragedy. "

H225 Hayes, Richard. "The Stage: The Children's Hour. "
       Commonweal, 57 (Jan. 16, 1953), 377. A review
       of the "striking revival. "

H226 "Hellman. " Stage, 12 (Jan. , 1935), 34. A portrait
       of LH that tells of her writing Children's Hour
       and of opening night.

H227 Hewes, Henry. "Broadway Postscripts Between the
       Dark and the Dark, Dark Darkness. " Saturday Re-
       view, 36 (Jan. 10, 1953), 30. A review of the pro-
       duction, play, and direction. Play should be titled
       The McCarthyites' Hour.

H228 Hohenberg, John. The Pulitzer Prizes: A History of
       The Awards in Books, Drama, Music and Journalism
       Based on the Private Files Over Six Decades. New
       York: Columbia University Press, 1974.

H229 Houghton, Norris. The Exploding Stage, An Introduction
       to Twentieth-Century Drama. New York: Weybright
       and Talley, 1971. About the capitalization of Child-
       ren's Hour.

H230 "How Goes the Bill of Rights, The Story of The Fight
       for Civil Liberty, 1935-1936. " American Civil Lib-
       erties' Union Annual Reports, Volume 2 (June, 1930-
       37), New York: Arno Press, 1970.

H231 "Hurdle on Play Ban Hunted, Stage Outside Hub Sought. "
       Boston American, Dec. 16, 1935, p. 3.

H232 Isaacs, Edith J. R.   "Without Benefit of Ingenue. "   Thea-
      tre Arts Monthly, 19 (Jan. , 1935), 13-15.   illus.
      The best of the month's "realistic plays" for which
      you make your own ending if displeased with LH's.

H233 Jordan, Elizabeth.   "The Season's Best Plays. "   Ameri-
      ca, 53 (July 27, 1935), 376-77.   A review of Child-
      ren's Hour as third on her list of the season's best;
      comments on the fine craftsmanship in writing and on
      the Pulitzer Award.

H234 _____.   "Valley Forge and Other Plays. "   America,
      52 (Dec. 29, 1934), 280.   A review of the play "that
      holds a big problem for reviewers and public alike"
      because of the theme.

H235 Kerr, Walter F.   "The Children's Hour. "   New York
      Herald Tribune, Dec. 19, 1952, p. 18.   A review
      of the revival: it "remains a remarkably shrewd
      and incisive melodrama. "

H236 Krutch, Joseph Wood.   The American Drama Since
      1918.   New York: Random House, 1939.   Commen-
      tary on.   Use also with Foxes.   Writes of LH's
      great skill.

H237 _____.   "The Best Play. "   Nation, 140 (May 22,
      1935), 610.   Of several years past, too.

H238 _____.   "The Heart of a Child. "   Nation, 139 (Dec.
      5, 1934), 656-57.   The review states the play is
      "unusually well-written, " but notes the defective last
      act.

H239 Laufe, Abe.   Anatomy of a Hit: Long-Run Plays on
      Broadway from 1900 to the Present Day.   New York:
      Hawthorn Books, Inc. , 1966.   Use also with Toys.

H240 _____.   The Wicked Stage, A History of Theater
      Censorship and Harassment in the United States.
      New York: Frederick Ungar Publishing Company, 1978.

H241 Lawson, John H.   Theory and Technique of Playwriting.
      New York: Hill and Wang, 1960.   Foxes and Watch
      mark "the highest development of dramatic thought in
      that period"; a full discussion of the obligatory scene
      and the climax of Children's Hour.

H242 Lewis, Felice Flanery. Literature, Obscenity, and
       Law. Carbondale, Illinois: Southern Illinois Uni-
       versity Press, 1976.

H243 "Library Club Hits Banning of Play, 600 From All Parts
       of State at Meeting." Boston Herald, Feb. 8, 1936,
       p. 3.

H244 Little, Stuart W. Off-Broadway: The Prophetic Theater.
       New York: Coward, McCann and Geoghegan, Inc.,
       1972.

H245 "London Success Seen for Children's Hour, Producer
       Regrets Action of Lord Chamberlain Banning Play
       and Considers Appealing." New York Times, Mar.
       15, 1935, p. 24. Comment by Alec L. Rea, pro-
       ducer.

H246 McCord, Bert. "Hellman Play at Coronet." New York
       Herald Tribune, Dec. 18, 1952, p. 26.

H247 McCoy, Ralph E. Banned in Boston: The Development
       of Literary Censorship in Massachusetts. Ph. D.
       dissertation. University of Illinois, 1956.

H248 McDermott, William F. "Children's Hour has an Unu-
       sual History in the Realm of Popular Plays." Cleve-
       land Plain Dealer, Nov. 22, 1936, WOMAG and A,
       p. 11.

H249 _____. "McDermott on Censorship: Small time
       Catos Busy ... Mayor Admits He Knows Art ...
       Theatergoers Silenced." Cleveland Plain Dealer,
       Dec. 18, 1935, p. 11. The drama critic writes of
       the banning of Children's Hour in Boston.

H250 Mantle, Burns. "Believe It or -- NO!" Stage, 12
       (May, 1935), 23. Explains how he can endorse a
       play "that has a cad for a hero."

H251 Marshall, Margaret. "Drama." Nation, 176 (Jan. 3,
       1953), 18-19. A review, "neither genuinely con-
       vincing nor genuinely moving."

H252 "Mary, What Are You Saying?" Life, 34 (Jan. 19, 1953),
       51+. illus. Pictorial story of the play.

H253 "May Stage Banned Hit in Suburbs, The Children's Hour
     Producer Told of Hub Disapproval. " Boston Sunday
     Post, Dec. 15, 1935, p. 19.

H254 "Mayor a Witness in Children's Hour Case, Producers
     of Play Ask U. S. Court to Restrain Him and Other
     Members of Censor Board. " Boston Evening Globe,
     Jan. 29, 1936, p. 8.

H255 "Mayor Bans Tragedy Here, Calls Play Children's Hour
     Unfit for People. " Boston Sunday Globe, Dec. 15,
     1935, p. 45.

H256 "Mayor Heard on Censorship, Calls Children's Hour an
     Immoral Play. " Boston Globe, Jan. 30, 1936, p.
     15. illus.

H257 Morgan, Charles. "American Week in London. " New
     York Times, Nov. 29, 1936, 12, p. 2.

H258 Motherwell, Hiram. "The Box Office Indicates: To
     Define the Trend of This Season's Theatre, Begin
     with an Analysis of the Public's Favor as Shown by
     the Weekly Gross. " Stage, 12 (May, 1935), 28-29.

H259 "Mrs. Hopkins Protests Ban on Children's Hour. " Bos-
     ton Globe, Feb. 8, 1936, p. 20. Director of the
     Massachusetts Branch of Foreign Policy Association.

H260 Nathan, George Jean. "The Theatre: A Play and Some
     Other Things. " Vanity Fair, 43 (Feb. , 1935), 37.
     A review of the play, "the one material contribution
     of the season to American playwriting. "

H261 _____. The Theatre in the Fifties. New York: Al-
     fred A. Knopf, 1953. On the revival of Children's
     Hour.

H262 _____. The Theatre of the Moment, A Journalistic
     Commentary. New York: Alfred A. Knopf, 1936.
     Material is found on pp. 248-50, unindexed.

H263 "No Hearing on Banned Show, Mayor Indicates He Will
     Turn Down Appeal. " Boston Post, Dec. 17, 1935,
     p. 26.

H264 Norton, Elliot. Broadway Down East: An Informal

Account of the Plays, Players and Playhouses of
Boston from Puritan Times to the Present. (Lec-
tures Delivered for the National Endowment of the
Humanities, Boston Public Library Learning Library
Program) Boston: Trustees of the Public Library,
1978.   illus.

H265 _____. "Second Thoughts of a First Nighter. " Boston Sunday Post, Feb. 2, 1936, p. 21.   A "powerful
tragedy not for anyone under 21. "

H266 "Old Play in Manhattan: The Children's Hour. " Time,
60 (Dec. 29, 1952), 55.   A brief review.

H267 "Other Current Shows. " New Masses, 13 (Dec. 25,
1934), 29.   An unsigned brief review (probably by
Stanley Burnshaw): "A near tragedy which is piling
them in partly because of its touching on the sac-
rosanct border of perversion ... Miss Hellman, the
author, covers many a technical hole with faultless
dialogue. "

H268 "Play Ban Fight Aired in Court, Mayor Defends Action
on Children's Hour. " Boston Herald, Jan. 29, 1936,
pp. 1, 4.

H269 "Plays and Pictures: Children's Hour at the Gate Theatre. " New Statesman and Nation, 12 (Nov. 21, 1936),
810.   The play "lacks all literary or permanent value. "
A review. See: H279.

H270 Reardon, William R.   Banned in Boston: A Study of
Theatrical Censorship in Boston from 1630-1950.
Ph. D. dissertation.   Stanford University, 1952.

H271 "Society Protests Play Ban, Many of Elite Have Children's Hour Tickets Now. " Boston Post, Dec. 16,
1935, p. 10.

H272 Stephens, Frances.   "The Children's Hour. " Theatre
World, 52 (Nov. , 1956), 7.   Interpretation of the
play.

H273 "Summer's Children: A History of Mr. Shumlin's
Bracken Search for Actresses. " New York Times,
Jan. 20, 1935, 10, p. 2.

H274 "The Children's Hour. " Times (London), Nov. 13, 1936,
     p. 14.   A review that discusses the "special merits
     of this extremely interesting play. "

H275 "The Children's Hour, A Modern Young Lady, Third
     Year High School, Helps Us Through Some of the
     More Esoteric Problems Raised by this succès de
     scandale. " Stage, 12 (Jan. , 1935), 28-29.   A re-
     view by a high school girl, who was not shocked,
     but found the play interesting, honest, convincing,
     "beautifully written. "

H276 "The Children's Hour at the Gate Theatre. " New States-
     man and Nation, Nov. 21, 1936, p. 810.

H277 "The Children's Hour, by Lillian Hellman. " Times
     (London), Nov. 22, 1950, p. 10.   A review of the
     London production.

H278 "The Children's Hour, by Lillian Hellman. " Times
     (London), Sept. 20, 1956, p. 5.   illus.   A review.

H279 "The Children's Hour Is Hailed in London, Production
     at Gate Theatre Studio Is Uncensored--Wins Critical
     Acclaim. " New York Times, Nov. 13, 1936, p. 27.
     See: H269.

H280 "The Children's Hour Is Weighed in Chicago, Theatre
     Guild Head Says It Has Been Barred, but City Offi-
     cial Denies Action. " New York Times, Jan. 10,
     1936, p. 17.

H281 "The Fruits of a New Symposium. " New York Times,
     Mar. 8, 1936, 9, p. 2.   Regarding the results of
     Herman Shumlin's poll of why patrons had seen The
     Children's Hour.

H282 "The New Books: Drama. " Saturday Review of Litera-
     ture, 11 (Mar. 2, 1935), 523.   A review of the
     Knopf edition.

H283 The New York Theatre Critics' Reviews, 13 (1952), 151-
     53.   (The Reviews begin with Volume 1 in 1940.)

     The reviews are listed in the following order:
     Kerr, Walter F.   "The Children's Hour. "   New York
     Herald Tribune, Dec. 19, 1952.

Watts, Richard, Jr. "The Children's Hour Scores
Again." New York Post, Dec. 19, 1952.
Atkinson, Brooks. "At the Theatre." New York
Times, Dec. 19, 1952.
Hawkins, William. "Children's Hour at 18, Still
Shocks." World-Telegram and The Sun, Dec. 19,
1952.
Chapman. John. "Revival of The Children's Hour
Strong in Plot, Weak in Acting." Daily News,
Dec. 19, 1952.
McClain, John. "A Welcome, Though Gruesome,
Addition." Journal-American, Dec. 19, 1952.
Winchell, Walter. "Children's Hour Revival A
Spellbinder as in '34." Daily Mirror Dec. 19,
1952.

H284 "The Theatre: New Plays in Manhattan." Time, 24
(Dec. 3, 1934), 24. illus. A review.

H285 "The Thunderbolt of Broadway." Literary Digest, 118
(Dec. 1, 1934), 20. illus. A review: "a play that
shines with integrity."

H286 "Theater: The Children's Hour." Newsweek, 40 (Dec.
29, 1952), 40. A review that points out LH shows
her hand "as director immediately."

H287 Thompson, Robert Wayne. A Production and Production Book of Lillian Hellman's "The Children's Hour."
M. F. A. thesis. University of Texas, 1964.

H288 Vernon, Grenville. "The Pulitzer Award." Commonweal, 22 (May 31, 1935), 134. Regarding the controversy over Children's Hour.

H289 Verschoyle, Derek. "The Theatre: The Children's
Hour." Spectator (London), 157 (Nov. 20, 1936), 905.
A review of the Gate Theatre production, an interpre-
tation, and a comment on the ban.

H290 Walbridge, Earle. "Closed Doors." Saturday Review
of Literature, 11 (Mar. 16, 1935), 548. A letter
regarding the earlier review (H282) stating his opinion of LH's basing her play on "The Great Drums-
heugh Case."

H291 Wyatt, Euphemia Van Rensselaer. "The Drama: The

Children's Hour. Catholic World, 140 (Jan., 1935), 466-67. A review and interpretation of the play for which the central question is "Have I ever or may I by hasty judgment bring so much suffering to anyone by an unjust word."

H292 _____. "Theater: The Children's Hour." Catholic World, 176 (Feb., 1953), 388. A review of the revival.

H293 "When Spring Comes to Paris." New York Times, June 7, 1936, 9, p. 1. A review of the Paris production, "a very ordinary melodrama."

H294 "Whisper Opposed in Play, Ruling on Injunction Against Children's Hour Ban Delayed." New York Times, Jan. 30, 1936, p. 14. Regarding the Boston ban.

H295 "Winter's Harvest, A Paean of Praise for Some of the Novas in Our Entertainment World This Season." Stage, 12 (Mar., 1935), 8-9. illus. About the play, but the emphasis is upon Miss McGee.

H296 "Would Stage Show for Mayor, Producer of Banned Play Is Extremely Disturbed by Action." Boston Herald, Dec. 17, 1935, p. 4.

H297 Young, Stark. "Two New Plays." New Republic, 81 (Dec. 19, 1934), 169. A brief review; "no play in town whose first acts hold the audience to so strict attention."

THE COLLECTED PLAYS

H298 Adler, Renata. "The Guest Word: A Review Revisited." New York Times, July 9, 1972, 7, p. 39. Writes of the critical "ineptitude" of Charles T. Samuels and his "high contempt" in response to his lead review of The Collected Plays (H303).

H299 Allen, Trevor. "Books in Brief." Books and Bookmen, 18 (Jan., 1973), 122. Brief review of the paperback.

H300 Durbin, James H., Jr. "The Collected Plays," in Frank N. Magill, ed., Survey of Contemporary Literature, rev. ed. Volume II. Englewood Cliffs, New Jersey: Salem Press, 1977. An essay-review.

H301 Knowlton, Keith. "Showtime at Your Leisure. " The
      Financial Post (Toronto), 67 (Mar. 10, 1973), 16.
      A review.

H302 Moers, Ellen. "Family Theater. " Commentary, 54
      (Sept. , 1972), 96-99.   Reviews of Richard Moody's
      Lillian Hellman, Playwright (F152) and The Collected
      Plays.   Writes of the two consuming obsessions in
      LH's plays, family and capital; her characters are
      "not sinners, just relatives. "

H303 Samuels, Charles Thomas.   "The Collected Plays by
      Lillian Hellman. " New York Times, June 18, 1972,
      7, pp. 2-3, 16-17.   A review of Moody's biography
      of LH (F152) and The Collected Plays, which he be-
      lieves belong in the "league of Neil Simon instead of
      Williams and Inge. " He comments on LH's narrow
      conception of drama; sees her plays as "forensic
      responses to contemporary problems. " See: H298
      and H304.

H304 _____.   "The Guest Word: The Reviewer Replies. "
      New York Times, July 23, 1972, 7, p. 27.   A re-
      ply to Renata Adler (H298) in which he says he is
      "bluntly disparaging" about LH's plays, but not about
      her.

H305 Sullivan, Dan.   "Volumes for Your Five-Foot Theater
      Shelf. " Los Angeles Times, Apr. 16, 1972, CAL,
      p. 28.   A brief review; the edition "reminds us how
      much our theater owes this fine playwright. "

H306 Szogyi, Alex.   "The Collected Plays, by Lillian Hell-
      man. " Saturday Review, 55 (Aug. 12, 1972), 51-52.
      illus.   LH is "one of the gurus of the American lit-
      erary scene. " A review of the collection.

H307 "The Best of 1972--for Giving and Getting. " Saturday
      Review, 55 (Dec. 2, 1972), 72.   A recommendation
      of the "definitive collection" of "this century's great-
      est American playwright. "

H308 Women: Their Changing Roles.   The Great Contempor-
      ary Issues Series, Set I, Volume 4.   New York:
      Arno Press, 1978.   Reviews the New York Times'
      review of The Collected Plays.

THE LARK

H309 "A Joan with Gumption. "   Newsweek, 46 (Nov. 28, 1955),
110.   A review.

H310 "Anne Frank Gets Award of Critics. "   New York Times,
Apr. 2, 1956, p. 20.   LH's adaptation was runner-
up in the foreign division.

H311 Atkinson, Brooks.   "New Joan of Arc, Julie Harris
Plays Her in The Lark. "   New York Times, Nov.
27, 1955, 2, p. 1.   "LH ... is keener theatrical
technician than Christopher Fry. "

H312 _____.   "Theatre: St. Joan with Radiance, Julie
Harris Stars in Lark at Longacre. "   New York Times,
Nov. 18, 1955, p. 20.   A review.   LH's "adaptation
has solid strength. "

H313 Bentley, Eric.   "Theatre. "   New Republic, 133 (Dec.
5, 1955), 21.   LH tries to rescue "Joan from Anouilh. "
Richard Hayes (H321) calls this "the most telling
commentary the play has yet occasioned. "

H314 Blum, Daniel, ed.   Theatre World Season 1955-1956.
New York: Greenberg Publishers, 1956.   Photos
of production and cast and credits.

H315 _____.   Theatre World Season 1956-1957.   New
York: Greenberg Publishers, 1957.   Photos of production and cast and credits.

H316 Calta, Louis.   "Prices at Lark to be Increased, Rates
for Orchestra Seats Will Rise $1. 15--Producer Cites
Big Operating Cost. "   New York Times, Nov. 18,
1955, 2, p. 1.

H317 Gassner, John.   "Broadway in Review. "   Educational
Theatre Journal, 8 (March, 1956), 32-33.   A review: "distinctly strengthened by Lillian Hellman's
energetic adaptation. "

H318 Gibbs, Wolcott.   "The Theatre: Miss Sullivan and Miss
Harris. "   New Yorker, 31 (Dec. 3, 1955), 112-118.
A review of the production with comment on the play.

H319 Griffin, Alice.   "Books: Of a Different Feather, the

Fry Translation and Hellman Adaptation of The Lark. "
Theatre Arts, 40 (May, 1956), 8-10.   LH's version
"is romantic ... Miss Hellman's appeals to the heart. "

H320 Hatch, Robert.   "Theater. "   Nation, 18 (Dec. 3, 1955),
        485-86.   A review.

H321 Hayes, Richard.   "The Stage: The Lark. "   Common-
        weal, 63 (Dec. 23, 1955), 304-05.   A review: "a
        genteel muddle. "   See: H313.

H322 Hewitt, Alan.   "The Lark, Theatrical Bird of Passage. "
        Theatre Arts, 40 (Mar. , 1956), 63-64+, 96.   illus.
        A review.   LH "has made it a bolder play, less
        intellectual, more obviously theatrical. "

H322a Johnson, Joann H.   A Production Study and Text of
         Jean Anouilh's "The Lark" adapted by Lillian Hellman
         as Presented at Catholic University.   Ph. D. disser-
         tation.   Catholic University, 1964.

H323 "Julie as a Memorable Joan. "   Life, 39 (Dec. 12, 1955),
        114+.   illus.

H324 Kerr, Walter F.   "Theater: The Lark. "   New York
        Herald Tribune, Nov. 18, 1955, p. 12.   illus.

H325 Knepler, Henry.   "Translation and Adaptation in the
        Contemporary Drama. "   Modern Drama, 4 (May,
        1961), 31-41.   A discussion of the changes LH made
        as significant "as they are extensive. "

H326 Lewis, Theophilus.   "Theatre: The Lark. "   America,
        94 (Dec. 24, 1955), 363-64.

H327 McCord, Bert.   "Julie Harris Will Open in The Lark
        Tonight. "   New York Herald Tribune, Nov. 17, 1955,
        p. 14.

H328 Mannes, Marya.   "Three Playwrights Compliment Their
        Audiences. "   The Reporter, 13 (Dec. 29, 1955), 31-
        32.   A commentary and review of the play that highly
        praises it.

H329 Millstein, Gilbert.   " 'Unexceptionable' Julie Harris. "
        New York Times, Nov. 4, 1955, 6, pp. 14, 19-20,
        22.   Chiefly comment on the production, but some
        evaluation of LH's adaptation.

H330 O'Connor, Frank. "St. Joan, from Arc to Lark."
      Holiday, 19 (Mar., 1956), 77, 88-89. A review of
      the play.

H331 O'Flaherty, Vincent J. "St. Joan Wouldn't Know Her-
      self." America, 95 (Apr. 28, 1956), 109-10. Per-
      tains more to Anouilh's Lark, but of peripheral ref-
      erence and interest.

H332 Peck, Seymour. "The Maid in Many Guises." New
      York Times, Dec. 4, 1955, 6, pp. 28-29. A por-
      trait of Julie Harris that includes commentary on
      the play and about the production.

H333 Schumach, Murray. "Shaping a New Joan." New York
      Times, Nov. 13, 1955, 2, pp. 1, 3. A commen-
      tary sub-titled: "Miss Hellman Discusses Adapting
      The Lark."

H334 Shipley, Joseph T. "Four Plays That Push Too Hard."
      New Leader, 38 (Dec. 5, 1955), 19. A review.

H335 "The Lark." Theatre Arts, 40 (Jan., 1956), 18-19.
      illus.

H336 The New York Theatre Critics' Reviews, 16 (1955),
      206-08.

          The reviews are listed in the following order:
          Kerr, Walter F. "Theater: The Lark." New York
              Herald Tribune, Nov. 18, 1955.
          Atkinson, Brooks. "Theatre: St. Joan With Radiance."
              New York Times, Nov. 18, 1955.
          Watts, Richard, Jr. "A Stirring Play About Joan of
              Arc." New York Post, Nov. 18, 1955.
          Coleman, Robert. "Theatre: The Lark Proves
              Spellbinding, Witty, Joan of Arc Story Retold in
              Fine Adaptation by Lillian Hellman." Daily Mir-
              or, Nov. 18, 1955.
          Hawkins, William. "Julie Harris Captures Inner
              Beauty of Joan." World-Telegram and The Sun,
              Nov. 18, 1955.
          McClain, John. "Julie Depicts a Vital Joan, Earthi-
              ness Adds to Dramatic Impact in Flashback Pat-
              tern." Journal-American, Nov. 18, 1955.
          Chapman, John. "Julie Harris Simply Magnificent in
              a Beautiful Drama, The Lark." Daily News, Nov.
              18, 1955.

H337 "The Theater: A Fiery Particle." Time, 66 (Nov.
      28, 1955), 76-78+. illus. An extended review of
      the play and the production that tells that LH cut
      "43 pages from Anouilh's version."

H338 Wyatt, Euphemia Van Rensselaer. "Theatre: The Lark."
      Catholic World, 182 (Jan. , 1956), 308-09.

THE LITTLE FOXES

H339 Aaron, Jules. "The Little Foxes." Educational Thea-
      ter Journal, 27 (Dec. , 1975), 553-54. A review
      and commentary on the production at the University
      of California, Santa Barbara.

H340 "Americans in London." New York Times, Nov. 1,
      1942, 8, p. 2. Comment on the London production
      of Foxes.

H341 Anderson, John. "The Season's Theater." Saturday
      Review of Literature, 20 (Apr. 29, 1939), 14-15,
      illus.

H342 Atkinson, Brooks. "Miss Bankhead Has a Play, Lillian
      Hellman's Stinging Drama About Rugged Individualism
      Provides a Number of Good Acting Parts." New
      York Times, Feb. 26, 1939, 9, p. 1. Found also
      in Brooks Atkinson, Broadway Scrapbook. New York:
      Theatre Arts, Inc. , 1947.

H343 _____. "The Play." New York Times, Feb. 16,
      1939, p. 16. A review of the opening at The Na-
      tional Theatre in Washington.

H344 Bankhead, Tallulah. "Miss Bankhead Objects." New
      York Times, Oct. 29, 1967, 2, p. 5. A letter in
      response to LH's essay of remembrance (D34) in
      which she contradicts Hellman's account of the 1938
      Foxes.

H345 Barnes, Clive. "Theater: Return of The Little Foxes,
      Hellman Play Staged by Lincoln Troupe." New York
      Times, Oct. 27, 1967, p. 53. illus.

H346 _____. "Theater: The Little Foxes Revisited, Leigh-
      ton and Marshall Appear in New Roles, Geraldine

Chaplin Acts with Spirit and Force." New York Times, Jan. 6, 1968, p. 24. A review of the production moved to The Barrymore Theater.

H347 Benchley, Robert. "The Theatre: The Little Foxes." New Yorker, 15 (Feb. 25, 1939), p. 25+. A review: "awfully, awfully good."

H348 "Bohemian Nights in New York." Times (London), Feb. 7, 1955, p. 11. Announcement of Foxes' opening on March 4.

H349 Brown, John Mason. "Miss Bankhead and The Little Foxes," Broadway in Review. New York: W.W. Norton and Company, Inc., 1940.

H350 Calta, Louis. "Lead Is Dropped by Miss Leighton, Actress Takes a Smaller Part in Little Foxes Here." New York Times, May 16, 1967, p. 49.

H351 Cambridge, John. "The Little Foxes, a Story of Southern Aristocrats." Daily Worker, Feb. 17, 1939, p. 7. illus. A review with commentary on Miss Hellman's viewpoint.

H352 Coe, Richard L. "Dated Little Foxes at ACTF." Washington Post, Apr. 22, 1972, B, p. 5.

H353 Cooke, Richard P. "The Theater: A Well-Acted Revival." Wall Street Journal, 170 (Oct. 30, 1967), p. 18. A review of the production.

H354 Drutman, Irving. Good Company. Boston: Little, Brown and Company, 1976. Unindexed pp. 190-91 concern Bankhead and Foxes.

H355 Eatman, James. "The Image of American Destiny: The Little Foxes." Players, 48 (Dec.-Jan., 1973), 70-73. illus. An assessment of Foxes in terms of the moral ambiguity of the characters and the political climate of the times; of Ibsen.

H356 Eaton, Walter Prichard. "Some Modern Plays in Print." New York Herald Tribune Books, July 23, 1939, p. 11.

H357 Falb, Lewis W. American Drama in Paris, 1945-1970.

Chapel Hill: University of North Carolina Press,
1973.   Foxes in Paris, 1962.

H358 Ferguson, Otis.   "A Play, a Picture. "   New Republic,
98 (Apr. 12, 1939), 279.   A review of the play that
suggests Foxes would have done better with a better
cast; "play is irresolute, but aims to please. "

H359 Freedman, Morris.   The Moral Impulse, Modern Drama
from Ibsen to the Present.   Preface by Henry T.
Moore.   Carbondale, Illinois: Southern Illinois University Press, 1967.   Interpretation, comparison with
Brecht.

H360 Gilliatt, Penelope.   "Lark Pie. "   The New York Review
of Books, 10 (Feb. 1, 1968), 30.   A letter about
Elizabeth Hardwick's review of the revival of Foxes,
which Gilliatt felt was a hideous attack (H365).

H361 Gassner, John.   Directions in Modern Theatre and Drama.   New York: Holt, Rinehart and Winston, Inc. ,
1966.   Writes of the "almost forensic form" of Foxes.

H362 Gilder, Rosamond.   "Sweet Creatures of Bombast. "
Theatre Arts, 23 (Apr. , 1939), 244, 246-47+.   illus.

H363 Goldman, William.   The Season, A Candid Look at
Broadway.   New York: Harcourt, Brace and World,
Inc. , 1969.   On Mike Nichols' Foxes.

H364 Gottfried, Martin.   "Theatre: The Little Foxes. "
Women's Wear Daily, Oct. 27, 1967, p. 84.   A
review of the Repertory Theater of Lincoln Center
revival: Foxes "fails the test of time. "

H365 Hardwick, Elizabeth.   "The Little Foxes Revived. "
The New York Review of Books, 9 (Dec. 21, 1967),
4-5.   A review of the revival of the play that provoked much discussion: See: H360, H387, H393.
and then Hardwick's replies (H366, H367).   Writes
of what Foxes reveals about "the left-wing popular
writers of the Thirties, " of LH's handling of the
conventions of the drawing room and of realism and
and protest.   Although Foxes is a "triumph of craftsmanship, " it lacks because LH failed to deal with the
complications of the industrial prosperity of the South.

H366 _____. "Raising Hellman. " The New York Review
       of Books, 9 (Jan. 18, 1968), 32. A letter in reply
       to Felicia Montealegre (H387) and Richard Poirier
       (H393) defending her position, giving her familiarity
       with the play, defending her right to analyze Foxes
       according to her own lights.

H367 _____. "Lark Pie. " The New York Review of Books,
       10 (Feb. 1, 1968), 30. A letter in reply to Penel-
       ope Gilliatt (H360) stating her interest in the work
       of the 30's and 40's and in LH account for her re-
       viewing Foxes.

H368 Hartley, Lodvick C.   Patterns in Modern Drama.
       Englewood Cliffs, New Jersey: Prentice-Hall, Inc.,
       1948.   The introduction to Foxes includes an over-
       view of and a forthright comment on her plays through
       Another Part of the Forest.

H369 Heilman, Robert B.   "Drama of Money. " Shenandoah,
       21 (Summer, 1970), 20-33.

H370/1 Hewes, Henry.   "The Crass Menagerie. " Saturday
       Review, 50 (Nov. 11, 1967), 26. A review of the
       revival.

H372 Kemper, Robert Graham.   "Evil Revisited. " The
       Christian Century, 85 (Mar. 13, 1968), 332. A re-
       view of "an actors' play. "

H373 Kerr, Walter.   "Slipping Through Our Fingers, " Thirty
       Plays Hath November. New York: Simon and Schus-
       ter, 1966.

H374 _____. "We Could Have Five Little Foxes. " New
       York Times, Nov. 5, 1967, 2, pp. 1, 3. Comment
       on the planning of the coming revival.

H375 Kroll, Jack.   "Chasing the Fox. " Newsweek, 70 (Nov.
       6, 1967), 86. A review of the Lincoln Center re-
       vival.

H376 Kronenberger, Louis.   "Greed. " Stage, 16 (Apr. 1,
       1939), 36-37+. Considers it the "simplest possible
       kind of melodrama. " Speaks of her moral aware-
       ness, of LH's "power, " of Foxes in comparison to
       Children's Hour.

H377 Krutch, Joseph Wood. "Unpleasant Play. " Nation,
      148 (Feb. 25, 1939), 244.

H378 Lewis, Theophilus. "A Play and a Point of View, The
      Tobacco Road Makers. " Interracial Review, 12
      (Oct. 30, 1939), 159-60.

H379 _____. "The Little Foxes. " America, 117 (Dec.
      9, 1967), 723.

H380 "Lillian Hellman Files Suit Over Little Foxes Telecast. "
      New York Times, Oct. 21, 1967, p. 17. Sues CBS.

H381 McCarten, John. "The Theatre: Low Jinks. " New
      Yorker, 43 (Nov. 4, 1967), 162-63.

H382 Martin, Judith. "Unsentimental Look at Politics, Life,
      Art. " Washington Post, Nov. 12, 1974, B, p. 2.
      Review of revival in Washington.

H383 Martin, Ralph G. Lincoln Center for the Performing
      Arts. Englewood Cliffs, New Jersey: Prentice-
      Hall, 1971. Regarding the revival in 1967.

H384 Miller, Jordan Y. American Dramatic Literature: Ten
      Modern Plays in Historical Perspective. New York:
      McGraw-Hill Book Company, Inc. , 1961. Introduc-
      tory material to the play, "a problem play, not a
      melodrama. "

H385 "Miss Leighton Says Shift Is for Nichols. " New York
      Times, May 17, 1967, p. 38.

H386 "Miss Signoret Seen in Play She Adapted. " New York
      Times, Dec. 6, 1962, p. 56. Paris production.

H387 Montealegre, Felicia. "Raising Hellman. " The New
      York Review of Books, 9 (Jan. 18, 1968), p. 32.
      A letter objecting to Elizabeth Hardwick's review
      (H365) in which she suggests Hardwick had not read
      the Foxes. See also: H393.

H388 "Name in Lights ... Lillian Hellman. " Stage, 16 (Mar.
      15, 1939), p. 46. illus. A review with praise for
      Hellman.

H389 Nathan, George Jean. "Theater Week: Dour Octopus. "

Newsweek, 13 (Feb. 27, 1939), 26.   An enthusiastic
review.

H390 "New Play in Manhattan. "   Time, 33 (Feb. 27, 1939),
38, 40.   illus.   A review of the season's "most
tense and biting drama" by a "moralist, " not a "mis-
anthrope. "

H391 O'Hara, Frank Hurburt.   "Comedies Without a Laugh, "
Today in American Drama.   Chicago: University of
Chicago Press, 1939.   Discusses Foxes as if it were
a novel, interprets the play and the characters; considers the social forces that "loom" behind the main
action.

H392 Phillips, Elizabeth C.   "Command of Human Destiny as
Exemplified in Two Plays: Lillian Hellman's The
Little Foxes and Lorraine Hansberry's A Raisin in
the Sun. "   Interpretations, 4 (1972), 29-39.

H393 Poirier, Richard.   "Raising Hellman. "   The New York
Review of Books, 9 (Jan. 18, 1968), 32.   A letter
in response to Elizabeth Hardwick's "disconcerting"
review of the revival that takes issue with her interpretation and picking.   See: H365, H366, H367,
H387.

H394 Robertson, T. H. B.   "The Little Foxes. "   Boston Trans-
cript, Apr. 22, 1939, p. 1.

H395 Shipley, Joseph T.   "This Week on the Stage: 'That
Spoil the Vine. ' "   New Leader, 22 (March 4, 1939),
6.   A review: "the play is a sharp, a bitter conflict; but as in most life's wars, our sympathies are
all on one side. "

H396 Simon, John.   "The Stage. "   Commonweal, 87 (Dec. 1,
1967), 304-05.

H397 _____.   Uneasy Stages, A Chronicle of New York
Theater, 1963-1973.   New York: Random House,
1975.

H398 "The Little Foxes. "   One Act Play Magazine, 2 (Feb. ,
1939), 748-49.

H399 "The Little Foxes: Ruth McKenney Hails the New Play

by Lillian Hellman. " New Masses, 30 (Feb. 28,
1939), 29+. A review: "The play is savage ...
Lillian Hellman comes into her own as one of America's most vigorous and exciting playwrights. "

H400 "The Little Foxes, Tallulah Bankhead Has Her First
U. S. Hit. " Life, 6 (Mar. 6, 1939), 70-73. illus.

H401 The New York Theatre Critics' Reviews, 1 (1940), 490-
92.

The reviews are listed in the following order:
Mantle, Burns.   "The Little Foxes, Taut Drama of
a Ruthless Southern Family. " Daily News, Feb.
16, 1939.
Atkinson, Brooks.   "Tallulah Bankhead Appearing in
Lillian Hellman's Drama of the South, The Little
Foxes. " New York Times, Feb. 16, 1939.
Watts, Richard, Jr.   "Dixie. " New York Herald
Tribune, Feb. 16, 1939.
Ross, George.   "Decay of the South Hellman Play
Theme. " World-Telegram, Feb. 16, 1939.
Lockridge, Richard.   "Lillian Hellman's The Little
Foxes Opens at the National Theatre. " New York
Sun, Feb. 16, 1939.
Waldorf, Wilella.   "The Little Foxes Opens at the
National Theatre. " New York Post, Feb. 16,
1939.

H402 The New York Theatre Critics' Reviews, 28 (1967) 237-
40.

The reviews are listed in the following order:
Kerr, Walter.   "We Could Have Five Little Foxes. "
New York Times, Nov. 5, 1967.
Barnes, Clive.   "Theater: Return of The Little
Foxes, Hellman's Play Staged by Lincoln Troupe. "
New York Times, Oct. 27, 1967.
Gottfried, Martin.   "Theatre: The Little Foxes. "
Women's Wear Daily, Oct. 27, 1967.
Chapman, John.   "Lincoln Center Rep Revival of
The Little Foxes a Humdinger. " Daily News,
Oct. 27, 1967.
Cooke, Richard P.   "The Theater: A Well-Acted
Revival. " Wall Street Journal, Oct. 30, 1967.
Watts, Richard, Jr.   "Ruthlessness of the Hubbards. "
New York Post, Oct. 27, 1967.

H403 "The Theater: Greedy Lot. " Time, 90 (Nov. 3, 1967),
      64+. illus.

H404 "The Theatres. " Times (London), Sept. 15, 1942, p.
      8. An announcement of Foxes' coming at end of
      October.

H405 "The Theatres. " Times (London), Sept. 15, 1942, p.
      8. Miss Fay Compton will play Regina.

H406 Vernon, Grenville. "The Stage and the Screen: The
      Little Foxes. " Commonweal, 29 (Mar. 3, 1939),
      525.

H407 Watts, Richard, Jr. "Dixie. " New York Herald Trib-
      une, Feb. 16, 1939, p. 14.

H408 Weales, Gerald. "What Kind of Fool Am I?" The Re-
      porter, 38 (Jan. 11, 1968), 36. A review that con-
      siders the revival "ridiculously over-praised. "

H409 Willis, John. Theatre World (1967-68 Season). New
      York: Crown Publishers, Inc., 1968. Pictures
      and cast information of the 1967 revival.

H410 Wilson, Edmund. "An Open Letter to Mike Nichols. "
      The New York Review of Books, 9 (Jan. 4, 1968),
      5-6+. An article regarding the life of the theater
      and his concern over Walter Kerr's Times' review
      of the revival.

H411 Wolak, William Joseph. A Production Book for "The
      Little Foxes. " M. A. thesis. St. Louis University,
      1961.

H412 Wyatt, Euphemia Van Rensselaer. "The Drama: The
      Little Foxes. " Catholic World, 149 (Apr. 19, 1939),
      87-88. An interpretation of the play, "better tech-
      nically than Children's Hour. "

H413 Zolotow, Sam. "Changes Coming in The Little Foxes. "
      New York Times, Nov. 2, 1967, p. 61. Cast changes
      announced for Barrymore Theater production.

H414 _____. "Equity Bars Role for Miss Chaplin, Union
      Rule on Aliens Keeps Her Out of The Little Foxes. "
      New York Times, Sept. 22, 1967, p. 55.

A musical adaptation of Foxes was done in 1949 by Marc
Blitzstein. The following few, but representative, reviews
are of interest particularly for their reference to LH.
>   Atkinson, Brooks. "At the Theatre." New York Times,
>   Nov. 1, 1949, p. 32. illus.
>   _____. "Musical Experiment, Marc Blitzstein's
>   Regina Fails to Add Stature to Original Little Foxes."
>   New York Times, Nov. 13, 1949, 2, p. 1.
>   Crawford, Cheryl. One Naked Individual, My Fifty
>   Years in the Theatre. Indianapolis: The Bobbs-
>   Merrill Company, Inc., 1977. pp. 172-74 are not
>   indexed.
>   Gibbs, Wolcott. "The Theatre: The Little Foxes as
>   Regina." New Yorker, 25 (Nov. 12, 1949), 56-58.
>   "New Plays: Regina." Theatre Arts, 34 (Jan., 1950),
>   12. illus.
>   Paramenter, Ross. "Regina Returns in Concert Form."
>   New York Times, June 2, 1952, p. 25.
>   Zolotow, Sam. "Regina Musical, Will Open Tonight."
>   New York Times, Oct. 31, 1949, p. 21.

THE SEARCHING WIND

H415 Barnes, Howard. "The Theatres: Perception and
     Poetry." New York Herald Tribune, Apr. 13, 1944,
     p. 16.

H416 "Broadway Report." PM, Dec. 14, 1944, p. 16. An
     announcement of the suspension of performances of
     Searching Wind for vacation.

H417 "Drama Critics Vote No Award for Best American
     Play This Season." PM, Apr. 26, 1944, p. 20.
     Searching Wind lacked one vote to win.

H418 Eaton, Walter Prichard. "The Pulitzer Prize." The
     Theatre Annual, 1944, pp. 24-30.

H419 Fleischman, Earl E. "The Searching Wind in the Mak-
     ing." Quarterly Journal of Speech, 31 (Feb., 1945),
     22-28. Fleischman appeared in a scene at the end
     of the play and writes about the emergence of the
     production, of Shumlin's method of directing, Bay's
     settings, LH; he discusses the nature of the play

and does throw light on the "creative process involved in the theatrical production. "

H420 Gibbs, Wolcott. "Miss Hellman Nods. " New Yorker, 20 (Apr. 22, 1944), 42+. A review which notes LH has "abandoned her usual precision of construction, " that the play is "loose as a haystack. "

H421 Gilder, Rosamond. "Search for a Play: The Sum of the Season. " Theatre Arts, 28 (June, 1944), 331-32. illus. A commentary on what the play accomplishes as one of the few serious plays then current.

H422 "How War Came. " New York Times, Apr. 23, 1944, 6, p. 19. illus. Comment.

H423 "It's a New Hit Because.... " Vogue, 103 (June 1, 1944), p. 110. illus. A brief comment on the double focus of the play.

H424 Jordan, Elizabeth. "Theatre: The Searching Wind. " America, 71 (Apr. 29, 1944), 108. A review of "the best play of the year. "

H425 Kronenberger, Louis. "A Drama with Teeth to It. " PM, Apr. 14, 1944, p. 20. Reprinted from the late edition Apr. 13, 1944. A review: the play resembles "Shaw in its incisive dialogue, its provocative ideas, its political awareness and its force of personality. "

H426 _____. "Going to the Theater: The Critics Circle's Vote. " PM, Apr. 28, 1944, p. 20. Accounts for his not voting and questions the Circle's standards.

H427 _____. "Going to the Theater: The Searching Wind. " PM, Apr. 23, 2944, p. 16. Analysis of the play.

H428 LaGuardia, Robert. Monty, The Biography of Montgomery Clift. New York: Arbor House, 1977.

H429 "Lillian Hellman. " PM, Apr. 12, 1944, p. 16. A picture of LH and a notice of the opening at the Fulton.

H430 Maney, Richard S. "From Hellman to Shumlin to Broadway. " New York Times, Apr. 9, 1944, 2, p. 1.

illus. Comments on the Shumlin production, that both Shumlin and Hellman look on the theater as an adult institution.

H431 Marshall, Margaret. "Drama." Nation, 158 (Apr. 22, 1944), 494-95. A review which develops the failure of the play as one of lack of clarity of thought and feeling; LH is "an expert at the cruel and knowing line."

H432 Nathan, George Jean. Theater Book of the Year, 1943-1944. New York: Alfred A. Knopf, 1944. Interprets the play, points out that LH departed from being the dramatist to becoming the "crusader" and so spoils the play; writes of her indignation and "public-spiritedness" in connection with the flawed play.

H433 "New York Drama Critics' Circle Award." New York Times, Apr. 26, 1944, p. 25.

H434 Nichols, Lewis. "The Searching Wind." New York Times, Apr. 13, 1944, p. 25. A review that discusses LH's remarkable craftsmanship, clarity of thought, integrity, crisp words as a "credit to the theatre."

H435 _____. "The Searching Wind: Lillian Hellman's Latest Play a Study of Appeasement and Love." New York Times, Apr. 23, 1944, 2, p. 1.

H436 Ormsbee, Helen. "Miss Hellman All But Dares Her Next Play to Succeed!" New York Herald Tribune, Apr. 9, 1944, 4, pp. 1-2. Includes the anecdote that accounts for the title.

H437 Phelan, Kappo. "The Stage and the Screen: The Searching Wind." Commonweal, 40 (Apr. 28, 1944), 40.

H438 Randolph, Alan F. "Dissent in the Drama Mailbag." New York Times, July 16, 1944, 2, p. 1. A letter disagreeing with the critics.

H439 "Scene Shifting Queried: Patent Infringement Is Alleged in Production of Play." New York Times, July 12, 1944, p. 21.

H440 "Scenes from a Political Drama...." New York Times,
June 23, 1946, 2, p. 3. illus.

H441 Shipley, Joseph T. "The Barren Years." New Leader,
26 (May 6, 1944), 8. A review of the play.

H442 Sillen, Samuel. "The Searching Wind." New Masses,
60 (May 2, 1944), 26-27. A review: "fails to rise
to the significance implicit in its anti-appeasement
theme."

H443 The New York Theatre Critics' Reviews, 5 (1944), 217-
20.

The reviews are listed in the following order:
Morehouse, Ward. "Lillian Hellman's Play, The
Searching Wind, Eloquent and Powerful." New
York Sun, Apr. 13, 1944.
Garland, Robert. "The Searching Wind on the Ful-
ton Stage." Journal-American, Apr. 13, 1944.
Waldorf, Wilella. "The Searching Wind a Mild Blast
at Compromise and Appeasers." New York Post,
Apr. 13, 1944.
Rascoe, Burton. "The Searching Wind, Miss Hell-
man's Finest." World-Telegram, Apr. 13, 1944.
Kronenberger, Louis. "A Drama with Teeth to It."
New York Newspaper PM, Apr. 13, 1944.
Barnes, Howard. "Perception and Poetry." New
York Herald Tribune, Apr. 13, 1944.
Chapman, John. "The Searching Wind, A Forceful
Drama about World Appeasers." Daily News,
April 13, 1944.
Nichols, Lewis. "The Play in Review: The Search-
ing Wind." New York Times, Apr. 13, 1944.

H444 "The Searching Wind." Life, 16 (May 1, 1944), 43-
44+. illus.

H445 "The Theater: New Plays in Manhattan." Time, 43
(Apr. 24, 1944), 72. illus. A review of the "first
really provocative play of the season."

H446 "Theater: Hellman's Blue Ribbon." Newsweek, 23
(Apr. 24, 1944), 86+. illus.

H447 Wilson, John S. "No First Night Jitters for Playwright
Lillian Hellman." PM, Nov. 17, 1946, pp. 16+. An
interview prior to opening of Searching Wind.

H448 Wyatt, Euphemia Van Rensselaer. "The Drama: The
      Searching Wind. " Catholic World, 159 (May, 1944),
      170-71.   A review that discusses the theme of the play
      as "the world's tragedy is the sum total of all of
      our personal weaknesses. "

H449 Young, Stark. "Behind the Beyond. " New Republic,
      110 (May 1, 1944), 604.

TOYS IN THE ATTIC

H450 "A Drama of Disastrous Love. " Life, 48 (Apr. 4,
      1960), 53-54+. illus.

H451 Adler, Jacob H. "Miss Hellman's Two Sisters. "
      Educational Theatre Journal, 15 (May, 1963), 112-
      117.

H452 Atkinson, Brooks. "One Revue: One Play, Thurber
      Carnival and Toys in the Attic. " New York Times,
      Mar. 6, 1960, 2, p. 1. "One of her minor works. "

H453 _____. "The Play: Toys in the Attic. " New York
      Times, Feb. 26, 1960, p. 23.

H454 Blum, Daniel, ed. Theatre World Season 1959-1960.
      Philadelphia: Chilton Company, 1960. Photos of
      production and cast and credits.

H455 Bohle, Bruce. "The Openings: Toys in the Attic. "
      Theatre Arts, 44 (May, 1960), 57-58+. A review.

H456 Brustein, Robert. "The Play and the Unplay. " New
      Republic, 142 (Mar. 14, 1960), 22-23. Writes of
      the play as in the "Ibsen tradition" by a true play-
      wright, perhaps overly crafted.

H457 Chapman, John. Broadway's Best: 1960. New York:
      Doubleday and Company, 1960. A synopsis and in-
      terpretation.

H458 Clurman, Harold. "Theatre. " Nation, 190 (Mar. 19,
      1960), 261-62. A review, "highly selective realism. "

H459 Downer, Alan S. Recent American Drama. Minnea-
      polis: University of Minnesota Press, 1961. Use al-
      so for The Searching Wind; unindexed pp. 41-42.

H460 Driver, Tom F. "Puppet Show." The Christian Century, 77 (Apr. 27, 1960), 511+. A review that discusses melodrama in connection with Toys.

H461 "English Finesse in an American Play." Times (London), Nov. 11, 1960, p. 16. Reviewed as an "intensely American play."

H462 "First Nights: Broadway Comes Alive" Newsweek, 55 (Mar. 7, 1960), 89. illus.

H463 Freedley, George. "Toys in the Attic." Library Journal, 85 (Aug., 1960), 2809. A brief review of the Random House edition.

H464 Gassner, John. "Broadway in Review, Toys in the Attic." Educational Theatre Journal, 12 (May, 1960), 113-15. Found also in Dramatic Soundings, Evaluations and Retractions Culled from 30 Years of Dramatic Criticism. New York: Crown Publishers, Inc., 1968, 481-84. Gassner's is high praise for Toys and LH's work. Writes of her previous decade of writing, of the special merit of her work, of her use of character.

H465 Hayes, Richard. "The Stage: Forecast." Commonweal, 71 (March 18, 1960), 677. Brief comment on the play.

H466 Hewes, Henry. "Love in the Ice Box." Saturday Review, 43 (Mar. 12, 1960), 71-72.

H467 Kerr, Walter. "First Night Report: Toys." New York Herald Tribune, Feb. 26, 1960, p. 12.

H468 Lewis, Theophilus. "Theatre: Toys in the Attic." America, 103 (May 28, 1960), 323.

H469 Magill, Frank N., ed. "Toys in the Attic," Survey of Contemporary Literature, rev. ed. Volume XI. Englewood Cliffs, New Jersey: Salem Press, 1977. An essay-review.

H470 Mannes, Marya. "Miss Hellman's 'Electra'." The Reporter, 22 (Mar. 31, 1960), 43.

H471 Shipley, Joseph T. "James Thurber's Empty Carnival

and Hellman's Crowded Attic. " New Leader, 43
(March 21, 1960), 21. A review.

H472 Szogyi, Alex. "The Collected Plays, by Lillian Hellman. " Saturday Review, 55 (Aug. 12, 1972), 51-
52. This review is concerned chiefly with Toys.

H473 The New York Theatre Critics' Reviews, 21 (1960),
345-48.

The reviews are listed in the following order:
Ashton, Frank. "Toys Takes Apart Lives of Five. "
World-Telegram and The Sun, Feb. 26, 1960.
Coleman, Robert. "Toys Sure-Fire Hit. " Mirror
Feb. 26, 1960.
McClain, John. "Top Writing--Top Acting. " Jour-
nal-American, Feb. 26, 1960.
Atkinson, Brooks. "Theatre: Hellman's Play. "
New York Times, Feb. 26, 1960.
Watts, Richard, Jr. "Lillian Hellman's Striking
Drama. " New York Post, Feb. 26, 1960.
Chapman, John. "Miss Hellman's Toys, Vigorous
and Absorbing Drama. " Daily News, Feb. 26,
1960.
Kerr, Walter. "First Night Report: Toys. " New
York Herald Tribune, Feb. 26, 1960.

H474 "The Theater: New Plays on Broadway. " Time, 75
(Mar. 7, 1960), 50. illus.

H475 Trewin, J. C. "Deep Down. " Illustrated London News,
237 (Nov. 26, 1960), 964. illus. A review that
considers the play over-written, "a parody of the
sultrier Deep South drama. "

H476 Tynan, Kenneth. "The Theatre, Deaths and Entrances. "
New Yorker, 36 (Mar. 5, 1960), 124-45. A review
that discusses the similarities of Toys to the work
of Tennessee Williams.

H477 Watts, Richard, Jr. "That 'Shabby Season' in Perspec-
tive. " Theatre Arts, 44 (July, 1960), 13+, 16, 63.

H478 Zolotow, Sam. "New York Drama Critics' Circle
Awards--Five Finger Exercise is named by Critics'
Circle. " New York Times, Apr. 20, 1960, p. 44.
illus. Toys voted best American drama of the 1959-
60 season.

WATCH ON THE RHINE

H479 "Aldwych Theatre: Watch on the Rhine. " Times (London), Apr. 23, 1942, p. 6. A review and comment.

H480 Atkinson, Brooks. "Critics' Prize Plays. " New York Times, Apr. 27, 1941, 9, p. 1. An account of the process by which Watch was chosen.

H481 _____. "Hellman's Watch on the Rhine: Author of The Children's Hour and The Little Foxes Writes of an American Family Drawn into the Nazi Orbit. " New York Times, Apr. 13, 1941, 9, p. 1. Found also in Broadway Scrapbook. New York: Theatre Arts, Inc. , 1947. Characterizes LH's talent and her mind.

H482 _____. "The Play: Lillian Hellman's Watch on the Rhine Acted with Paul Lukas in Leading Part. " New York Times, Apr. 2, 1941, p. 26. illus.

H483 _____. "Watch on the Rhine, After Five Months the Actors Are Giving a Notable Performance. " New York Times, Aug. 24, 1941, 9, p. 1. "the foremost theatrical achievement of the season. "

H484 "Autumn Plans. " Times (London), Sept. 1, 1941, p. 8. Watch to open.

H485 Berkowitz, Rozia. "No Rumanian Count. " New York Times, Apr. 13, 1941, 9, p. 3. A letter informing the editor.

H486 Bessie, Alvah. "Watch on the Rhine, Lillian Hellman's New Play Tells Story of a German Anti-Fascist. " New Masses, 39 (Apr. 15, 1941), 26-28. A review of LH's "dramatic evaluation of the central problem of our time--the struggle against the developing force of reaction. ... " Bessie believes LH skates around the issue.

H487 " 'Command' Performance for Watch on the Rhine. " New York Times, Jan. 6, 1942, p. 26. To be held at the National Theatre for President Roosevelt's birthday.

H488 "Critics Acclaim Watch on the Rhine. " PM, Apr. 2,

1941, p. 22.   A summary of the critics' views.

H489 "Critics' Prize Goes to <u>Watch on the Rhine</u>:   Lillian
      Hellman's Play Wins Annual American Award. "   <u>New</u>
      <u>York Times</u>, Apr. 23, 1941, p. 24.   An announce-
      ment of and a list of the critics who voted for the
      Award.

H490 Darlington, W. A.   "<u>Watch on the Rhine</u>, Miss Hellman's
      Play Provides London with Another Smash Hit. "   <u>New</u>
      <u>York Times</u>, May 3, 1942, 8, pp. 1-2.   A London
      review.

H491 "Drama Award Presented: Lillian Hellman Gets Critics'
      Plaque at Their Dinner. "   <u>New York Times</u>, Apr.
      28, 1941, p. 10.

H492 "Drama Critics' Circle Bows to Lillian Hellman. "   <u>PM</u>,
      Apr. 28, 1941, p. 23.   Acknowledgement of the
      Award for <u>Watch</u> given the previous night at the Al-
      gonquin.

H493 Eaton, Walter Prichard.   "Stage Plays in Print. "   New
      York <u>Herald Tribune Books</u>, Oct. 5, 1941, p. 28.

H494 Evans, Alice.   "Bits of Broadway. "   <u>New Theatre News,</u>
      May, 1941, p. 7.

H495 Fagin, Bryllion.   "Dramatists' Use of the American
      Stage for Democracy Finds Responsive Audiences. "
      <u>New Leader</u>, 24 (July 5, 1941), 4.

H496 "Footnotes on Headliners: Producer. "   <u>New York Times,</u>
      Apr. 27, 1941, 4, p. 2.

H497 "Footnotes on Headliners: <u>Watch</u> chosen for a 'Com-
      mand' Performance. "   <u>New York Times</u>, Jan. 11,
      1942, p. 2.   illus.

H498 Freedley, George.   "New Book Survey. "   <u>Library Jour-</u>
      <u>nal,</u> 66 (May 15, 1941), 462.   A brief review and
      recommendation of the Random House edition.

H499 French, Warren, ed.   <u>The Forties: Fiction, Poetry,</u>
      <u>Drama</u>.   DeLand, Florida: Everett/Edward, Inc.,
      1969.   Use also for <u>The Searching Wind</u>; information
      also given on those elected to National Institute of
      Arts and Letters at the same time LH was.

H500 Gibbs, Wolcott. "The Theatre: This Is It." New
       Yorker, 17 (Apr. 12, 1941), p. 32.

H501 Gilder, Rosamond. "Prizes That Bloom in the Spring."
       Theatre Arts, 25 (June, 1941), 409-11.

H502 _____. "The Kingdom of War." Theatre Arts, 25
       (Nov., 1941), 791-92.

H503 _____. "War Plays: There Shall be No Night and
       Watch on the Rhine," in Rosamond Gilder and others,
       eds., Theatre Arts Anthology. New York: Theatre
       Arts, 1950, pp. 649-51.

H504 Gould, Jack. "Paul Lukas, Late of Hollywood: Ran-
       dom Notes on the Central Figure in Lillian Hellman's
       New Drama, Watch on the Rhine." New York Times,
       Apr. 6, 1941, 9, pp. 1, 2.

H505 Heilman, Robert Bechtold. Tragedy and Melodrama,
       Versions of Experience. Seattle: University of
       Washington Press, 1968.

H506 "Hellman Play Opens in Moscow." New York Times,
       Feb. 26, 1945, p. 10. Under the title Trouble in
       the Parolly Family.

H507 Irwin, Ben. "Editorial." New Theatre News, Nov.,
       1940, pp. 1-2.

H508 Jordan, Elizabeth. "Theatre: Watch on the Rhine."
       America, 65 (April 19, 1941), 54. A review: In
       Watch, "a certain warming humanity in her recent
       outlook has been a special feature of her latest play's
       appeal."

H509 Kronenberger, Louis. "Critics Vote Watch on the Rhine
       Season's Best." PM, Apr. 23, 1941, p. 21. illus.
       An account of the balloting.

H510 _____. "Watch on the Rhine--The Best Play of the
       Season, a Melodrama of Anti-Nazism." PM, Apr.
       2, 1941, p. 23. illus. A review: "The theater
       found its voice last night ... exciting melodrama"
       that "ends on a deeply human and moving" note.
       Picture of a smiling LH with Herman Shumlin between
       acts.

H511 Krutch, Joseph Wood. "No Such Animal." Nation,
       152 (Apr. 12, 1941), 453. A review of a not very
       "convincing play."

H512 "Lillian Hellman in Moscow." New York Times, Nov.
       16, 1944, p. 18.

H513 Martin, Kingsley. "A Fine Play, Watch on the Rhine."
       New Statesman and Nation, 23 (May 2, 1942), 258.

H514 "Message Without Hysteria: Watch on the Rhine Pre-
       sents Subtle Indictment of the Nazis." Newsweek,
       17 (Apr. 14, 1941), 70.

H515 Nathan, George Jean. "Playwrights in Petticoats."
       American Mercury, 52 (June, 1941), 750-52. Watch
       proves LH "the best of our American women play-
       wrights."

H516 "New Broadway Hit, Watch on the Rhine, Brings Nazi
       Danger Close." Life, 10 (Apr. 14, 1941), 81-82+.
       illus.

H517 Noble, Peter. Hollywood Scapegoat, The Biography of
       Erich von Stroheim. New York: Arno Press, 1972.
       An account of LH's asking von Stroheim to see Shum-
       lin about the role of Kurt Müller.

H518 O'Hara, John. "Prize Collection." Newsweek, 17
       (Apr. 28, 1941), p. 64. illus. Comment on the
       PM poll and the standing of Watch.

H519 "Opera and Drama Given in Baltimore: Watch on the
       Rhine Première." New York Times, Mar. 25, 1941,
       p. 26.

H520 "Radio: The U.S. Short Wave." Time, 38 (Nov. 3,
       1941), 56. illus. Excerpt from Watch read in Ger-
       man and shortwaved to Europe.

H521 Sillen, Samuel. "The Merchants of Alibis." New Mass-
       es, 39 (May 6, 1941), 22. Watch mentioned in re-
       view of Michael Gold's The Hollow Men.

H522 Sobel, Bernard. "Drama: Propaganda and the Play."
       Saturday Review, 25 (March 7, 1942), 13.

H523 "Stage Holidays, Two London Elevens in London Thea-
      tres. " Times (London), Aug. 5, 1943, p. 6.   Tour-
      ing company to take over the London production for
      two weeks.

H524 The New York Theatre Critics' Reviews, 2 (1941), 341-
      44.

         The reviews are listed in the following order:
      Atkinson, Brooks.   "Lillian Hellman's Watch on the
         Rhine Acted with Paul Lukas in the Leading Part. "
         New York Times, Apr. 2, 1941.
      Brown, John Mason.   "Lillian Hellman's Watch on
         the Rhine Presented. " New York Post, Apr. 2,
         1941.
      Anderson, John.   "Watch on the Rhine at the Mar-
         tin Beck, Lillian Hellman's New Play Concerns
         Conflict in U. S. Over Fascism; Paul Lukas' Act-
         ing Brilliant. " Journal-American, Apr. 2, 1941.
      Watts, Richard, Jr.   "Portrait of a German. " New
         York Herald Tribune, Apr. 2, 1941.
      Kronenberger, Louis.   "Watch on the Rhine--The
         Best Play of the Season, A Melodrama of Anti-
         Naziism. " New York Newspaper PM, Apr. 2,
         1941.
      Whipple, Sidney B.   "Watch on the Rhine Avoids the
         Soap-Box. " World-Telegram, Apr. 2, 1941.
      Mantle, Burns.   "Watch on the Rhine Stirring Drama
         of a Family of Refugees. " Daily News, Apr. 2,
         1941.
      Lockridge, Richard.   "Lillian Hellman's Watch on
         Rhine Opens at the Martin Beck. " New York Sun
         Apr. 2, 1941.

H525 "The Theater: New Play in Manhattan. " Time, 37
      (Apr. 14, 1941), 64. illus. A review.

H526 "The Theatres. " Times (London), Aug. 2, 1943, p. 8.
      Watch to change cast in second year.

H527 "The Theatres: Autumn Plays. " Times (London), Sept.
      1, 1941, p. 8.   An announcement of its coming to
      London.

H528 "Theater. " Newsweek, 17 (May 5, 1941), 67.   New
      York Drama Critics' Circle Award announced.

H529 "To Show Hellman Manuscript." New York Times,
      Jan. 25, 1942, p. 37. The original ms. with pro-
      duction notes and corrections to be displayed at Li-
      brary of Congress.

H530 Toohey, John L. A History of the Pulitzer Prize Plays.
      New York: Citadel Press, 1967.

H531 "Topics of the Times, Laughter Against Hitler." New
      York Times, Apr. 24, 1941, p. 20. An editorial.

H532 Van Gelder, Robert. "Of Lillian Hellman." New York
      Times, Apr. 20, 1941, 9, pp. 1, 3. Sub-titled
      "Being a Conversation with the Author of Watch on
      the Rhine." LH talks of how she works and writes,
      of Dear Queen (E1).

H533 Vernon, Grenville. "The Stage and Screen: Watch on
      the Rhine." Commonweal, 34 (Apr. 25, 1941), 15-
      16. The reviewer found Watch "a come-down after
      Foxes," poorly constructed, and the dialogue strained.

H534 "Watch on the Rhine." Times (London), June 22, 1942,
      p. 8. An announcement of a matinee benefit for the
      Actors' Orphanage.

H535 "Watch on the Rhine." Times (London), Apr. 23, 1942,
      p. 6. A review of the London performance.

H536 "Watch on the Rhine Seen by President." New York
      Times, Jan. 26, 1942, p. 18.

H537 Watts, Richard, Jr. "Portrait of a German." New
      York Herald Tribune, Apr. 2, 1941, p. 20.

H538 "What Is Life Worth?" New York Times, Apr. 6, 1941,
      4, p. 8. An editorial on Brooks Atkinson's interpre-
      tation of Watch as meaning "the death of fascism is
      more desirable than the lives and well-being of the
      people who hate it." See: H482.

H539 Will, George F. The Pursuit of Happiness, and Other
      Sobering Thoughts. New York: Harper and Row,
      Publishers, 1978.

H540 Wright, Basil. "The Theatre: Watch on the Rhine."
      Spectator (London), 168 (May 1, 1942), 419. An in-
      terpretation.

H541 Wyatt, Euphemia Van Rensselaer. "The Drama: Watch
     on the Rhine. " Catholic World, 153 (May, 1941),
     215-15.

H542 Young, Stark. 'Watch on the Rhine. " New Republic,
     104 (Apr. 14, 1941), 498-99. Commentary and re-
     view: "essentially a melodrama. "

Films

ANOTHER PART OF THE FOREST

H543 Agee, James. "Films." Nation, 166 (June 19, 1948), 697. A review: "a saber-toothed play."

H544 Ager, Cecelia. "Lillian Hellman in the Forest Primeval." PM, May 19, 1948, p. 15. A review: "an exceptionally interesting drama."

H545 Hartung, Philip T. "Theater-into-Cinema." Commonweal, 48 (June 4, 1948), 185. A review: LH "understands people."

H546 Hatch, Robert. "Movies: Broadway in Hollywood." New Republic, 118 (June 7, 1948), 29.

H547 McCarten, John. "The Current Cinema: Another Part of the Forest." New Yorker, 24 (May 29, 1948), 66.

H548 Pryor, Thomas M. "At the Rivoli: Another Part of the Forest." New York Times, May 19, 1948, p. 30. illus.

H549 _____. "Reviews in Brief: Another Part of the Forest." New York Times, May 23, 1948, 2, p. 1.

H550 "Television Play: Another Part of the Forest." Times (London), Jan. 17, 1957, p. 3.

H551 Walsh, Moira. "Films: Another Part of the Forest." America, 79 (May 22, 1948), 178. A review: "transferred to the screen with integrity."

DEAD END

H552 "Brazil Bans Two U.S. Movies." New York Times, Oct. 31, 1937, p. 32. Because it imparts "wrong practices of gunplay."

H553 Casty, Alan. Development of the Film, An Interpretive

History. New York: Harcourt, Brace, Jovanovich,
Inc., 1973. Use also with other of her films.

H554 Churchill, Douglas W. "Leg Art: Hollywood's New
Crisis." New York Times, May 30, 1937, 10, p.
3. Comments on the juvenile cast and on the sets.

H555 Cunningham, James P. "The Screen." Commonweal,
26 (Aug. 20, 1937), 406. A review.

H556 Ferguson, Otis. " 'And There Were Giants on the
Earth'." New Republic, 92 (Sept. 1, 1937), 103+.
Use also with The Spanish Earth.

H557 Ferguson, Donita. "Movie of the Week: Dead End." Literary Digest, Sept. 4, 1937, p. 30. A review: "Towering
obstacles faced the scenarist and director of this
bold, unblushing drama."

H558 Fitzmorris, Thomas J. "Films: Dead End." America,
57 (Aug. 28, 1937), 504. A review of "a distinctly
adult production."

H559 Galway, Peter. "The Movies: Dead End." New Statesman and Nation, 14 (Nov. 20, 1937), 836.

H560 Garbicz, Adam, and Jacek Klinowski. Cinema, The
Magic Vehicle: A Guide to Its Achievement. Journey One: The Cinema Through 1949. Metuchen,
New Jersey: The Scarecrow Press, 1975. Use also
for film Foxes.

H561 Hurley, Neil P. The Reel Revolution, A Film Primer
on Liberation. Maryknoll, New York: Orbis Books,
1978.

H562 "Just Like the Movies." Literary Digest, Dec. 11, 1937,
4. Pictures of and a discussion of the effects of the
movie upon a group of school children.

H563 Kauffmann, Stanley, with Bruce Henstell. American
Film Criticism, from The Beginnings to "Citizen
Kane." New York: Liveright, 1972.

H564 McManus, John T. "At the Rivoli: Dead End." New
York Times, Aug. 25, 1937, p. 25. illus.

H565 _____. "East River Chiaroscuro, A Modest Camera
        Records for the Screen The Stark Contrasts of Dead
        End." New York Times, Aug. 29, 1937, 10, p. 3.

H566 _____. "The Screen: The Rivoli's Dead End Pre-
        sents Anew a Prima Facie Case for Revision of the
        Social Scheme." New York Times, Aug. 25, 1937,
        p. 25. illus.

H567 "Memphis Bans Dead End: Not a Proper Picture for
        Youth of Today, Board Says." New York Times,
        Aug. 4, 1945, p. 7.

H568 "Movie of the Week: Dead End." Life, 3 (Aug. 30,
        1937), pp. 62-64. illus.

H569 Nicoll, Allardyce. "Film Reality: The Cinema and
        the Theatre," in James Hurt, ed., Focus on Film
        and Theatre. Englewood Cliffs, New Jersey: Pren-
        tice-Hall, Inc., 1974.

H570 "News of the Stage: Film Rights to Dead End Bought
        by Goldwyn for $165,000." New York Times, Feb.
        28, 1936, p. 19.

H571 Nugent, Frank S. "Home Is the Sailor." New York
        Times, Sept. 12, 1937, 11, p. 3.

H572 Orme, Michael. "The World of the Cinema." Illus-
        trated London News, 191 (Nov. 27, 1937), 955.

H573 Pryor, Thomas M. "Local Boys Make Good in Films."
        New York Times, Aug. 22, 1937, 10, p. 3.

H574 "Screen: New York Tenements Provide Melodrama and
        Moral." Newsweek, 10 (Aug. 28, 1937), p. 24.
        illus.

H575 Seldes, Gilbert. "Another Sockeroo...." Scribner's,
        52 (Nov., 1937), 63+.

JULIA

H576 Arnold, Gary. "A Faithful, Elegant But Evasive Julia."
        Washington Post, Oct. 12, 1977, B, pp. 1, 3. illus.

H577 Blake, Richard A. "Women: Friends to Each Other."
America, 137 (Oct. 22, 1977), 268+. Review of the
film.

H578 Blume, Mary. "A Friendship for All Seasons in Julia."
Los Angeles Times, Dec. 26, 1976, CAL, p. 48+.

H579 Canby, Vincent. "Julia Tries to Define Friendship."
New York Times, Oct. 3, 1977, p. 40. illus. A
review.

H580 Champlin, Charles. "Julia: Through a Memoir Dearly."
Los Angeles Times, Oct. 2, 1977, CAL, pp. 1, 38.
illus.

H581 Dunning, Jennifer. "Valentino and Julia Bring Stars
Out in the Rain." New York Times, Oct. 3, 1977,
p. 26. illus. An account of the pre-release screening of Julia, Oct. 1, 1977, at Cinema 1 and of the
party that followed. Photo of LH and Leonard Bernstein.

H582 Ferris, Susan. "Making of Julia." Horizon, 20 (Oct.,
1977), 86-90, 91-94. illus.

H583 Fosburgh, Laceey. "Why More Top Novelists Don't
Go to Hollywood." New York Times, Nov. 21, 1976,
2, pp. 1, 13. illus.

H584 Hatch, Robert. "Film." Nation, 225 (Nov. 5, 1977),
475-76. A review of the production with remarks
about the prose version.

H585 Kael, Pauline. "A Woman for All Seasons?" New
Yorker, 53 (Oct. 10, 1977), 94, 99-102.

H586 Kalb, Bernard. "Remembering the Dashiell Hammett
of Julia." New York Times, Sept. 25, 1977, 2,
pp. 15-16. Includes some comment about LH.

H587 Kauffmann, Stanley. "Julia." New Republic, 177
(Oct. 15, 1977), 32-33. A review: "irresistible."

H588 Kay, Karyn, and Gerald Peary, eds. Women and the
Cinema, A Critical Anthology. New York: E. P.
Dutton and Company, Inc., 1977. An interview with
Jane Fonda.

H589 Klemesrud, Judy. "Vanessa Redgrave--'The Only Per-
       son Who Could Play Julia'." New York Times, Oct.
       2, 1977, 2, pp. 15, 30. An interview with Redgrave
       in which she speaks of preparing for the role, of the
       relationship between LH and Julia.

H590 Knelman, Martin. "Starring ... The Writer." Atlantic,
       240 (Nov., 1977), 96-98. Use also with An Unfinished
       Woman.

H591 Lutze, Peter. "Julia and Lilly." The Christian Century,
       94 (Dec. 21, 1977), 1198+. Review and comment
       on theme of Julia.

H592 Oakes, Philip. "Looking for the Lady." Sunday Times
       (London), Nov. 6, 1977, p. 35. illus.

H593 Reilly, Charles Phillips. "Film Reviews: Julia."
       Films in Review, 28 (Nov., 1977), 565. A review:
       emphasizes "the expository quality of Miss Hellman's
       short story."

H594 Schlesinger, Arthur M., Jr. "The Duplicitous Art."
       Saturday Review, 5 (Oct. 29, 1977), 46-47. An
       article on how films have changed; a review of Julia.

H595 Shalit, Gene. "Movie Screen Scene." Ladies' Home
       Journal, 94 (Dec., 1977), 10.

H596 Weinraub, Judith. "Two Feisty Feminists Filming
       Hellman's Pentimento." New York Times, Oct. 31,
       1976, 2, p. 17.

H597 Westerbeck, Colin L., Jr. "The Screen." Common-
       weal, 105 (Feb. 17, 1978), 117. Review: the trou-
       ble with Julia "is that it is not in control of its own
       implications."

H598 Wilson, Jane. "Hollywood Flirts with the New Woman."
       New York Times, May 29, 1977, 2, pp. 1, 11.

THE CHASE

H599 Alpert, Hollis. "Peyton Chase." Saturday Review, 49
       (Feb. 19, 1966), 64. A review.

H600 Bart, Peter. "On a Grim 'Chase' with Sound and Fury. "
New York Times, June 20, 1965, 2, p. 11.

H601 Crowther, Bosley. "The I. Q. of Hollywood Films. "
New York Times, Feb. 20, 1966, 2, p. 1.

H602 _____. "The Chase. " New York Times, Feb. 19,
1966, p. 24.

H603 _____. "The Screen: The Chase, Overheated West-
ern Is Served at 2 Theaters. " New York Times,
Feb. 19, 1966, p. 12. illus.

H604 Drutman, Irving. "Questioning Miss Hellman on Movies. "
New York Times, Feb. 27, 1966, 2, p. 5.

H605 Gill, Brendan. "The Current Cinema. " New Yorker,
42 (Feb. 26, 1966), 108. A review: "over-plotted. "

H606 Hartung, Philip T. "The Screen. " Commonweal, 84
(Apr. 1, 1966), 55. A review: a "melodramatic
script. "

H607 Hatch, Robert. "Film. " Nation, 202 (Mar. 7, 1966),
280. A review: " ... it could have been a great
picture. "

H608 Kael, Pauline. Kiss, Kiss, Bang, Bang. Boston: An
Atlantic Monthly Press Book, Little, Brown and Company, 1968.

H609 Tudor, Andrew. Image and Influence, Studies in the
Sociology of the Film. New York: St. Martin's
Press, 1974.

H610 Walsh, Moira. "Films: The Chase. " America, 114
(Mar. 5, 1966), 337+. A review: the "characters
never got beyond the point of being caricatures of
grotesque misbehavior. "

THE CHILDREN'S HOUR

H611 Crowther, Bosley. "Not-So-New Films From Old Ones. "
New York Times, Mar. 18, 1962, 2, p. 1.

H612 _____. "The Children's Hour. " New York Times,
Mar. 15, 1962, p. 28. illus.

H613 Dick, Bernard F.   Anatomy of Film.   New York: St. Martin's Press, 1978.   illus.   Use with These Three.

H614 Gill, Brendan.   "True and False: The Children's Hour. " New Yorker, 38 (Mar. 17, 1962), 123.

H615 Kael, Pauline.   I Lost It at the Movies.   Boston: Little, Brown and Company, 1965.

H616 Mekas, Jonas.   "The Children's Hour. "   Village Voice, 7 (Mar. 1, 1962), 11.

H617 "The Children's Hour. "   Films in Review, 13 (Apr. , 1962), 236-37.   illus.

H618 Walsh, Moira.   "Films: Additional 'Adult' Material. " America, 107 (June 2, 1962), 360.   A brief review.

H619 Whitehall, Richard.   "The Children's Hour. "   Films and Filming, 8 (Sept. , 1962), 31-32.

THE DARK ANGEL

H620 "A Train Without a Country. "   New York Times, Aug. 18, 1935, 9, p. 2.

H621 M[cCarten], J[ohn] C.   "The Current Cinema. "   New Yorker, 11 (Sept. 7, 1935), 62.   Brief note about the film.

H622 "On the Current Cinema: The Dark Angel. "   Literary Digest, 120 (Sept. 14, 1935), 33.

H623 Richards, Jeffrey.   Visions of Yesterday.   London: Routledge and Kegan Paul, 1973.

H624 Sennwald, Andre.   "The Screen: Samuel Goldwyn Presents a New Edition of The Dark Angel at the Rivoli Theatre. "   New York Times, Sept. 6, 1935, p. 12.

H625 "The Dark Angel at the Leicester Square. "   New Statesman and Nation, 11 (Oct. 5, 1935), 447.

H626 Vernon, Grenville.   "The Dark Angel. "   Commonweal, 22 (Sept. 20, 1935), 499.   Review.

THE LITTLE FOXES

H627 Bazin, André. <u>What Is Cinema</u>? Berkeley: University of California Press, 1967. Considers <u>Foxes</u> a
drama of manners.

H628 Brady, Thomas. "Peace Comes to <u>The Little Foxes</u>. "
<u>New York Times</u>, June 22, 1941, 9, p. 4.

H629 Churchill, Douglas W. "A House Divided: The Warner-
Goldwyn Dispute Headlines Hollywood's All-Star Word
Battle. " <u>New York Times</u>, June 1, 1941, 9, p. 3.

H630 Crowther, Bosley. "In the Charmed Circle, ... The
Outstanding Film of the Year. " <u>New York Times</u>,
Dec. 28, 1941, 9, p. 5. <u>Foxes</u> listed in the "sec-
ond-string 'ten'. "

H631 _____. "Mildly Unpleasant: Samuel Goldwyn's <u>The
Little Foxes</u> Raises the Question of Ugliness on the
Screen. " <u>New York Times</u>, Aug. 24, 1941, 9, p.
3.

H632 _____. "The Screen in Review: <u>The Little Foxes</u>,
Full of Evil, Reaches the Screen at the Music Hall. "
<u>New York Times</u>, Aug. 22, 1941, p. 19.

H633 Ferguson, Otis. "Happy Endings. " <u>New Republic</u>, 105
(Oct. 10, 1941), 622.

H634 _____. "The Man in the Movies. " <u>New Republic</u>,
105 (Sept. 1, 1941), 278.

H635 "Film Version of <u>The Little Foxes</u> Opens at Music Hall. "
<u>New Leader</u>, 24 (Aug. 23, 1941), 6. Comment on
the film.

H636 Fitzmorris, Thomas J. "Films: <u>The Little Foxes</u>. "
<u>America</u>, 65 (Sept. 13, 1941), 643. A brief review.

H637 "<u>Little Foxes</u> Stays on at Music Hall. " <u>New Leader</u>,
24 (Aug. 30, 1941), 6. Comment: <u>Foxes</u> "takes its
place with the most successful attractions in the
theatre's history. "

H638 McManus, John T. "<u>The Little Foxes</u> Is a Great Movie,
but Not Great Enough. " <u>PM</u>, Aug. 22, 1941, p. 22.
illus. A review: until LH "came along with her <u>The</u>

Little Foxes" Hollywood had not paid much attention
to the "basic anti-social fault" of greed.

H639 "Miss Hellman Loses Little Foxes Plea. " New York
Times, Feb. 27, 1970, p. 26.

H640 Mosher, John.   "The Current Cinema: The Season
Opens. " New Yorker, 17 (Aug. 23, 1941), 63.

H641 "Movie of the Week: The Little Foxes, Famed Stage
Hit Makes Fine Film for Bette Davis. " Life, 11
(Sept. 1, 1941), 47-50.

H642 "Plays and Pictures: The Little Foxes. " New Statesman and Nation, 24 (Nov. 7, 1942), 304.

H643 Wilson, Robert, ed.   The Film Criticism of Otis Ferguson. Philadelphia: Temple University Press,
1971.

THE NEGRO SOLDIER

H644 Barnouw, Erik.   Documentary, A History of the Non-
Fiction Film. New York: Oxford University Press,
1974.

H645 Barsam, Richard Meran.   Nonfiction Film, A Critical
History. Foreword by Richard Dyer MacCann. New
York: E. P. Dutton and Company, Inc. , 1973.

H646 Bogle, Donald.   Toms, Coons, Mulattoes, Mammies,
and Bucks, An Interpretive History of Blacks in
American Films. New York: The Viking Press,
1973.

H647 Crowther, Bosley.   "4 Theatres Show Negro War Film:
Documentary Picture Issued by War Department Opens
in Broadway Houses. " New York Times, Apr. 22,
1944, p. 8.

H648 Foster, Joseph.   "The Negro Soldier. " New Masses,
60 (Apr. 11, 1944), 28+.   A review of the film for
which LH had written the story and Carleton Moss
the script: a "beautifully constructed film. "

H649 Lardner, David.   "The Current Cinema: Two-Gun Salute. " New Yorker, 20 (May 6, 1944), 71.   Review.

H650 MacCann, Richard Dyer. The People's Films, The
      Political History of U. S. Government Motion Pic-
      tures. Studies in Public Communication, New York:
      Hastings House Publishers, 1973.

H651 McManus, John T. "The Negro Soldier, at Four B'way
     Theaters Today ... Salute Negro Greatness Through-
     out U. S. History. " PM, Apr. 21, 1944, pp. 14-15.
     A review of the film, not only "distinguished for its
     presentation of the Negro in U. S. war and peace,
     but for a warm story which threads through it and
     for moments of incomparable satisfaction for all
     Americans. . . . "

H652 Noble, Peter. The Negro in Films. Port Washington,
     New York: Kennikat Press, 1948, reissued 1969.

H653 "Would Ban Army Film. " New York Times, Apr. 22,
     1944, p. 8.

THE NORTH STAR

H654 Agee, James. Agee on Film, Reviews and Comments.
     Volume I. New York: Grosset and Dunlap Publish-
     ers, 1958.

H655 Crowther, Bosley. "Fiction or Fact? Russian War
     Documentaries Provide a Bearing on The North Star. "
     New York Times, Nov. 7, 1943, 2, p. 3.

H656 _____. "Films in Words: A Cheery Welcome to
     Two New Volumes of Published Screen-Play Scripts. "
     New York Times, Nov. 14, 1943, 2, p. 5.

H657 _____. "The Screen in Review: "The North Star,
     Invasion Drama, With Walter Huston, Opens in Four
     Theatres Here. " New York Times, Nov. 5, 1943,
     p. 23.

H658 Farber, Manny. "Movies in Wartime. " New Republic,
     110 (Jan. 3, 1944), 16-20.

H659 _____. "Mrs. Parsons, etc. " New Republic, 110
     (Jan. 10, 1944), 53. Comment on the Viking edition:
     a "pat on the back for the Russians. "

H660 _____. The Cardboard Star. " New Republic, 109
        (Nov. 8, 1943), 653. A review: admires the film,
        but the "characters are undifferentiated. "

H661 "Films on TV. " Film in Review, 9 (Feb. , 1958), 93+.
        Concerning the release of North Star as Armored
        Attack, much edited and shorter by 25 minutes.

H662 Hartung, Philip T. "All That I Know of a Certain Star. "
        Commonweal, 39 (Nov. 19, 1943), 117-18. A re-
        view: "A paean of praise sung to the people of
        Russia--not the bigwigs who were featured in Mission
        to Moscow ... Lillian Hellman's story comes through. "

H663 "Hearst Orders Anti-Soviet Smear of North Star Movie. "
        PM, Nov. 4, 1943, p. 9. An account of W. R.
        Hearst's dropping Frank Quinn's complimentary review
        of the film from the New York Mirror, Nov. 7, 1943,
        and replacing it with a description of the film as
        Bolshevist propaganda.

H664 Jacobs, Jack. "James Wong Howe. " Film in Review,
        12 (April, 1961), 226. Regarding the Lillian Hellman
        written North Star released for TV. See: H670.

H665 Kazin, Alfred. New York Jew. New York: Alfred A.
        Knopf, 1978.

H666 Kronenberger, Louis. "Introduction" to The North Star,
        by Lillian Hellman. New York: The Viking Press,
        1943.

H667 McManus, John T. "North Star Gleams With Under-
        standing. " PM, Nov. 5, 1943, p. 16. A review
        of the film that counters the attacks of W. R. Hearst
        and George Sokolsky: "a superfine film about Russia,
        by and for Americans ... a moving script by Lillian
        Hellman. "

H668 _____. "Speaking of Movies: San Simeon-Berlin
        Axis. " PM, Nov. 30, 1943, p. 25. Commentary:
        regards W. R. Hearst's "smear order to all Hearst
        editors against The North Star" as an aid to Hitler.

H669 Milestone, Lewis. "Mr. Milestone Beats a Plowshare
        into a Sword. " New York Times, Mar. 14, 1943, 2,
        p. 3.

H670 Mitchell, George. "James Wong Howe." Film in Review, 12 (June/July, 1961), 381. A letter correcting Jack Jacobs' title of North Star release from Counter Attack to Armored Attack. See: H664.

H671 "North Star Under Fire: Killing Without 'Judicial Process' Scored by Legion of Decency." New York Times, Nov. 8, 1943, p. 24.

H672 "Peasant Epic of Russia." New York Times, Oct. 10, 1943, 6, p. 16. illus.

H673 Pryor, Thomas M. "At Peace with the World." New York Times, July 7, 1946, p. 3.

H674 Rotha, Paul. The Film Till Now, A Survey of World Cinema. New York: Funk and Wagnalls Company, 1949. Use also with The Spanish Earth.

H675 Simon, Henry. "Themes and Variations: North Star Music." PM, Nov. 7, 1943, p. 16. Commentary principally on Aaron Copland's music.

H676 Stanley, Fred. "Hollywood Views the Russian Front." New York Times, Oct. 3, 1943, 2, p. 3.

H677 _____. "Hollywood's New Slant on the Soviet Union: Three Pictures Being Recorded on Russian Civilians at War--Advice from the OWL." New York Times, Feb. 28, 1943, 2, p. 3.

H678 Strauss, Theodore. "The Author's Case: Post-Première Cogitations of Lillian Hellman on The North Star." New York Times, Dec. 19, 1943, 2, p. 5.

H679 "The North Star." PM, Nov. 3, 1943, p. 16. illus. Brief comment.

THE SEARCHING WIND

H680 Agee, James. "Films." Nation, 162 (July 6, 1946), 25. Review: "People as highly civilized as these are seldom seen in the movies, and are still more seldom played with understanding."

H681 Ager, Cecelia. "A Timely and Stirring Theme Dimmed

by Bloodless People. " PM, June 27, 1946, p. 18.
A review: "The base of The Searching Wind is solid,
honest, and tough. "

H682 Crowther, Bosley.   "Ladies Know Best, An Observation
Upon the Persuasive Powers of Females in Films. "
New York Times, June 30, 1946, 2, p. 1.

H683 _____.   "The Screen in Review: The Searching Wind
Paramount Film Based on Stage Play by Lillian Hellman Opens Here. " New York Times, June 27, 1946,
p. 29.

H684 Farber, Manny.   "Hellman's Movietone News. "   New
Republic, 115 (Aug. 5, 1946), 142.

H685 Fitzmorris, Thomas J.   "Films: The Searching Wind. "
America, 75 (July 6, 1946), 313.   A brief review.

H686 Gassner, John.   "The Theatre Arts. "   Forum, 106
(Aug. , 1946), 177.   Brief comment.

H687 Hartung, Philip T.   "The Screen: A Time to Remem-
ber. "   Commonweal, 44 (July 12, 1946), 308+.   A
review of the film and comment on the script by
Miss Hellman.

H687aMcCarten, John.   "The Current Cinema: Look Out,
They're Coming in the Window. " New Yorker, 22
(June 29, 1946), 64.

H688 McGrath, Thomas.   "Films of the Week. "   New Masses,
60 (July 23, 1946), 28+.   A review: a "fine and
exciting achievement. "

H688aManvell, Roger.   "The Searching Wind. "   Sight and
Sound, 15 (Autumn, 1946), 98.

H689 "The New Pictures. " Time, 48 (July 1, 1946), 94.

H689a"The Searching Wind. " PM, June 25, 1946, p. 16.
illus.   An announcement of the opening of the film.

THE SPANISH EARTH

H690 "Cinema: The New Pictures. " Time, 30 (Aug. 23,

1937), 48-49. illus.

H691 Galway, Peter. "The Movies: The Spanish Earth. "
New Statesman and Nation, 14 (Nov. 13, 1937), 495.

H692 Hemingway, Ernest. "The War in Spain Makes a Movie
with Captions by Ernest Hemingway. " Life, 3 (July
12, 1937), 20-23. illus.

H693 "Hemingway Film Banned by Censor in London. " New
York Times, Oct. 24, 1937, p. 32.

H694 "Hemingway Film Seen, Spanish Earth Drastically Cut
by British Censor's Order. " New York Times, Nov.
9, 1937, p. 27.

H695 Jacobs, Lewis, ed. The Documentary Tradition from
'Nanook' to 'Woodstock. ' New York: Hopkinson and
Blake, Publishers, 1971.

H696 Lawson, John Howard. Film: The Creative Process,
The Search for an Audio-Visual Language and Structure. New York: Hill and Wang, 1967.

H697 McManus, John T. "At the 55th Street Playhouse: The
Spanish Earth. " New York Times, Aug. 21, 1937,
p. 7.

H698 _____. "Down to Earth in Spain. " New York Times,
July 25, 1937, 10, p. 4.

H699 _____. "Realism Invades Gotham. " New York Times,
Aug. 22, 1937, 10, p. 3.

H700 Mosher, John. "The Current Cinema: Madrid and
Thereabouts. " New Yorker, 8 (Aug. 21, 1937), 51+.
A review.

H701 "Providence Bans Spanish Earth. " New York Times,
Dec. 11, 1937, p. 22.

H702 "The Shape of Things. " Nation, 145 (Aug. 28, 1937),
210+. A commentary and recommendation: an
"utterly compelling study of a people struggling to
hold the land which a democratic government had
after centuries wrested for them from a decayed
feudal aristocracy. "

H703 "The Week. " New Republic, 92 (Aug. 18, 1937), 31.
     Brief review.

H704 W, H.   "Long Heralded, The Spanish Earth Opens 55th
     Street Playhouse. " New Leader, 20 (Aug. 21, 1937),
     4.   A review and commentary on significance and on
     Miss Hellman's collaboration.   An ad on the same
     page notes Lillian Hellman's collaboration.

THESE THREE

H705 Best, Katharine.   "Seen in the Dark. " Stage, 13 (April,
     1936), 8.   Comment on the success of the film and
     on the challenge of recasting Children's Hour as
     These Three.

H706 _____.   "Stage Awards the Palm Pictures. " Stage,
     13 (May, 1936), 41-43.   Awarded the Palm for the
     scenario writing of this "genuine screen tragedy. "

H707 Churchill, Douglas W.   "Pot Pourri from the Wonder
     City. " New York Times, Mar. 1, 1936, 9, p. 4.

H708 Cunningham, James P.   "These Three. " Commonweal,
     23 (Apr. 3, 1936), 636.   Comment on this "generally
     fine and superbly balanced motion picture" and an
     account of the changes required by the "self-imposed
     prohibitions of Hollywood. "

H709 Farrell, James T.   "Theatre Chronicle. " Partisan
     Review, 3 (Apr., 1936), 24.   Brief mention of a
     film "worth mentioning. "

H710 Farber, Manny.   "Films: Yes and No. " New Republic,
     86 (Apr. 1, 1936) 222.   A positive review: "Lillian
     Hellman's very clever rewrite of her Children's
     Hour. "

H711 Mosher, John.   "The Current Cinema: A Children's
     Hour. " New Yorker, 12 (Mar. 28, 1936), 55+.   A
     review, with comment on LH's handling of the script.

H712 Nugent, Frank S.   "Guerdons Well Earned, Being the
     Reelector of the Year's Best Ten, or Eleven, Pic-
     tures. " New York Times, Jan. 3, 1937, 10, p. 5.

H713 _____. "The Screen: Heralding the Arrival of These Three, at the Rivoli." New York Times, Mar. 19, 1936, p. 22.

H714 _____. "These Three, These Five, The Children's Hour and the Dionnes Alike Have Whispering Campaigns." New York Times, Mar. 22, 1936, 11, p. 3.

H715 "On the Current Screen: The Children's Hour Superbly Adapted Into Deeply Affecting Film." Literary Digest, Mar. 14, 1936, p. 22.

H716 "Pictures Now Showing." Stage, 13 (April, 1936), 10. A brief review.

H717 Tyler, Parker. Screening the Sexes, Homosexuality in the Movies. New York: Holt, Rinehart and Winston, 1972.

H718 Van Doren, Mark. "Films: These Three." Nation, 142 (Apr. 15, 1936), 492. A Brief review: "succeeds rather well in translating The Children's Hour."

TOYS IN THE ATTIC

H719 "Broadway Plays to Be Filmed." Times (London), Aug. 2, 1960, p. 11.

H720 "Cinema: Steel Butterfly." Time, 81 (Aug. 9, 1963), 73.

H721 Comerford, Adelaide. "Toys in the Attic." Film in Review, 14 (Aug.-Sept., 1963), 439. A review: "Lillian Hellman worked off her personal hatred of the South more effectively in The Little Foxes .... Toys is not a success."

H722 Crowther, Bosley. "Old Familiar Faces and Farces, New Films Manifest the Difficulty of Making Them Look New." New York Times, Aug. 11, 1963, 2, p. 1.

H723 _____. "Toys in the Attic." New York Times, Aug. 1, 1963, p, 17. illus.

H724 Kauffmann, Stanley. "Films: Gold, Golding, Gilt. "
      New Republic, 149 (Aug. 17, 1963), 28.   Found also
      in A World on Film, Criticism and Comment.   New
      York: Delta Book, Dell Publishing Company, 1966.

H725 Mapp, Edward.   Blacks in American Films.   Metuchen,
      New Jersey: The Scarecrow Press, 1971.

H726 Miller, Jonathon. "The Current Cinema: Toys in the
      Attic. " New Yorker, 39 (Aug. 10, 1963), 60-61.

WATCH ON THE RHINE

H727 Agee, James. "Films. " Nation, 156 (Sept. 25, 1943),
      360.   A brief review: "plays better on the screen"
      than on the stage.

H728 Crowther, Bosley. "The Cream of the 1943 Crop. "
      New York Times, Dec. 26, 1943, 2, p. 3.

H729 _____. "Watch on the Rhine, A Fine Screen Ver-
      sion of the Lillian Hellman Play, Opens at the Strand. "
      New York Times, Aug. 28, 1943, p. 15.

H730 Farber, Manny. "Parting Is Such Sweet Sorrow. " New
      Republic, 109 (Sept. 13, 1943), 364.   A review:
      "One of Miss Hellman's greatest virtues is an ability
      to spread a rich, human group of characters over
      her plays. "

H731 _____. "The Happiness Boys. " New Republic, 110
      (Feb. 28, 1944), 280.   Commentary on the film:
      "Watch is not in the category of filmgoers who go
      only to be entertained. "

H732 Gassner, John, and Dudley Nichols, eds.   Best Film
      Plays of 1943-44.   New York: Crown Publishers,
      Inc. , 1945.

H733 Gould, Harriet. "Portrait of an Anti-Fascist. " PM,
      Aug. 29, 1943, pp. 2-5.   illus.   Comments with
      excerpts from the filmscript: "The great virtue of
      the movie, as in the play, lies in the fact that it
      presents a clear, sharp portrait of an extremely im-
      portant kind of person--an anti-Fascist. "

H734 Hartung, Philip T. "Watch!" Commonweal, 38 (Sept. 24, 1943), 563. A review: "one of the most pro- vocative pictures to be made on the themes of war."

H735 Lardner, David. "The Current Cinema: No Deprecia- tion." New Yorker, 19 (Aug. 28, 1943), 44.

H736 Lawrence, Paul. Actor, The Life and Times of Paul Muni. New York: G. P. Putnam's Sons, 1974.

H737 Maltz, Albert. "What Shall We Ask of Writers?" New Masses, 57 (Feb. 12, 1946), pp. 19-20. Questions reviewing policy and standards of New Masses' cri- tics; refers to different estimates of acceptance of Watch as play and Watch as film. See: Alvah Bes- sie H486 and Daniel Prentiss H738.

H738 Prentiss, Daniel. "Watch on the Rhine." New Masses, 47 (Sept. 14, 1943), 30. illus. A review of great praise: "one of the film's chief merits is that it makes payment on humanity's long-standing debt to the heroes of the Spanish republic." See also: H486 and H737.

H739 Sheridan, Mary. "Films: Watch on the Rhine." Ameri- ca, 69 (Sept. 11, 1943), 642. A brief review.

H740 Simon, Henry. "Watch on the Rhine Still Packs Its Wallop on Screen." PM, Aug. 29, 1943, p. 22. A review.

H741 Strauss, Theodore. "Of Lillian Hellman, A Lady of Principle, The Author of Watch on the Rhine and North Star Stands by Her Guns." New York Times, Aug. 29, 1943, 2, p. 3.

H742 "Watch on the Rhine at RKO Theatres." New Leader, 26 (Oct. 9, 1943), 6.

Books

AN UNFINISHED WOMAN

H743 "An Unfinished Woman--A Memoir. " American Jewish
      Archives, 23 (Apr. , 1971), 105.

H744 "An Unfinished Woman--A Memoir. " Executive (Ontario),
      12 (Jan. , 1970), 51.

H745 "An Unfinished Woman--A Memoir. " Best Sellers, 34
      (Dec. 15, 1974), 429.

H746 "An Unfinished Woman--A Memoir. " Booklist, 66
      (Sept. 1, 1969), 25.

H747 "An Unfinished Woman--A Memoir. " Publishers' Week-
      ly, 195 (Apr. 14, 1969), 94.

H748 Bailey, Paul.   "Beyond the Veil: An Unfinished Woman. "
      Listener (London), 82 (Oct. 23, 1969), 567.   A re-
      view that includes comment on the quality of LH's
      life and mind.

H749 Beaufort, John.   "She Cast a Shrewd Eye ... Not Least
      on Herself. "   Chrisitan Science Monitor, July 24,
      1969, p. 7.

H750 Blakeston, Oswell.   "In Love with Books. "   Books and
      Bookmen, 15 (Jan. , 1970), 48-49.   illus.

H751 Bogan, Louise.   What the Woman Lived, Selected Let-
      ters of Louise Bogan, 1920-1970.   Edited by Ruth
      Simmer.   New York: Harcourt, Brace, Jovanovich,
      Inc. , 1973.

H752 Coles, Robert, M. D.   "Lillian Hellman. "   Atlantic,
      224 (July, 1969), 28.   A letter to the Atlantic where
      pre-publication of a section of Unfinished Woman
      had appeared (C3) :   writes of Lillian Hellman's mix
      of "crystal clear rationality with a great deal of
      warmth and feeling. "   See: H767, H776.

H753 Cook, Bruce,   "The Expanding Arts: Judging the Judges. " National Observer, 9 (Mar. 9, 1970), 23.

H754 Duffy, Sister M. Gregory, O. P. "An Unfinished Woman. " Best Sellers, 29 (July 1, 1969), 132+.

H755 Epstein, Joseph. "No Punches Pulled. " New Republic, 161 (July 26, 1969), 27-29.

H756 Evans, John W. "An Unfinished Woman, " in Frank N. Magill, ed. , Survey of Contemporary Literature, rev. ed. Volume XII. Englewood Cliffs, New Jersey: Salem Press, 1977. An essay-review.

H757 French, Philip. "A Different Woman. " New Statesmen, 78 (Oct. 24, 1969), 580.

H758 Fuller, Edmund. "The Bookshelf: Shy, Solitary Writer as a Difficult Woman. " Wall Street Journal, 174 (July 8, 1969), 16.

H759 Grant, Annette. "Lively Lady: An Unfinished Woman. " Newsweek, 73 (June 30, 1969), 89-90. illus.

H760 Grumbach, Doris. "Extraordinary Autobiography: Taking Pride in Falling. " National Catholic Reporter, 6 (Dec. 17, 1969), 4.

H761 Kotlowitz, Robert. "Rebel as Writer. " Harper's, 238 (June, 1969), 87-88, 89-91.

H762 Lasson, Robert. "Something Old, Something New, Something Borrowed. An Unfinished Woman: A Memoir. " Washington Post Book World, June 22, 1969, p. 5. illus. A review of a "disappointing book" of which the Hammett piece is the best writing.

H763 Lehmann-Haupt, Christopher. "The Incompleat Lillian Hellman. " New York Times, June 30, 1969, p. 37. illus. A review that also reveals the essential Hellman.

H764 Morton, James. "Lillian Hellman's Memoirs. " Contemporary Review, 216 (Mar. , 1970), 165+.

H765 Nelson, Elizabeth R. "Lillian Hellman's An Unfinished Woman. " Library Journal, 94 (June 15, 1969), 2460.

H766 Noble, Jeanne. <u>Beautiful, Also, Are the Souls of My</u>
      <u>Black Sisters: A History of the Black Women in</u>
      <u>America.</u> Englewood Cliffs, New Jersey: Prentice-
      Hall, Inc. , 1978. Regarding LH's treatment of
      Sophronia and Helen.

H767 _____. "Lillian Hellman. " <u>Atlantic,</u> 224 (July, 1969),
      28. Letter praising LH's "sensitive description of her
      relationship with Sophronia and Helen" and her cap-
      turing the "inner world of domestics. " (Ms. Noble
      was Vice President, National Council of Negro Wo-
      men, New York University, New York, at the time.)
      <u>See:</u> C3, H752, H776.

H768 "Paperbooks: <u>An Unfinished Woman. </u>" <u>Times</u> (London),
      Feb. 22, 1973, p. 11. A brief review: "The only
      internationally known woman playwright gives ...
      some deep insight into her nature. "

H769 "Playwright Reminisces. " <u>Chatelaine</u> (Toronto), 42
      (Oct. , 1969), 6. A brief review.

H770 Pritchett, V. S. "Stern Self-Portrait of Lady. " <u>Life,</u>
      66 (June 27, 1969), 12. A review; "a good-humored
      but drastic search for what she has been and is. "

H771 "Probing Without Pattern. " <u>Times Literary Supplement,</u>
      Jan. 22, 1970, p. 75. "Not so much reviewing a
      book as reviewing a woman. "

H772 Rabinowitz, Dorothy. "Experience as Drama. " <u>Commen-</u>
      <u>tary,</u> 48 (Dec. , 1969), 95-96.

H773 Rogers, W. G. "Personal History, a Review of <u>An Un-</u>
      <u>finished Woman. </u>" <u>Saturday Review,</u> 52 (July 5, 1969),
      30+. illus. A review; "the whole book is vividly
      thrilling theater. "

H774 Saal, Rollene W. "Pick of the Paperbacks. " <u>Saturday</u>
      <u>Review,</u> 53 (Nov. 28, 1970), 39.

H775 Seligson, Marcia. "Parties. " <u>Washington Post Book</u>
      <u>World,</u> Aug. 31, 1969, p. 2.

H776 Shaw, Irwin. "Lillian Hellman. " <u>Atlantic,</u> 224 (July,
      1969), 28. A letter praising LH's piece in the April
      edition (C3): "evocative and womanly and strong ...

written with honesty and without frills or deception
... it's just like her.... " <u>See</u>:   H752, H767.

H777 Stephens, Jan.   "One Happy, Two Not. "   <u>Times</u> (London), Aug. 6, 1977, p. 7.

H778 Symons, Julian.   "Special Notices: <u>An Unfinished Wo-man,</u> "   <u>London Magazine</u>, 10 (Apr. , 1970), 108.

H779 Toomey, Philippa.   "Paperbacks. "   <u>Times</u> (London), Feb. 22, 1973, p. 11.

H780 Tynan, Kenneth.   "Tough and Tender. "   <u>Observer</u>, Oct. 19, 1969, p. 34.   A review that interprets LH's work, compares her with Joan Littlewood ("the vulnerable women"), writes of <u>Unfinished Woman</u> as work of American realism.

H781 Weeks, Edward.   "The Peripatetic Reviewer: <u>An Un-finished Woman</u>. "   <u>Atlantic Monthly</u>, 224 (June, 1969), 106.

H782 Williams, Michaela.   "Miss Hellman's Personal Fragments Merge Into Personality of Beauty. "   <u>National Observer</u>, 8 (July 14, 1969), 17.   illus.

H783 Young, Stanley.   "<u>An Unfinished Woman: A Memoir</u>. " <u>New York Times,</u> June 29, 1969, 7, p. 8.   illus. "A public person's view of her private self. "   A comprehensive review.

PENTIMENTO

H784 Annan, Gabriele.   "Professional Portraits. "   <u>Listener</u> (London), 91 (Apr. 25, 1974), 535-36.   Likens LH to Maugham in craftsmanship and professionalism. "It is the book of a doyenne. "

H785 Butcher, Mary Vonne.   "Their Americas, A Review of <u>Burr</u> and <u>Pentimento</u>. "   <u>Tablet</u> (London), June 8, 1974, 554-55.

H786 Coleman, John.   "Exits and Entrances. "   <u>Observer</u>, Apr. 28, 1974, p. 36.

H787 Cosgrove, Mary Silva.   "Outlook Tower: <u>Pentimento</u>. "

The Horn Book Magazine, 50 (Feb. , 1974), 76.

H788 Dees, Robert. "Pentimento, a Book of Portraits, " in
Frank N. Magill, ed. , Survey of Contemporary Literature, revised edition. Volume IX. Englewood
Cliffs, New Jersey: Salem Press, 1977. An essay-
review of the criticism of the book.

H789 Duffy, Martha. "Half-Told Tales, " Time, 102 (Oct.
1, 1973), 114-16. illus.

H790 "Flashback, a Review of Pentimento. " Economist, 251
(May 25, 1974), 143. "A remarkable form of autobiography. "

H791 Fremont-Smith, Eliot. "Lillian Hellman: Portrait of
a Lady. " New York Magazine, Sept. 17, 1973, p.
82.

H792 French, Philip. "A Difficult Woman. " Times (London), Apr. 25, 1974, p. 12. "A masterly writer
of prose and a major witness of our times. "

H793 Grossman, Ellen. "Pentimento: A Book of Portraits
by Lillian Hellman. " Commentary, 57 (Feb. , 1974),
88-90.

H794 Haynes, Muriel. "More on the Unfinished Woman. "
Ms. 2 (Jan. , 1974), 31-33. A review of Pentimento,
"a triumphant vindication of the stories the author
threw away in her twenties because they were 'no
good'. "

H795 Hirsch, Foster. "Pentimento: A Book of Portraits. "
America, 129 (Dec. 29, 1973), 508. A review, like
many others, that found Pentimento lacking because
LH told so little about herself and the theater, but
appreciative of the honesty in what she did tell.

H796 Hoover, Francis X. J. "Pentimento: A Book of Portraits. " America, 129 (Nov. 17, 1973), 379. A
brief review of "an outstanding book. "

H797 Horwitz, Carey A. "Pentimento. " Library Journal,
98 (Nov. 15, 1973), 3369. A brief review.

H798 James, Clive. "Stars and Stripes. " The New Review

(London), 1 (May, 1974), 88-90.   An analysis of LH's
style in Pentimento and her approach to her material:
"an attitudinizing mind of which her mannered prose
was the logically consequent expression. "   Writes
of the influence of E. B. White and Hemingway in
Hellman's approach.   Wishes LH revealed her thinking and opinions to complement her account of her
feelings.

H799 Keith, Don Lee.   "A Playwright Sorts, Shares Her
      Memories. "   New Orleans Times-Picayune, Oct. 7,
      1973, p. 10.   illus.   "She reaffirms just how extra-
      ordinary a woman she is. "

H800 Kirsch, Robert.   "Three Authors and Their Second
      Thoughts. "   Los Angeles Times, Sept. 23, 1973,
      CAL, p. 54.   illus.   A review of Pentimento.

H801 Kupferberg, Herbert.   "Hellman Memoir Summons Peo-
      ple for an Encore. "   National Observer, 12 (Oct. 13,
      1973), 19.

H802 Lehmann-Haupt, Christopher.   "Seeing Others to See
      Oneself. "   New York Times, Sept. 17. 1973, p. 31.
      illus.

H803 Leonard, John.   "1973: An Apology and 38 Consolations. "
      New York Times, Dec. 2, 1973, 7, p. 2.   A re-
      view of Pentimento and high praise.

H804 "Looking Back. "   Chatelaine (Toronto), 46 (Dec. , 1973),
      4.   illus.   A brief review.

H805 McLellan, Joseph.   "Paperbacks: Pentimento. "   Wash-
      ington Post Book World, Oct. 20, 1974, p. 4.

H806 _____.   "Pick of the Paperbacks, 1974. "   Washing-
      ton Post Book World, Dec. 22, 1974, p. 3.

H807 Mesic, Penelope.   "Reliving the Chance of a Full and
      Happy Life. "   Chicago Tribune Book World, Sept.
      23, 1973, p. 3.   illus.   A review: "Pentimento is
      a marvel, the kind of book that happens only once. "

H808 Nordell, Roderick.   "Best Seller, Pentimento. "   Chris-
      tian Science Monitor, Nov. 14, 1973, p. 17.

H809 "Painted Over, Lillian Hellman: Pentimento. " Times
      Literary Supplement, 26 (Apr. 26, 1974), 440. illus.
      A review; "the most important statements about her-
      self tend to come in parentheses. "

H810 "Pentimento. " MD Medical Newsmagazine, April, 1974,
      p. 207. A review.

H811 "Pentimento. " Library Journal, 98 (July, 1973), 2157.

H812 "Pentimento: A Book of Portraits. " Publishers' Week-
      ly, 204 (July 16, 1973), 106.

H813 "Pentimento. " Booklist, 70 (Oct. 15, 1973), 204.

H814 "Pentimento. " New York Times, Oct. 13, 1974, 7,
      p. 46. A review of the New American Library edi-
      tion.

H815 Poirier, Richard. "Pentimento. " Washington Post
      Book World, Sept. 16, 1973, pp. 1, 4-5. An ex-
      tended review; " 'Julia' is the most accomplished
      piece in the book. "

H816 Prescott, Peter S. "Leftover Life. " Newsweek, 82
      (Oct. 1, 1973), 95-96. illus. A review.

H817 Rabinowitz, Dorothy, "Current Books in Short Compass:
      Pentimento. " World, 2 (Aug. 28, 1973), 39. The
      masterpeices of the work are "Julia" and "Arthur
      W. A. Cowan. " At the heart "of all the portraits is
      a somberness that lives side by side with a most
      profound wit. "

H818 Raphael, Frederic. "Under Fire: Pentimento. " The
      Sunday Times (London), Apr. 28, 1974, 389. A
      mixed review, with comment about LH.

H819 Roud, Richard. "What Lillian Left Off Broadway. "
      The Guardian Weekly (Manchester), 110 (May, 11,
      1974), 22. A review of Pentimento.

H820 Schorer, Mark. "Pentimento. " New York Times,
      Sept. 23, 1973, 7, pp. 1-2. illus. A review that
      talks also of the character of an "extraordinary wo-
      man. "

H821 Siggins, Clara M. "Pentimento: A Book of Portraits."
Best Sellers, 33 (Oct. 1, 1973), 303. Pentimento
"could be seen as a palimpsest to her memoirs."

H822 Simon, John. "Pentimental Journey." Hudson Review,
26 (Winter, 1973-74), 743-52. Of them all, this is
the most comprehensive review of the book. Dis-
claims any connection with Charles Thomas Samuel's
New York Times' review of The Collected Plays
(H303).

H823 Stone, Laurie. "Pentimento." Viva, 5 (Aug., 1978),
40.

H824 Symons, Julian. "Drunk, but Not Disorderly." London Magazine, 14 (Aug., -Sept., 1974), 137-38. The
effect of the book "is one of charm and candor," not
a masterpiece.

H825 Theroux, Paul. "Dowager Empress." New Statesman,
87 (Apr. 26, 1974), 587-88. A review, "writes as
a survivor with elegance."

H826 Walt, James. "An Honest Memoir: Pentimento: A
Book of Portraits." New Republic, 169 (Oct. 20,
1973), 27-28.

H827 Wolff, Geoffrey. "The Find-Out Kicks." New Times,
6 (Apr. 30, 1976), 64-65. A review of the three
memoirs, which "make connections and light dark
places with a grace and to a degree that Miss Hellman's plays never managed."

SCOUNDREL TIME

H828 Abrahams, William. "Scoundrel Time." Times Literary,
Supplement, Jan. 7, 1977, p. 13. A letter on the
Richard Mayne review (H880).

H829 Adler, Larry. "The Lady Who Refused to Sing." The
Sunday Times (London), Nov. 7, 1976, p. 40. A
review.

H830 Baker, John F. "Lillian Hellman." Publishers' Weekly,
209 (Apr. 26, 1976), 6-7.

H831 Beichman, Arnold. "Different Value Systems Seen Opera-
      ting: Playwright Lillian Hellman's Memoir: Scound-
      rel Time." Christian Science Monitor, May 17, 1976,
      p. 23. A review that expresses regret that LH does
      not explain the difference between her value system
      and that of other intellectuals "like the Trillings."

H832 "Being Too Comfortable." Economist, 261 (Nov. 20,
      1976), 140. A review of the British edition with
      James Cameron's introduction.

H833 "Books Briefly." Progressive, 40 (Aug., 1976), 44.
      A review.

H834 "Brief Reviews." Critic, 35 (Winter, 1976), 87.

H835 Buchanan, Patrick. "A Writer Flatters Herself." Chi-
      cago Tribune, June 20, 1976, 2. p. 6. A critical
      review, gives background of the times and concludes
      the book might "better have been titled 'Gullible's
      Travels'."

H836 Buckley, William F., Jr. "Night of the Cuckoo."
      National Review, 29 (Apr. 29, 1977), 513+. A re-
      view that disputes LH's remark that she has nothing
      to be ashamed of in her life and points up the dif-
      ference between LH and Albert Speer's service in
      the interest of totalitarianism in Speer's favor.

H837 _____. "Scoundrel Time. And Who Is the Ugliest
      of Them All?" National Review, 29 (Jan. 21, 1977),
      101-06. Buckley believes the title should have been
      Scoundrel Time, by Lillian Hellman, as Told to Gar-
      ry Wills. He questions her credibility; he thinks the
      book serves her self-pity, self-righteousness; he be-
      lieves Scoundrel Time is disorderly and tasteless.
      He gives the account of Little, Brown cancelling its
      contract with Diana Trilling when she would not de-
      lete her essay on LH and quotes Arthur Thornkill's
      account of the Trilling cancellation.

H838 Campenni, Frank. "Hellman Looks Back in Anger."
      Milwaukee Journal, May 16, 1976, 5, p. 4. A re-
      view of the memoirs built around "one 67 minute
      event."

H839 Caute, David. "Un-American Activities." Observer,

Nov. 7, 1976, p. 27. A review of the edition with the "off-the-cuff preface by James Cameron and a background essay by Garry Wills." The book irritates the reviewer, but he concludes with high praise and mention of her wit and sharp ear.

H840 Clemons, Walter. "Way It Was: Scoundrel Time." Newsweek, 87 (Apr. 26, 1976), 96-97. illus. "Her most sustained piece of narrative."

H841 Coles, Robert. "Are You Now or Have You Ever Been ...." Washington Post Book World, May 9, 1976, p. 5. The review remarks LH "can't stop asking herself what is right."

H842 Cook, Bruce. "Notes on a Shameful Era: Scoundrel Time." Saturday Review, 3 (Apr. 17, 1976), 28-29. illus. "A triumph of tone."

H843 Croce, Arlene. "Comments on 'The Blacklist'." New York Times, Oct. 17, 1976, 2, p. 12. A letter in support of Hilton Kramer's article (H867).

H844 Cushman, Kathleen. "Hellman on HUAC, One Woman's Record of a Terrible Time." National Observer, 15 (May 1, 1976), p. 19. illus. A background essay and review of Scoundrel Time.

H845 Edwards, Thomas R. "Provocative Moral Voice." New York Times, May 29, 1977, 7, p. 1. A review of We Must March My Darlings, by Diana Trilling, that includes discussion of the Little, Brown affair and of Scoundrel Time.

H846 Edwards, Verne E. , Jr. "Book Reviews: Scoundrel Time." Journalism Quarterly, 53 (Winter, 1976), 751-52.

H847 Falk, Richard A. "Scoundrel Time: Mobilizing the Intelligentsia for the Cold War." Performing Arts Journal, 1 (Winter, 1977), 97-102.

H848 Fremont-Smith, Eliot. "Making Book." Village Voice, 21 (Feb. 16, 1976), 52. illus. A preview of Scoundrel Time; Little, Brown brought out the book in April. A photo with Woodward and Bernstein.

H849 _____ . "Making Book on a Cranky Spring. " Village
      Voice, 21 (Mar. 29, 1976), 42. A brief comment
      on.

H850 French, Philip. "I Puritani. " New Statesman, 92
      (Nov. 5, 1976), 635+. A review of the edition with
      the Cameron essay; not "a useful guide to the period
      or a particularly enlightening essay upon it. " The
      reviewer quarrels with LH, but sees the value of
      the book; believes LH's politics are emotion and mor-
      al based.

H851 Fussell, Paul. "Treason of the Clerks. " Spectator
      (London), 237 (Nov. 13, 1976), 20-21. A review.

H852 Gillam, Richard. "Intellectuals and Power. " The
      Center Magazine, 10 (May-June, 1977), 27-28.

H853 Glazer, Nathan. "An Answer to Lillian Hellman. "
      Commentary, 61 (June, 1976), 36-39. Reviews
      Scoundrel Time and recounts LH's challenge of those
      who did not go to her defense and the defense of
      others who were punished by the HUAC. He still
      thinks that those who believed in freedom belonged
      outside the Waldorf Conference, not inside. He
      writes that LH never dreams of asking herself what
      her responsibility to truth was; Glazer thinks LH is
      righteous only because of what she did and not be-
      cause of actually helping to extend freedom. Wills'
      introduction disgraces the book because he straight-
      forwardly favors Communist totalitarianism to de-
      mocracy.

H854 Goodman, Walter. "Fair Game. " New Leader, 59
      (May, 24, 1976), 10-11. A review that gives back-
      ground of the times and reminds the reader that LH
      was accused only of "hobnobbing with the Communists, "
      not ever accused of being one.

H855 Gornick, Virginia. "Neither Forgotten nor Forgiven. "
      Ms. , 5 (Aug. , 1976), 46-47. Commends the book
      for the voice behind the words, the spirit, the style,
      the warmth, the anger, but Wills' introduction is
      "bad, very bad. "

H856 Gray, Paul. "An Unfinished Woman. " Time, 107
      (May 10, 1976), 83. illus. A review of Scoundrel
      Time.

H857 Hartnett, Robert C. "Scoundrel Time. " America, 135
     (Sept. 4, 1976), 102. Reviewed with Men Against
     McCarthy, by Richard M. Fried.

H858 Hentoff, Nat. "The Politics of Self. " Social Policy,
     7 (Jan. -Feb. , 1977), 55-57.

H859 Hogan, William. "Hellman Time. " San Francisco
     Chronicle, Apr. 12, 1976, p. 37.

H860 Hook, Sidney. "Lillian Hellman's Scoundrel Time. "
     Encounter, 48 (Feb. , 1977), 82-91. In his review
     article Hook gives historical perspective and back-
     ground to LH's "self-serving book. " He writes that
     LH is unjust to Henry Wallace, that her action is
     of the type helping "to destroy the open society whose
     benefits and freedom she enjoys. "

H861 Hoover, Francis X. J. "Scoundrel Time. " America,
     135 (Nov. 13, 1976), 336. A brief review.

H862 Howard, Maureen. "Scoundrel Time. " New York Times,
     Apr. 25, 1976, 7, pp. 1-2. illus. Unlike Patrick
     Buchanan's (H835) and Buckley's (H836, H837), How-
     ard's critical review is of Scoundrel Time as a mem-
     oir: "a beautiful work of self-definition, " "not a
     confessional book, " "in the tradition of a fine moral
     essay like Emerson's The American Scholar. " How-
     ard responds to the autobiographical material and
     style, to the drama of the memoir, rather than take
     issue with the righteousness of Hellman's position
     or motivation.

H863 Howe, Irving. "Lillian Hellman and the McCarthy
     Years. " Dissent, 23 (Fall, 1976), 378-82. His
     review article faults the vulgar Garry Wills' essay,
     the shoddiness of LH's argument, the untrue account.

H864 Hunt, David. "Clean Conscience. " Listener (London),
     96 (Nov. 18, 1976), 656. A review of the book and
     of the period; writes of James Cameron's "fairly
     smug British line" in his introduction and of Garry
     Wills' "sterner stuff. "

H865 Kazin, Alfred. "Comments on 'The Blacklist'. " New
     York Times, Oct. 17, 1976, 2, p. 12. A letter
     after Hilton Kramer's article (H867).

H866 Kempton, Murray. "Review of Scoundrel Time." The
       New York Review of Books, 23 (June 10, 1976), 22-
       25. Writes of the style LH developed for the re-
       telling as that of the ideal style of letters, as from
       an aunt who is enjoyed for her candor when it is
       turned on others rather than on oneself. In a foot-
       note, he takes issue with LH's rancor and personal
       feelings in designating James Wechsler a friendly
       witness when in fact he was not and was instead an
       openly hostile one.

H867 Kramer, Hilton. "The Blacklist and the Cold War, Cul-
       tural Revisionism Is 'in' Among Film Makers, Wri-
       ters, and Producers." New York Times, Oct. 3,
       1976, 2, pp. 1, 16-17. See: H865, H882, H889,
       H891.

H868 _____. "Reply." New York Times, Oct. 17, 1976,
       2, p. 28. See: H867.

H869 Lehmann-Haupt, Christopher. "Going One's Own Way."
       New York Times, Apr. 15, 1976, p. 31. This re-
       view appeared under the title "The Voice of McCarthy-
       ism--A Curious Personal Meditation." San Francisco
       Chronicle, Apr. 24, 1976, WOR, p. 34. illus.

H870 Leonard, John. "Critic's Notebook: An Evening with
       2 Walking Anachronisms." New York Times, May
       26, 1976, p. 24. Comment on Scoundrel Time in
       terms of Augustinian sin and guilt.

H871 Lewis, Jeremy. "Memoirs: All the Better to Know
       You With." Times (London), Nov. 18, 1976, p. 11.
       A brief comment.

H872 Lipsius, Frank. "American Mean Time." Books and
       Bookmen, 22 (June, 1977), p. 54. A review.

H873 McCarthy, Eugene J. "A Time of Betrayal: On Hell-
       man and HUAC." American Film, 1 (July-Aug.,
       1976), 70+. A review and comment that had more
       spoken up as Hellman, had the press had covered
       the actions of McCarthy more fully, had those in
       legislative responsibility spoken up against McCarthy,
       the Era would not have developed.

H874 McWilliams, Carey. "Time Is the Scoundrel." Nation,

222 (June 19, 1976), 741-42. Reviewed as a "fascinating memoir. "

H875 Maclean, A. "Scoundrel Time. " Times Literary Supplement, Dec. 13, 1976, p. 1516. A letter responding to Richard Mayne's review essay (H880).

H876 Magill, Frank N. , ed. "Scoundrel Time, " Magill's Literary Annual 1977. Volume II. Englewood Cliffs, New Jersey: Salem Press, 1977. An essay-review of Scoundrel Time.

H877 Maloff, Saul. "Jewel without Price. " Commonweal, 103 (July 1, 1976), 438-42. illus. A portrait of LH through the review of Scoundrel Time, "a matchless work of autobiography by the most exacting standards. "

H878 Marcus, Greil. "Undercover: Remembering the Witch-Hunts. " Rolling Stone, May 20, 1976, p. 97.

H879 Marvin, John R. "Scoundrel Time. " Library Journal, 101 (May 1, 1976), 1110.

H880 Mayne, Richard. "Ishmael and the Inquisitors. " Times Literary Supplement, Nov. 12, 1976, 1413. This review article also provoked response: See: H828, H864, H875, H884, H903, H906. Mayne considers the book "a tainted sandwich, " writes of LH's reproach of Lionel Trilling, believes LH got the best of both worlds; gives comprehensive picture of the times and people involved.

H881 _____. "To the Editor. " Times Literary Supplement, Dec. 10, 1976), 1560. A letter responding to other letters: "Pace. "

H882 Meeropol, Michael. "Comments on 'The Blacklist'. " New York Times, Oct. 17, 1976, 2, p. 12. A letter disagreeing with Hilton Kramer's column (H867) and objecting to his "snide remarks about" LH.

H883 Mitford, Jessica. A Fine Old Conflict. New York: Alfred A. Knopf, 1977. In the acknowledgement and the sources, Mitford cites Scoundrel Time as particularly helpful about the witch-hunts. In Chapter 9 ("HUAC"), she refers to LH's experience and of being forced into taking the Fifth Amendment.

H884 Nathan, Otto. "Scoundrel Time." Times Literary
      Supplement, Dec. 3, 1976, 1516. A letter in re-
      sponse to Richard Mayne's essay (H880).

H885 "New York Intelligencer: Bantam Raises Hellman."
      New York, 9 (Aug. 2, 1976), 56. illus. Details
      of the financial arrangement for paperback rights
      of Scoundrel Time.

H886 "Notes on Current Books: Scoundrel Time." Virginia
      Quarterly Review, 53 (Winter, 1977), 28. A brief
      comment.

H887 Owen, Gary. "Scoundrel Time," in Frank N. Magill,
      ed., Magill's Literary Annual 1977. Englewood
      Cliffs, New Jersey: Salem Press, 1977. An essay-
      review of reviews.

H888 Phillips, William. "What Happened in the Fifties."
      Partisan Review, 43, no. 3 (1976), 337-40. Cor-
      rects some of the facts and political conclusions of
      LH in Scoundrel Time.

H889 Radosh, Ronald, and Louis Menashe. "Comments on
      'The Blacklist'." New York Times, Oct. 17, 1976,
      2, p. 28. A letter on Hilton Kramer's article about
      the revisionists' view of the McCarthy Period (H867).

H890 Rosenthal, Marshall. " 'Thank God Somebody Finally
      Had the Guts to Do It " Chicago Tribune Book
      World, May 9, 1976, p. 3. illus. "Scoundrel Time
      will endure as a written measure of probity to which
      human beings may aspire."

H891 Schlesinger, Arthur, Jr. "Comments on 'The Black-
      list'." New York Times, Oct. 17, 1976, 2, p. 12.
      A letter in response to Hilton Kramer (H867).

H892 "Scoundrel Time." Publishers' Weekly, 209 (Mar. 1,
      1976), 90.

H893 "Scoundrel Time." Booklist, 72 (Apr. 1, 1976), 1083.

H894 "Scoundrel Time." New Yorker, 52 (Apr. 26, 1976),
      147.

H895 "Scoundrel Time." Playboy, 23 (June, 1976), 40+.

H896 "Scoundrel Time. " MD Medical Newsmagazine, Jan. ,
       1977, p. 196. A review.

H897 Shattan, J. "Scoundrel Time. " Midstream, 22 (Oct. ,
       1976), 67-77.

H898 Sherrill, Robert. "Wisdom and Its Price. " Nation,
       226 (June 19, 1976), 757-58. The background of
       her appearance before HUAC, a review of Scoundrel
       Time.

H899 Sigal, Clancy. "True Grit. " The Guardian Weekly
       (Manchester) 115 (Nov. 14, 1976), 22. A reveiw
       of LH's "icily angry essay about her historic appear-
       ance" and Garry Wills' "excellent commentary. "
       "What is missing from her story is the sheer scale
       of the inquisition. "

H900 Simon, John. Uneasy Stages: A Chronicle of the New
       York Theater, 1963-1973. New York: Random
       House, 1975.

H901 Smith, Jeannette. "Scoundrel Time. " Washington Post,
       Apr. 29, 1976, B, pp. 1, 3. illus. An account of
       the party given at Four Seasons in honor of Scoundrel
       Time with snippets of the guests' remarks.

H902 Sperry, Ralph A. "Scoundrel Time. " Best Sellers,
       36 (July, 1976), 116. A brief review, noting the
       "dreadful" Wills' introduction, "the bad" flaws "the
       excellent, " "the true writing begins on page 37. "

H903 Symons, Julian. " 'Ishmael and the Inquisitors'. "
       Times Literary Supplement, Dec. 17, 1976, 1586.
       A letter lamenting Richard Mayne's brisk dismissal
       of Dashiell Hammett in his review of Scoundrel Time
       (H880).

H904 "Their Lives and Times. " Washington Post Book World,
       Dec. 12, 1976, p. 9. A brief review, noting the
       value of Scoundrel Time is in its vivid "recapturing
       of an episode in our history that many Americans
       still would rather forget. "

H905 Traves, Mary. "Soundrel Time. " San Francisco, 18
       (July, 1976), 92-93. A review.

H906 Trilling, Diana. "Scoundrel Time. " Times Literary
        Supplement, Dec. 3, 1976, 1516. A letter that de-
        fines the liberal intellectual's responsibility in re-
        sponse to Richard Mayne's review (H880, H881).

H907 _____. We Must March My Darlings. New York:
        Harcourt, Brace, Jovanovich, 1977, 42-54. Mrs.
        Trilling writes to bring political clarification to some
        of the issues mentioned in Scoundrel Time, which on
        the whole "has been uncritically received as histori-
        cal statement, " places LH's politics, questions Garry
        Wills' moral authority and judgment, concludes both
        Hellman and Wills are opportunists. The material
        concerning Hellman is the most important in the en-
        tire controversy concerning Scoundrel Time.

THE BIG KNOCKOVER

H908 Alvarez, A. "The Thin Man. " Spectator (London),
        Feb. 11, 1966, p. 169. A review of The Big Knock-
        over.

H909 Boucher, Anthony. "Criminals at Large. " New York
        Times, June 26, 1966, 2, pp. 22, 24. A review.

H910 "Continental Op. " Newsweek, 68 (July 25, 1966), 93.

H911 Cuff, Sergeant. "Criminal Record: The Big Knockover. "
        Saturday Review, 49 (July 30, 1966), 40.

H912 Dawson, Helen. "Paperbacks: The Big Knockover. "
        Observer, Apr. 26, 1970, p. 27.

H913 Gardner, Frederick H. "The Return of the Continental
        Op. " Nation, 203 (Oct. 31, 1966), 454-56.

H914 Handlin, Oscar. "Reader's Choice. " Atlantic Monthly,
        218 (June, 1966), 137-38. The "introduction may be
        the best piece of writing Miss Hellman has ever done. "

H915 Malin, Irving. "The Big Knockover. " Commonweal,
        85 (Feb. 10, 1967), 535-36.

H916 Perlmutter, Emanuel. "End Papers. " New York Times,
        July 29, 1966), p. 29. A review of The Big Knock-
        over.

H917 Phelps, Donald. "Dashiell Hammett's Microcosmos. "
    National Review, 18 (Sept. 20, 1966), 941-42.

H918 Saal, Rollene W. "Pick of the Paperbacks: Fiction. "
    Saturday Review, 50 (July 29, 1967), 32.

H919 Schickel, Richard. "Dirty Work: The Big Knockover. "
    New York Herald Tribune Book Week, Aug. 28, 1966,
    14-15.

THE SELECTED LETTERS OF ANTON CHEKHOV

H920 Butler, Hubert. "The Selected Letters of Anton Chek-
    hov. " The Guardian (Manchester), July 22, 1955,
    p. 4.

H921 Halsband, Robert. "Notes: The Selected Letters. "
    Saturday Review, 38 (July 9, 1955), 33. A brief
    review that mentions the "somewhat casual introduc-
    tion. "

H922 Korg, Jacob. "The Selected Letters of Anton Chekhov. "
    Nation, 181 (July 30, 1955), 102.

H923 "Letters from Chekhov. "   Times Literary Supplement,
    Sept. 2, 1955, p. 506.   LH's introduction is "indivi-
    dual and well done. "

H924 Lowenthal, Marvin. "Anton Chekhov 'Characters'. "
    New York Herald Tribune Book Review, May 1, 1955,
    p. 2. A comprehensive review.

H925 O'Connor, Frank. "He Had an Unerring Nose for Hum-
    bug of Any Sort, The Selected Letters of Anton Chek-
    hov. " New York Times, Apr. 24, 1955, 7, pp. 4-
    5. It is "more comprehensive and better balanced
    than Mrs. Garnett's, and it contains an excellent in-
    troduction" by Lillian Hellman.

H926 Popkin, Henry. "Self-Portrait: The Selected Letters
    of Anton Chekhov. " Commonweal, 62 (June 24, 1955),
    310-11.

H927 "Power of Negative Thinking. " Time, 65 (May 9, 1955),
    114+. illus. "Deftly introduced and edited. "

H928 Rahv, Philip.   "The Education of Anton Chekhov. "
       New Republic, 133 (June 18, 1955), 18-19.   "The
       fullest and best edition of its kind" so far in English.

H929 Saal, Rollene W.   "Pick of the Paperbacks. "   Saturday
       Review, 49 (Dec. 17, 1966), 38.   A brief comment.

H930 "The Selected Letters of Anton Chekhov. "   Booklist,
       51 (June 15, 1955), 426.

H931 V[oiles], J[ane].   "Among the New Books: The Selected
       Letters of Anton Chekhov. " San Francisco Chronicle,
       Aug. 21, 1955, p. 18.   LH also shows "why Chekhov
       was without the final spiritual violence which only a
       creative genius like Tolstoi possesses. "

H932 Warner, Rex.   "The Selected Letters of Anton Chekhov. "
       London Magazine, 2:2 (Nov. , 1955), 82-84.   A re-
       view and a comparison with the Garnett translation
       and preface.

J

ADDENDUM

J1 "The Little War, " in Whitney Burnett, ed. , <u>This Is My</u>
   <u>Best</u>. Cleveland: The World Publishing Company,
   1945.
   "Pieces from a diary written on a long trip to Europe
   in 1937 ... "; about Civil War Spain and a "Blonde
   Lady. "

J2 A brief biographical note about Hammett and commentary
   signed by Lillian Hellman appears as a prologue to
   <u>The Novels of Dashiell Hammett</u>. New York: Alfred
   A. Knopf, 1965.

J3 "How Lillian Hellman Writes a Play. " <u>PM</u>, Mar. 12,
   1944, pp. 11-12.
   An interview after <u>The Searching Wind</u> went into rehearsal: "slender and smart looking. " "I'm unable
   to say where I start. But I know I <u>don't</u> start by
   telling myself to write a play about War. "

J4 "Some of the Popular Playwrights Returning to Broadway
   This Season. " New York <u>Herald Tribune</u>, Aug. 1,
   1948, 5, p. 2.
   A note announcing that LH is planning <u>The Naked and</u>
   <u>the Dead</u>.

J5 Crosby, John. "Radio In Review: The Totalitarian Individual. " New York <u>Herald Tribune</u>, Sept. 21, 1948,
   p. 18.
   A review of the Lux Radio Theater production and a
   significant analysis of the characters: "Miss Hellman
   professes to loathe totalitarianism ... but she never-
   theless understands the totalitarian individual better
   than she understands the human or maleable individual.
   Her humans, incidentally, are invariably idiots. "

J6 Beaufort, John. "Openings on Broadway. " <u>Christian</u>
   <u>Science Monitor,</u> Mar. 17, 1951, p. 8.
   A review and commentary: "an unfairly slanted view
   of American life. "

J7 Walcutt, Charles Child. <u>Man's Changing Mask: Modes</u>
   <u>of Characterization in Fiction.</u> Minneapolis: University of Minnesota Press, 1966.
   Concerning the characterization of Carrie in <u>Toys</u>.

J8 Beebe, Lucius. "Stage Asides: Miss Hellman Speaks
   Up. " New York <u>Herald Tribune</u>, Apr. 27, 1941, 6,
   pp. 1, 4.

An interview: "I'm not filled with moral indignation or a great yen for reform when I take pen in hand, ... but somewhere along the way the subject begins to assume a 'significance' ... may have cribbed the idea for Watch from Henry James' Europeans. "

J9 Watts, Richard, Jr. "A Tribute to Miss Hellman's Departed Play. " New York Herald Tribune, Mar. 1, 1942, 6, p. 1.

J10 "The Theater: Who's to Write Next Season's Drama?" New York Herald Tribune, May 18, 1941, 6, p. 1. Concerning the novel-like three-dimensional quality of Watch.

J11 Weales, Gerald. Clifford Odets, Playwright. New York: Pegasus, Bobbs-Merrill Company, Inc. , 1971.

J12 Stillman, Deanne, and Anne Beatts, eds. "Pimento: Lillian Hellman Reaches Into the Pickle Jar for Her Past, " in Titters. New York: Colliers, 1976, pp. 56-60.
A parody of Pentimento.

INDEX

Unless page numbers are indicated, the location citations refer to sections listed in the Table of Contents and then to the individual item within the section. For example, F20 is the citation to the section "Books about ... LH, " and is found in numerical order there.